Manx Brothers in Arms

World War I 'from a father's perspective'

Julie Quine

First published 2016

Revised 2017

ISBN: 978 1536838794

Cover design: Christina Quine

(Vess, Lardy and Dono Quine)

Also available as an (Amazon) e-book

Other related Amazon E-books

Anecdotes written by John Lindsay Quine (Dono), edited by Julie Quine:

Odyssey of a Marine Engineer (Odyssey 1): Dono's life in the Merchant Navy and Royal Navy (1906 to 1918)

Marine Engineer to MHK (Odyssey 2): 1919 to 1980

Print version: Odyssey of a Marine Engineer 1886 to 1980

Contents

How fleet is a glance of the mind
Compared with the speed of its flight,
The tempest itself lags behind
And the swift winged arrows of light.
When I think of my own native land
In a moment I seem to be there,
But alas! Recollection at hand
Soon hurries me back to despair.

Oh pardon me thou bleeding piece of earth
That I am meek and gentle with these butchers.

Written by
Dono

Preface

'World War I' conjures up the thought of trenches and battlefields... It is a subject which I avoided, until recently...

Unlike World War I books recounting the personal experiences of soldiers on the battlefield or important public figures of the time, this book relates a father's war-time experiences and perceptions regarding the impact of war on the Isle of Man and shores beyond. John Quine wrote copious letters to his son, Dono, throughout the war. Extracts from these form the basis of the book, together with anecdotes and memoirs written by his three sons, as well as some added background information.

The project began with a view to writing the biography of Canon John Quine. What I discovered in his letters from 1914 to 1919 was a complete surprise – I was inspired to read on and discover more regarding John's thoughts and the experiences of his family.

Their stable, complacent Edwardian world suddenly faced unknown and frightening threats: spies on the hillside behind the Vicarage signalling to ships; submarine activity in the Irish Sea; strange contraptions discovered on the beaches; the sound of bombing from across the water; the creation of two large internment camps filled with Germans and Austrians, and not least, the threat of invasion from the sea and the air, including the sight of airships. Seeing these through John's eyes and hearing his reactions to them through his letters was fascinating.

Surprisingly, John had a keen interest in helping his sons devise new methods of defeating the enemy – on land, at sea, and in the air...

War is something I never really understood: why men enlisted, and why they continued to go out to fight when millions had already lost their lives. It seems that increasingly it became a game of cat and mouse – 'kill' or 'be killed', with countries implementing more rigorous game plans to outwit their opponents – including cutting off food supplies, and spying on the enemy to find out what their next move might be.

I never realised how much happened in those long war years, but the letters give some understanding and insight, telling a different, but very interesting side of the story.

Note: The letters of Canon John Quine, written 1906 to 1920, reside in the Manx Museum Archives, I.O.M. [1]. The extracts incorporate minor modifications to confer greater coherency for the reader. John's handwriting was indecipherable in places, resulting in possible misspellings... John's letters were obviously solely for his son's interest, not for the man in the street; despite the fact that he was a Clergyman, John did have some strong views which may offend some readers.

Reference Map of the Isle of Man

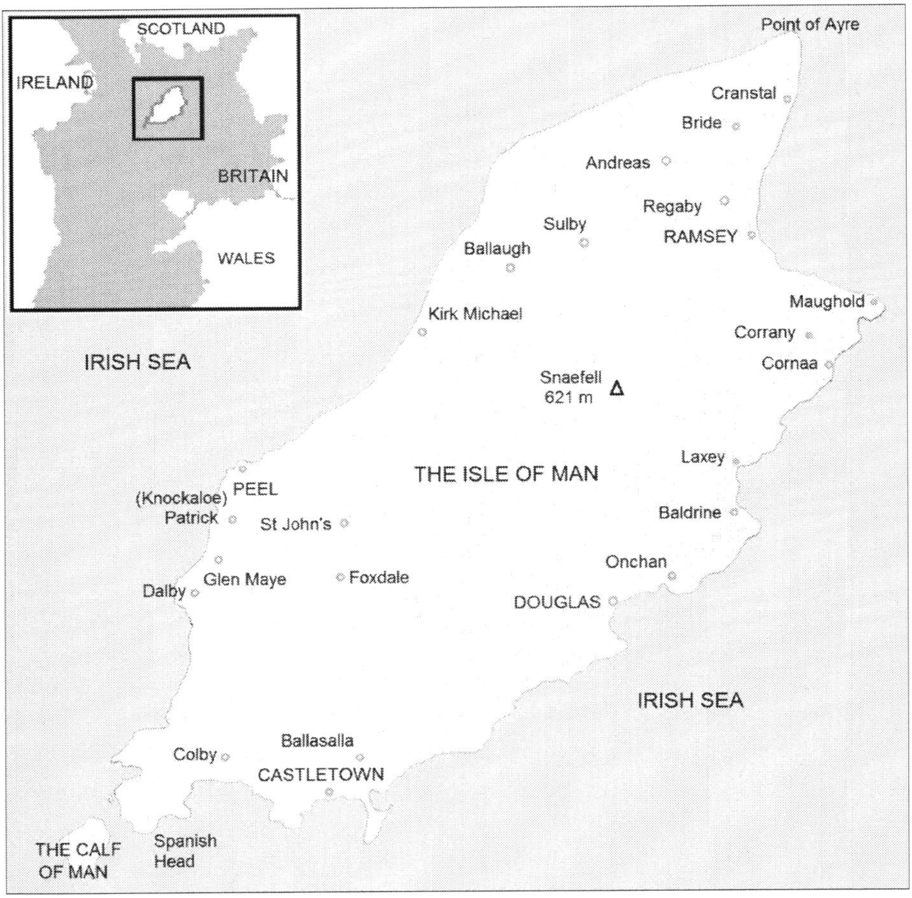

Drawn: Julie Quine (not to scale)

The Island

For those who do not know, the Isle of Man is a small beautiful island situated in the Irish Sea between Ireland and the U.K. It is approximately 33 miles long and 12 miles wide, covering approximately 227 square miles of land. Just before the outbreak of World War I the population of the island was in the region of 50,000. A hundred years later, it stands at around 85,000.

Although agriculture and fishing were prevalent industries at the start of the twentieth century, tourism was the mainstay of the Manx economy. This era preceded the cheap foreign holiday, and throughout the holiday season, people flocked to the island in their droves, especially from the textile towns of Lancashire. Thousands of people travelled daily on the fifteen Steam Packet ships in service, and the Douglas promenade was crowded with people arriving and departing – the boarding houses along the bustling promenade, full to capacity.

Between May and September 1913 there were a staggering 615,726 visitors. During the same period in 1914 the number of visitors fell to around 404,000 as the outbreak of war began to have an impact. [Figures from Isle of Man Examiner 16.10.1915]

Regarding the government of the island, the Isle of Man is not part of the United Kingdom, but is a Crown Dependency with its own independent Parliament called 'Tynwald', which creates the laws of the island.

The *Legislative Council* is the upper branch of Manx Parliament and the *House of Keys* the lower, and the two branches meet to form the Tynwald Court. The head of this Government is the Lieutenant Governor, the representative on the island of the Lord of Mann (currently Queen Elizabeth II).

In August 1914, Lord Raglan held the position of Lieutenant Governor and had much greater power over the island than the man in the same post today.

During the four and a half years of war, the Isle of Man did not suffer as greatly as mainland Britain, certainly as far as lack of food went (there was no rationing on the island), but war did destroy the tourist industry and had other significant impacts upon the welfare of the people.

John

John was an outstanding individual, born on the Isle of Man in 1857 – the son of a Manx miller. He won an open scholarship to Merton College Oxford where he studied mathematics, and took additional courses in Greek, Latin Literature and Divinity. Returning to the Isle of Man, John secured the Headship of the Douglas Grammar School in 1883, and married Mary Jane Lindsay the following year.

In 1895 John became the Vicar of All Saints Church in Lonan, and his growing family moved to the Vicarage there.

The Vicarage, situated in a rather bleak location, had a clear view up towards the island's highest mountain – Snaefell, and in the opposite direction, down to the sea. Here John found more time for his literary interests and published his novel *Captain of the Parish* in 1897, which was based around his observations of the people of the island and its beauty.

John was elected Chaplain to the *House of Keys* in 1906, requiring his presence at the sittings of the House for prayers, and at the Tynwald ceremony held in the first week of July every year in St John's. Through this position, John became acquainted with Members of the House and other local dignitaries, particularly Lord Raglan, Lt. Governor, who held John in high esteem. John's brother, Thomas Frederick Quine, was also a member of the House for Rushen, and following their father's death in 1907, Thomas ran the Silverdale Mill, tea-rooms and boating lake in Ballasalla (in the south of the island) with his wife Eva.

So, we know that John was an intelligent and educated man with wide ranging interests. He was also an antiquarian, historian, and friend of the artist Archibald Knox.

Family photo circa 1899 – (left to right) Dono, Marge, Mary, Vess, Mary Jane Lindsay, Margaret, Lardy, Patrick (born 1896, died 1907), and John Quine.

Victoria Pier, Douglas M.N.H. circa 1900 [1]

John's Pre-war Notions

By 1909 John was generally well regarded in the community and attained his Canonry that year. He was a keen political observer, an avid reader of newspapers, and learnt much from the people around him; his thirst for knowledge and news was insatiable. From these sources he formed ideas about what was happening in politics as well as from listening to his counterparts in the *House of Keys*, and passed this knowledge on to his family.

The following extracts written by John to his eldest son Dono indicate these ideas and his feeling of the rapidly encroaching war.

In July 1909 John wrote:

> *'It is coming to it that we shall have universal military service...*
>
> *Enthusiasts talk about an era of unusual peace, but the condition of human nature, face to face with the struggle for existence in nations, promise many wars yet... The Governor* (of the Isle of Man) *made a speech arguing for the necessity of adopting the idea of universal military service.'*

John was for the latter idea, suggesting to Dono that ranges could be easily made on the island for firing practice:

> *'A good range could be made in Laxey Valley towards Snaefell base. The mine is now disused with a 2-mile range...'*
>
> ...Some rifle-ranges were opened in the early 1900's around the island at Ballaugh, Michael & Cronk Auld – pictured, M.N.H. [1]

In January 1910, John explained to Dono that it was important for countries to have colonies for emigration and expansion. John clearly understood Germany's colonial ambitions as one of the drivers towards war and wrote:

> *'England has had emigration as a safety valve and place of expansion for its excess energy, and its colonies have remained part of England, forming Greater Britain.*
>
> *Germany too has had emigration, but with the difference that its people have gone mainly to the U.S.A., become Americans & are lost to Germany. Germany has had practically no colonies to which people may go and still remain part of Germany, and an expansion place for its superfluous energy and trade development – greater than that drawn off by emigration. The result is that Germany has reached a point when it must have colonies...*
>
> *We have colonies almost in excess of our requirements, and they want a redistribution of them between themselves. This is their present purpose; and they mean war – not as against England itself with hate, but as a means to an end – which would leave England with less colonies and themselves with more...*
>
> *They have no milk-and-water sentiments about war being wrong. Fortunately for Germany they have no religious sects – which are the chief cause of internal dissension.'*

In March 1910 there was a great deal of discussion between Dono and his father regarding ships and guns:

> *'I think what you have said as to what might be possible in an Anglo-German war, of German ships producing a few guns, mounting them, and destroying the English ships of a like sort, a very good point, because – the never ready English, who allowed guns to go into the Transvaal in piano-cases and would not listen to anyone, will not now believe anything as to Germany possibly preparing surprises of the unexpected sort. Tell the English public the truth and you are certain of one thing – that you will not be believed.*
>
> *I do not say that guns on merchant ships, is likely, but it is possible. English have become unreal people. Unreality is what has gone down with them for four generations past.*
>
> *Speak a word as to war and all the liberal papers and nonconformist papers shout out that you are preaching the Gospel of Hate! The only hate in the matter is their own hate of England – of their betters, of*

the classes that have as yet any spirit left. Germany does not hate England – it merely wants a big part of our colonies, of our trade, and the leadership of things.

We who look war in the face do not hate Germany: we only look at facts...'

By February 1912, the prospect of a war appeared greater, and John's knowledge and understanding of the unification of Germany by Bismarck is striking in the following excerpt:

'I see some very grave speeches delivered by Officers at Manchester regarding a European war. I have absolutely no doubt about it. And this country is preparing itself for war – viz. inviting it, if ever a country did.

To answer that Germany has its own internal difficulties is no answer: because to Germany that would be the very reason of its embarking on war. It is impossible for German Statesmen not to believe in war – since its three wars – Danish, Austrian, and French – contributed to make Germany what she is! Germany was a chaos of small states, practically independent of each other; Prussia the most important!

The genius of Bismarck saw that the aggregate of force must be directed to one end, and engineered three important wars – against Denmark, and added Schleswig-Holstein to Prussia, and against Austria, which practically unified Germany against France.

A fourth successful war would make her undisputed arbiter and monopolist of Europe – with a quadrupled foreign trade, and world interest.

The German Chancellor in a recent speech in the Reichstag, discouraging internal dissension, ended by an utterance inspired I feel sure by the picture in his mind's eye of England as it at present is. He said that Nations should learn from the ruthless verdict of history, that to have internal dissensions is to be trampled underfoot in the irresistible march of fate!'

Watching from his study window, John rarely missed anything happening out at sea. He wrote on August 12th:

'A squadron of warships has been in Ramsey for several days – Monday to today. They had practice off here, with several sorts of guns, and I saw two of them off the bay, one dragging a string of

targets, the other (I think) firing. But while I could see the spray thrown up by the shot around the targets, I could see no smoke from either ship... They were not more than four miles from here...

Above 20 shots evidently missed; then a target was sent... this is the only hit I saw made.'

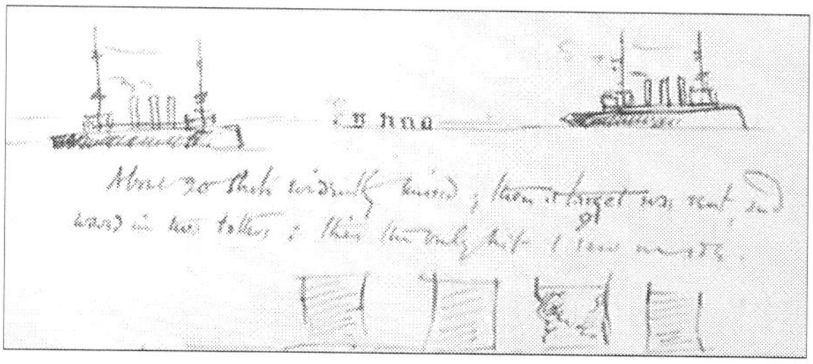

In 1912 John realised that people were becoming nervous of a war.

He wrote:

'I went to Baldrine yesterday to baptize a weak infant, the child of Mr & Mrs Lightbody. Afterwards I had a talk with him and found him an intelligent man. He said that he was a Commercial Traveller and went all over the country, north and south. He is convinced that the present time is a time of crisis, which will end in either a revolution or a foreign war. He had so seriously feared trouble in England this August that he took the house at Baldrine, so that his wife and children might be out of it...'

Later in October 1912 John wrote:

'We hear of work 'day and night' in English dockyards, and emergency preparations against what may develop out of the present Balkan war. I am not without hope that Turkey will yet show a good fight: but evidently those small states have been making preparations for a long time...'

Germany had certainly been making preparations for the past twenty years. In 1892, France and Russia had signed an alliance, leaving Germany feeling rather vulnerable against these military rivals. Germany began equipping itself and preparing plans in the event of future war, to make a pre-emptive strike on France (a plan developed by Schlieffen), followed by preparations on the Eastern Front to guard against Russian attacks (Germany assumed that Russia would be slow to organise its forces).

The Three Sons

The Canon's three sons – **Dono**, **Lardy** and **Vess** are the key individuals in this factual account.

Dono

The eldest son was John Lindsay Quine, born in January 1886; the family called him '**Dono**'. It is thought that this was due to the fact that his answer to everything in his youth was: "Don't know!"

In his early years Dono became fascinated by the Manx Steam Packet paddle steamers, inspiring him to want to learn more about the working of ships...

At the age of 14, Dono began a five-year apprenticeship at William Knox's firm in Douglas where he gained mechanical and electrical engineering experience, and in his spare time in his final year, he ran the lighting system in the Gaiety Theatre in Douglas.

In 1906 Dono left the island and went to sea as an engineer in the Merchant Navy with the Harrison Line, travelling around the world.

By 1912 he had completed his 'Extra 1st Class' Board of Trade qualification in marine engineering and was working in Liverpool at Cammell Laird shipbuilders with a view to employment with the Board of Trade as a ship surveyor or some such work.

Dono kept diaries regarding his work at sea, which he later transformed into short stories or anecdotes [Amazon e-book: 'Odyssey of a Marine Engineer'].

Lardy

Lawrence Lindsay Quine, known as **'Lardy'**, was born in August 1887.

Lardy proved that he was a determined character at the age of 14 when he dismissed the prospect of further education at King William's College; he felt his strength lay in the practical world of engineering.

His father therefore insisted that he undertook an apprenticeship on the local railway, hoping that the back-breaking work would change his mind. It didn't.

Lardy gained valuable experience of narrow-gauge railway work through his apprenticeship with the Isle of Man Railway Company.

...There were around 50 miles of such narrow-gauge (2 feet in width) track on the island at that time.

Following in the footsteps of Dono, after the completion of his apprenticeship at the age of 20, Lardy began work in the Merchant Navy on the Nelson Line as a refrigerating engineer, but was not as eager as Dono to complete examinations to further his career.

Lardy, like his brother, was at sea for months on end with brief visits home. As a result of this, he learnt to speak other languages including some Spanish.

He was a quiet young man who enjoyed playing football rather than studying, and perhaps felt at a disadvantage being the middle son of the family.

Vess

Sylvester Lindsay Quine, known as '**Vess**', was born in 1894, the youngest of John's sons, and the only one to attend King William's College in the south of the island, from 1909 until 1911. Whilst studying there, Vess stayed at Silverdale in Ballasalla with his Aunt Eva and Uncle Thomas.

His passion was making model aeroplanes. Flight was in its infancy, and as Vess was growing up, he was obviously influenced by this new idea.

His father, John, was sceptical about flight, and in 1909, wrote to Dono:

'I am very doubtful if anything practical will come out of aeroplanes.'

Nevertheless later in the summer of 1910, John reported:

'I see that a Liverpool man has succeeded in flying on a new machine at his first attempt, but on a 2nd/3rd trial – from the planes not flying true, he sailed into the sand-hills on the coast near Liverpool and smashed his machine, to the damage of £200-£300. Still it shows that they now know how to make a machine that will fly at the first attempt.'

Vess was about to return to King William's in 1910 and wrote:

'Dear Dono,

I go back to College tomorrow... I enclose some cuttings about the London to Manchester flight... I am going to make a model aeroplane at the College workshops this term...'

Complete letter: *[Appendix a]*.

So, both Dono and Vess were fascinated by anything technical, and Lardy was interested in engineering. At the time, wireless telegraphy, as well as flight, was just evolving; both were to become an integral part of operations in World War I.

Wireless Telegraphy

Dono was at sea between 1906 and 1911, and the impact of Wireless telegraphy (W/T) on the control of ships was discussed. When Dono later suggested to his father the idea of setting up a wireless telegraphy system at the Vicarage in the Isle of Man, John found the idea appealing.

The Vicarage study was quiet with the children away from home. John settled down, dipped his quill into his ink well, and wrote a letter to Dono in June 1912...

'My Dear Dono...

I do not see why we should not get a wireless receiver here – you'll know best what end of the stick to take hold...'

Dono explained in his memoirs how his interest in wireless telegraphy began:

'First spark stations were present on the I.O.M. Steam Packet Company ships circa 1909 or 1910, and the transmissions were to Seaforth Station on the side of the Mersey estuary, Liverpool, as there was no Post-Office station on the Isle of Man. The sparks took place between two metal spheres about one inch diameter placed outside the Telegraphists cabin or office. All messages were transcoded by Morse code and could easily be read by passengers who had the training and ability to read it.'

When Dono left Harrison's in 1911 and began working in Laird's shipyard, he had access to the few technical details of W/T that existed at that time and decided to make a W/T receiver. He wrote in his memoirs:

'Here, my practice of the Morse code at sea with the signal lamp and with a heliograph which I had made came in useful.

The story of my heliograph is worth narrating. On one of my voyages to South Africa in the S.S. Magician, we called at Port Louis on the island of Mauritius in the Indian Ocean.

On a Sunday afternoon with a friend, we climbed one of the cactus clad mountains overlooking the island, and on a small top at the end of the narrow stony path up the mountain, we came upon a military signal party of three men. They had a heliograph and were signalling to an island 20 miles away. The flashes from the distant station were remarkably good; the Morse signals were entirely readable.

On introducing ourselves and indicating our ship in the docks far below, they were most friendly and explained the details of the helio-instrument.

When we resumed our voyage I set to work and made two complete heliographs and eventually brought them home to the Isle of Man – to Lonan Vicarage. During brief visits home I was able to get some practice.

I remember one sunny Good Friday afternoon, a fine hazy day; Banks Howe above Groudle was faintly visible from the field in front of Lonan Vicarage. Leaving my father in charge of one set at the Vicarage, we (Vess & I) took the other set to a position on the Howe and established communication.

Although this was my father's first introduction to signalling, we received his message: his sister – our Aunt Marion, had turned up on a visit (meaning we had to return home).

Signalling by lamp at sea among ourselves was a recreation and in the engine room we made our own lamp with the necessary shutters to give the flashes.

The very first message I sent was 'send a man aft' over the length of the ship. Reading the messages sent in flashes by Morse code from ships was useful practice.'

In the summer of 1912, Dono sent some W/T apparatus to be set up in the Vicarage, carried over to the Isle of Man on the boat by his older sister, Mary. John met the boat and later wrote to Dono:

'...The boat arrived about 7pm. There was a great crowd, but they had had a good passage, including Mary, who had your wireless parcel for Vess – which arrived all right...'

The wireless required an aerial. Regarding this, John wrote:

'I got a 30 foot pole from Glover of Axenfell, but we found it far too heavy to drag home, so I am going to get Willy Kermode to drag it home with a horse. Since that however I have thought to mention the plan – which I think ought to work – but possibly not – of using trees only! It would be much easier to fix the system of wires if the trees only were used!

These trees can all be stripped of branches, with no disadvantage to the tree, and the average height of the wires would be as high as in your system...'

The W/T set-up was really starting to take shape at the Vicarage, and work was well in hand regarding fixing up the aerial. In July, John wrote:

> *'Yesterday I got Christian* (a local gentleman) *to cut off the branches of the fir tree – leaving only one tuft of foliage at the top... Mother was very angry when she found the fir tree topped of its branches, but it was no use wasting words on it!'*

Obviously the idea did not quite work as planned, as John wrote to Dono later in July saying:

> *'...Do not allow yourself to be disappointed over the lack of complete success of the wireless installation here... the topmast is still far too small; at least 7' must be got above the present height...'*

Lonan Vicarage and Church

...The photograph was probably taken prior to 1912 judging by the fir-tree! John undoubtedly spent much of his time with his 'glasses' pressed to the windows of his study in the Vicarage, looking out to the sea beyond, studiously watching for any unusual activities...

As Dono was working in Liverpool and made infrequent visits back to the island, he asked his youngest brother Vess for some assistance in the matter of setting up the wireless – Vess was now living back at home after finishing his studies at King William's College and was working as a Law student in the offices of Dickinson, Cruickshank & Co.

John was still sceptical about Vess making model planes in his spare time at home, and wrote to Dono in February 1913:

'I do not wish to interfere with his amusements. The place is dull enough, but I do think this everlasting making of gliders, model aeroplanes etc., is futile. At Law he has a chance of making money – in a few years, enough to get himself a motor car, and attend aeroplane meetings, etc.; meantime he should lie low and work away till he gets on his feet.'

...Although flight was now possible, it was only ten years since the Wright brothers had experimented and proved that flight of small planes could be controlled. Over the next few years great progress was made, integrating W/T into the machines, as the necessity of this was suddenly realised with the threat of war, not necessarily for combat, but for reconnaissance and defence.

Vess became very interested in the W/T task in hand at the Vicarage in his spare time, and great progress was made. Dono wrote in his memoirs:

'A splendid twin wire aerial was suspended from the top of the Church tower – passing to a high fir tree in the Vicarage garden and then down leads to the W/T set in the house. The average height of the aerial was not less than 50 feet directed from east to west.'

Meanwhile, John spoke to Lord Raglan regarding making an application for a wireless receiving station at the Vicarage, but until it was up and running, if this were possible, there was not much point.

At the end of March 1913, life at the Vicarage became a little more exciting. John wrote:

'Last evening Albert Christian, a retired telegraphist who lives in Laxey, to whom I had spoken about the wireless, came up about 7pm. He stayed till 10pm getting 'letters' only, and finding the sounds rather weak. Vess wished to go on watching for messages, and Christian was evidently wishful for some better results and inclined to stay... They succeeded wonderfully; it was a great success and went on till 1.30am.

The tuning up of the machine which Vess had to attend to, and Christian not having read anything for 4 years, and the sounds being quite different from those of the telegraph, could not give perfect results! Many times messages were coming – 3 or 4 at the same time.'

Vess wrote to Dono the following day:

'Dear Dono, I am almost too excited to write coherently. So many things seem to have rushed on us all together. An application form has arrived from the Post M.G. (Master General) *from London. We send it*

on herewith. I think you had better get it filled in and sent up to London by Tuesday. It is a formidable document but don't be afraid of it...

Last night all the doubts (if any) that could exist as to whether we had really a Wireless Station, were removed in a startling manner.

Albert Christian, a retired Post Office man – a telegraphist who reports for the Times or something, came to the house about 6.30pm. Pater thought we might as well show him the machines...

He was some time getting the hang of it but at last about 11pm he started writing down letters.

Towards 11.30, I got him on to Poldhu (Wireless Station in Cornwall until 1933) *and tuned carefully and altered my detector – and then things happened. He stiffened like 'a pointer on the meat', and from then till 1.20 he was a machine or Morse inker...*

He wrote down news of the world like fun: political, social, sporting, commercial, home and foreign, New York – Germany, all and everything.

Who won the Alexandra handicap? I know, though at this moment there are not 10 people in the island who do: Angel Clare. What does Germany think of Winston Churchill's Holiday? I know.

We are posting the full statement in the note book to you today. Keep it carefully; read, mark, learn and inwardly digest it... It is valuable – priceless to us – rush off and post that application.'

Albert Christian was sworn to secrecy, but obviously couldn't contain his excitement. He reported the achievement to the newspaper the following day! The lengthy piece in the *I.O.M. Times* included the following:

'The honour of establishing the first wireless receiving station in the island belongs to the sons of the Rev. Canon J. Quine, M.A., Vicar of Lonan – Mr John Lindsay Quine and Mr Sylvester Lindsay Quine...

Mr Sylvester Quine took charge of the wave measuring side, while our correspondent fixed the receiver to his ear with pencil and paper before him... towards midnight a distinct tone loomed out of the chaos of sounds... from Cornwall (Poldhu)... Paris and Germany, communications from the liner Oceanic... the death of Pierpont Morgan, and the disappointment of the Prince of Wales in being unable to go up in the Zeppelin airship.

At last the reward has come to these two clever amateur inventors...

They have demonstrated that it is possible to work wireless from the Isle of Man even in the present elementary state of the apparatus, but nevertheless with astonishing results... A.M.C.'

The Chief Constable of the island, Colonel Madoc and his wife visited John at the Vicarage after the publication of the news. Local interest was suddenly keen, but until a W/T licence was received, its future was uncertain.

On April 4th, John wrote to Dono:

> *'I think the visit* (by Madoc) *was intended friendly, and rather to avoid anything arising. As the newspaper (through Albert Christian's folly) had made the matter public, in a sense that the system had been installed and at work, I rather think the authorities had to do something to protect themselves.*
>
> *It is an exceedingly important fact as you point out, that the post office recognize the fact that one cannot apply for a licence until you have actually got a machine to licence – hence their request for description of machine, aerial etc. But Albert Christian had made things seem more than this!*
>
> *It has caused a great deal of amusement, as everybody has got the idea that something very splendid has been achieved, for they know no more about wireless than about other mysteries.'*

Photograph of the wireless set-up in the Vicarage at Lonan

A Government Office Order by B.E. Sargeaunt, Government Secretary, was posted in the Manx newspaper as follows:

> 'Wireless Telegraph Station – Last week a contemporary contained an account of the establishment of wireless telegraph apparatus in Lonan by the sons of Canon Quine... It was by means of this wireless station that the first news of the death of Mr Piermont Morgan reached the island.

The interesting enterprise, however, is likely to be stopped.

A few days ago the Government Secretary issued the following notice: Public attention is directed to the Wireless Telegraphy Act 1904 (an Act of the Imperial Parliament) which makes it an offence for any person to establish a wireless station, or to install or work any apparatus for wireless telegraphy, without a licence granted by the Postmaster-General.

The establishment, without a licence, of such station or apparatus within the Isle of Man renders the person offending liable to a penalty of £100, or to imprisonment, with or without hard labour for twelve months, and to the forfeiture, in either case of the apparatus – By order.'

Dono was obviously worried that the equipment would be taken away, as well as any secrets being divulged. Dono made some suggestions to Vess, who wrote back to Dono on April 4th 1913:

'I have carried out your ideas as to removing surplus apparatus to a place of safety.

Also, as to me telling anyone how it really works, I am ready for that. I have been asked by several already, but have waited until they gave me their idea and then said I supposed it was 'something like that'.

One chap asked me or rather told me that the wind must blow the sound away on stormy nights. "Of course," I said. I supposed it did. But I didn't tell him 'what sound'.'

Dono, aged 27, made a brief visit back to the island in May 1913.

He married his sweetheart, Margaret Ottewell, known simply as 'Daisy' (pictured), and they returned on the *Ben-My-Chree* to rented accommodation near to Dono's work in Liverpool.

Whilst at home on the island, Dono was able to experience the positive W/T accomplishment and wrote in his memoirs:

'With a tuned circuit, rectifier and head phones, we received 'Eiffel Tower', 'Poldu' in Cornwall, 'Cleethorpes' in Lincolnshire, 'Clifden' in Ireland, and some German stations.

The I.O.M. steamers and others in the area could also be heard at good readable strengths.

In thunderstorms accompanied by hailstones, the aerial could be dangerous; fast moving storms of hail could be heard coming and the aerial disconnected from the set; big sparks of dangerous volting often occurred in the house.'

A Licence for the wireless apparatus was eventually issued in June 1913.

It was a while before Albert Christian came back to the Vicarage to try receiving messages again, but he did.

John related his July visit to Dono:

'Albert Christian came up on Friday evening and took down a few pages of messages. He was a long time in getting into the swing of it again, or Vess had some difficulty in tuning up.

The installation is now in the store-room window – which is an advantage in several ways.

Vess thinks Christian has got deaf, and he is certainly insane on some points. He believes in being able to intercept wireless waves by means of the receiver or ear-piece of a telephone and an 'earth' as he calls it. I don't know what an 'earth' is; but I think it is something like this:

Excerpt from John's letter showing his sense of humour

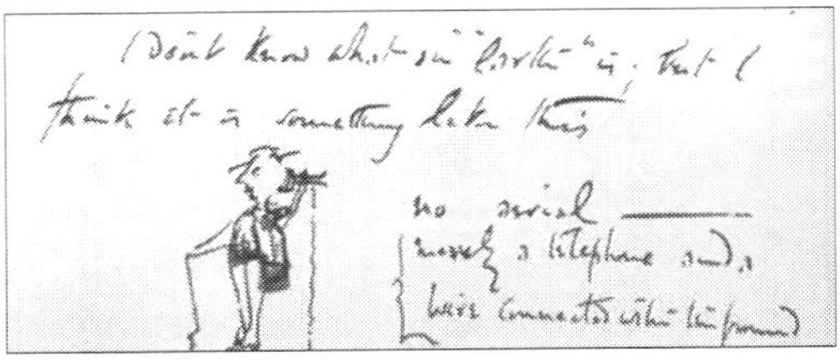
(Don't know what an "earth" is; but I think it is something like this

no aerial —
merely a telephone and a wire connected with the ground)

...No aerial – merely a telephone and a wire connected with the ground.

Christian, I think, was about to attempt to tell me that he could even do without the telephone and 'earth', but I looked at him and he modified his intended statement. He is not so enthusiastic now that sending paragraphs to the press is precluded.'

An inspection of the apparatus was not made until September 1913, when John wrote:

'The inspector of wireless came here yesterday accompanied by Tom Longden, the man who has charge of the pole and wire system of the Electric Tel. Co... He looked at the aerial and made some rough sketches, and at the interior apparatus. I could give him no information beyond vague generalities.'

To the average person, some written correspondence between the two brothers, Dono and Vess, would seem incomprehensible…

The following letter extract written by Vess in February 1914 is a good example, and caused some controversy later in 1915:

> *'Dear Dono, thanks for your letter & the information therein. I have for a long time been of the opinion that 'the Spanish Stn.' is Norddeich KAV. Perhaps our X* might hear his call some evening about 10pm W.L. about 900m. My coil is progressing favourably but of course slowly, as I am doing about 1 to 2 hours per night on my law now…'*

*Abbreviation for 'Christian'.

…Full letter: [Appendix b].

Work Prospects 1914

Lardy was determined to enjoy life – not take things too seriously, which at the age of 27 was hardly surprising. During a brief visit home from work in the Merchant Navy early in 1914, Lardy's behaviour was of some concern to John who wrote to Dono:

> *'Lardy's proclivity for the street in the evening, and his utter want of any wish within himself to push on his drawing etc., is a thing I do not know how to overcome: he cannot take a hint, any more than can a block of wood. Even if he attends to a thing for a time, he by and bye slips back into apparent forgetfulness of what was said.'*

However, soon after this, Lardy applied for work with the Manx Steam Packet Company, and at the beginning of June, he became one of their engineering crew. John wrote:

> *'I went to Douglas yesterday to meet Lardy – Mother had gone on by an earlier tram to meet Marge, and I found them at the boat about 2.30. When I went on board, Captain Keig, Blackburn, & Kelly Christian – Chief, were in a group together – though I did not notice them there. Keig caught me by the arm in a friendly way.*
>
> *After some chat, Blackburn said – "Your son is going to give us satisfaction; he shapes very well…!"*
>
> *Lardy seemed in good form. He said it was a fine change in the way of a job.'*

In the summer of 1914, Vess, aged 20, was working in the offices of Dickinson, Cruickshank & Co., taking the necessary exams leading to a career in Law, and he expected a further three years of such study.

Dono was living with his wife, Daisy, in Cheshire, working at Laird's in the Engineering Drawing Office as an engineer draughtsman. Their house, River View, New Ferry, was on the bank of the Mersey with a good view down to the river. Dono had an indoor aerial there with a crystal W/T set; during his lunch hour he could see the Isle of Man Steam Packet ships coming in and listened to their messages in Morse and their final call to Seaforth.

Dono's holidays began in the last week of July 1914 and he carried a new W/T receiver back to the Isle of Man and erected it in the Vicarage in time to hear the Kaiser's address to his troops after the declaration of war.

John, his wife, Dono and Vess were certainly amongst the first people in the Isle of Man to hear the news...

At the time, all three sons had good work prospects and a stock of experience, but their lives were about to take a dramatic turn with the outbreak of World War I.

Dono was recalled immediately to Laird's, sailing on the old Manx paddle ship *Mona's Queen*. Within a day or two the Post Office collected his W/T apparatus from Lonan Vicarage – never to be reinstated there again.

Already their complacent Edwardian existence was changing, but was this a good thing? Was the war viewed by young men as a great opportunity, and a way to break away from the doldrums of everyday life?

John's wife, Mary Jane Lindsay, was a forthright lady of Scottish descent who possessed some second-sighted intuition; apparently she foretold that her sons would survive the war and return home, but would her predictions hold true...?

...Mary Jane Lindsay was always referred to as 'Mother' in John's letters.

1914 Map

A rough guide to place names mentioned in John's early war letters

(Drawn by Julie Quine)

1914: War Breaks Out

On 28th June 1914 Archduke Franz Ferdinand of Austria-Hungary was assassinated by a Serbian nationalist. So entangled were the great powers in their alliances and military plans, that the conflict between Austria-Hungary and Serbia rapidly embroiled the whole of Europe with catastrophic consequences. It launched a war that would kill over 16 million men and wound at least another 20 million.

Due to an agreement drawn up in 1839, Britain had a duty to protect Belgium in the event of war, and as Germany invaded neutral Belgium, Britain too was drawn in on August 4th.

Many Manx men enlisted for training at the outbreak of war. John did not wish to tell his three sons that they should enlist, but he felt very strongly that they should do so... to fight for their country.

John went into Dickinson & Cruickshank's in Douglas to ask Mr Dickinson's approval for Vess to sign up with the Manx Volunteer Corps.

The only military units belonging to the Isle of Man in 1914 were the Officers Training Corps at King William's College, (two platoons formed in 1911), and one Company of the Isle of Man Volunteer Corps. The men were immediately mobilised and new recruits were quartered in the Drill Hall, Douglas.

Within days of the war announcement, the Home Office in London sent a deputation to the Isle of Man asking the Manx Government if accommodation could be found – for the internment of enemy aliens: Germans and Austrians who were resident in Britain. Cunningham's Holiday Camp in Douglas was suggested. The Isle of Man Volunteers were to be employed in guarding the first prisoners of war and escorting the men from the Manx ships to the Camp.

To provide some protection for the island, the naval authorities requested that Volunteer Corps manned war signal stations which were set up on Spanish Head in the south of the island, and at Port Cranstal in the north, as well as the existing Coast-guard stations at Knockaloe, Peel, Castletown, Ramsey, and Douglas. A guard was also required to protect the landing point of the sub-marine telegraph cable where it came ashore at Port Cornaa (near Corrany in the north east). Due to the extra trained men required around the island and for the Douglas Internment Camp, the

Lieutenant Governor requested the authority to raise a second Volunteer Company on August 15th. [3]

Regarding Vess joining the Volunteer Corps, John wrote:

> *'Mr Dickinson cordially approved! He said that his time would count as in office and that I need not concern myself further. Mr Dickinson even said he would be good for the cost of his outfit to some extent.'*

John told Vess to get a grip of all the details, to be ready for any special enlistment later.

On Dono's return to Laird's, he anticipated some hard work on new ships urgently required for war service... but it was not to be. He wrote in his memoirs:

> *'...instead a wonderful exciting phase of experience was to begin. I was appointed to the staff of Engineer, Captain J.D. Rees R.N., stationed in Sheffield (Cammell Laird). My work was the inspection of materials in Yorkshire for war ships building at the time. I was responsible for all the engineering materials for four destroyers and two light cruisers.'*

Dono was testing and passing materials for the new ships hurriedly being turned out for the Admiralty who had a limited number of destroyers at that time. John wrote to Dono suggesting that the new job suited him well:

> *'...it might have been made for you at this stage: it will give you a pull in experience, plus proof in the most tangible form of Laird's idea of you: their testimonial concrete. You are now in the employ of the Admiralty, or in effect on the Royal Naval Construction Corps Reserve.*
>
> *Lardy said to you that you could serve the country best with your professional knowledge in the construction of their ships – far more than with a rifle in a regiment. Now comes the opportunity to get the thoroughness of your capacities noticed... the trust in you by the Admiralty is not misplaced.*
>
> *Those firms must produce the right sort of stuff or you are not going to pass it!'*

John avidly read local newspapers, but definite news on the war front was not forthcoming. At the outbreak of war the Manx Press consisted of – *The I.O.M. Times*, *Examiner*, *Mona's Herald*, *The Ramsey Courier*, and the *Peel City Guardian*. Under the Defence of Realm Regulations, nothing was to be published which was seen to be of assistance to the enemy. [3]

John also read national and international papers and from these he surmised that:

> '...*these* (British) *Army Corps of ours, say 12,000, are already in Belgium.'*

> ...Germany had formulated the 'Schlieffen Plan' to cut off the Channel ports from Paris; the initial idea was to go through neutral Belgium to avoid fortifications along the French-German border.

John saw that the Germans were quickly advancing through France and Belgium. Operations had begun to halt the German advance, but it was obvious that stopping the formidable German Army was going to require an enormous effort, and that a quick German victory was a real possibility. John told Dono:

> *'All exaggerations allowed for, the Belgians have held up the German advance for a fortnight, and have forced a change of plan – viz. to enter France via south of the Ardennes.*
>
> *Thus – 100 miles due S.E. of Dunkirk in the Mense with Namur – a fortress, where the Mense bends from N. to E.N.E. They meant a strong army to pass round north of this through open country. This has not come off.*
>
> *Now they are going to drive a vast army through Luxembourg south of the Ardennes, south of Namur – part of their original plan. But is there room? For 100 miles from Namur is Verdun, the north end of the French 'Wall of China' line of fortresses.*
>
> *A significant report in today's newspapers says the Germans are entrenching Dusseldorf – on the Rhine. The place is a dozen miles below Cologne, and Cologne (on the Rhine) is about 100 miles due east of Ardennes. This seems to mean that they think it possible they may be driven back, and that the French may reach the Rhine.'*

John suggested that:

> *'A flying column, if it were possible, should dynamite the Cologne bridges. To my mind the feeling of security of which the English have been rightly accused, is less than the feeling of the security of the Germans – who have taken it for granted that all will be on French soil! Germany has had in view this absorbing of Holland & Belgium – and a seaboard from the Kiel Canal to the Straits of Dover.*
>
> *The French will use the bayonet on every opportunity. Their artillery is said to be good. My idea is they are best at offensive operations.'*

On August 14th the Battle of the Frontiers began between the French and German armies. The war was also widening in the East, as Russia invaded East Prussia on the 17th August; Japan declared war on Germany on 23rd, and Austria-Hungary began its offensive in Galicia (Russian Poland).

In the West, the British Expeditionary Force (BEF) had moved to Mons where the advancing Germans were encountered. The Battle of Mons took place on August 23rd, and the BEF withdrew from Mons towards Le Cateau and Landrecies.

John was speculating on what the Dutch might do:

> *'...Holland & Belgium – that and nothing else – is what Germany wants. The Dutch ought to throw in their lot with Belgium in the hour of strain: they ought to be in it now. They ought to have been in it already.'*

In August, Lardy, working on the Steam Packet ships, was paid off at Barrow, but told by Mr Kelly to report to Mr Blackburn, with assurances that his work had given the highest satisfaction. Blackburn required him at the beginning of September for overhaul of a steamer laid up in Douglas, and then to go across to Barrow.

Vess was training with the Manx Territorials in the Drill Hall Camp, and John wrote:

> *'He had his first day shooting at the range – 100 – 200 & 300 yards on Tuesday: ten rounds at each, total possible 40 points at each. Out of the 120 points possible he made 68.*
>
> *He is having his second day's shooting at the range today, and expects to go to a little picket camp at Cornaa next week.'*

John made frequent trips into Douglas by tram, and called at the Government Office and spoke to Lord Raglan – telling him of Vess's wish to go to the Front as a despatch rider, or in the signalling service. Lord Raglan said that he would do his best, and would write to his friend Col. Morgan of the Regiment of Engineers.

Recruiting on the island was well underway and John reported to Dono:

> *'Col. Thompson, the Recruiting Officer, visited Laxey* (mining village) *looking for men who were accustomed to working with explosives for the Sappers Corps... they raised not a man. Three had heard it was 36/- a week and went to Douglas, but they found it was 1/1 per day and did not join.'*

Regarding Vess, things were not looking very optimistic; he had developed pneumonia through his new work; he had only been in the Drill Hall Camp for two weeks. He was sent to Nobles Hospital in Douglas as the Officers thought he would get proper care there. On August 25th 1914, John wrote:

> *'I went in this morning to see Vess. Mother and Marge saw him this afternoon. His temperature was 104 degrees yesterday but had dropped considerably today. Dr Godson went in to see him today. This pneumonia is always to be regarded with anxiety.'*

Towards the end of August the newspapers reported the fall of the Belgian fortified city of Namur which John saw as:

> *'...serious if it means the forts, all and singular. Indeed it is not explicable, if it was certain that they were stronger than those of Liège. Either Colonel Leman was an exceptionally good commandant or the commandant of Namur exceptionally deficient; or – one knows not what to think! I assume the plan of the Allies will be a defensive one, shifting a bit back and fighting every position. The farther the Germans advance, the more laborious their supply.*
>
> *There ought to be reinforcements in a few weeks, enough to enable them to assume the offensive.'*
>
> ...Regarding British forces available, Britain's regular army of voluntary recruits was highly trained, but small. In August 1914 it consisted of 247,432 men. The army reserve of former soldiers who had completed service and could be called up – totalled 145,347, and Special Reserve – men with 6 months training, topped up with 2 weeks every year – totalled 63,933. By the end of the month nearly 300,000 British men had enlisted. [8]

John felt that every Parish district in the Isle of Man should be compelled to send its quota of men: e.g. Lonan Parish of 2,600 – 52; he wrote:

> *'Surely it is high time for a lightening Act of Parliament, enforcing conscription and the formation of a bigger force here. It is the right moment to do it. For the Isle of Man, population of 52,000 we should have 1040; we do not send a third of this.*
>
> *...I'm sorry to say that while I hear of about six or eight men from the Parish that have offered themselves, there is not one from Laxey. There might I think be a larger wage offered, and men up to 35 or so accepted. The absence of that offer does not excuse the lack of spirit.'*

On August 28th, WWI spread from land to sea with the first battle between British and German ships near Heligoland. Three German ships were sunk with 1200 German casualties. This battle intimidated the German Navy at the outset of war and led Kaiser Wilhelm to believe that his fleet should be used for defence rather than attack on the open seas.

John wrote:

> *'The affair on the right of Heligoland is satisfactory so far – though not a big affair – two or three cruisers and two destroyers accounted for, with no actual loss of a vessel on our side.*
>
> *I infer from the audacity of the 'scoop' right up to the fens of Heligoland, that the mine-sweeping by pairs of linked trawlers or so, has been going on vigorously for three weeks past.*
>
> *They would never have arranged a scoop which involved taking little cruisers into the Elbe approaches if they had not cleared it of mines!*
>
> *The moral effect of the scoop must be immense.'*

At the outbreak of war, two other German cruisers in the Mediterranean, the *Goeben* and *Breslau*, found themselves outnumbered by British ships.

It was imperative to stop German ships joining the Austrian fleet (to intercept French transport bringing colonial troops from Algeria to France) so British ships trailed the *Goeben* & *Breslau*. Gunfire broke out between *H.M.S Gloucester* and the two cruisers.

More British ships joined the pursuit, but thinking that the cruisers were trapped in the eastern Mediterranean, the chase was called off by Milne, Commander of the British Fleet, not suspecting that the German ships would head for Constantinople – where they became part of the Turkish Navy (Turkey was still a neutral country at this time).

John wrote:

> *'I hear the Goeben had her furnaces ruined, and that the Breslau was a good deal broken with shell. But as the English Admiral has been recalled from the Mediterranean, and the French Admiral taking command, some mismanagement took place!*
>
> *A store ship called the Emir is now at Gibraltar as a prize; I noticed it mentioned as what the Goeben & Breslau relied on.'*

German ships were intercepting merchant shipping to cut off fuel and food supplies being transported into Britain, and so British ships were sent to intercept them to try to stop their destruction of merchant shipping.

German cruisers in foreign waters had the advantage of speed; the British cruisers did not. John wrote:

'It is clear that there are 5 cruisers in the Pacific and several in the Atlantic, which when once found, are immediately lost again by virtue of their advantage in speed. The toll of merchant vessels must be considerable.'

...In the British Empire alone during the month of August 1914, the loss of merchant ships was over 46,000 gross tonnage. 'From the early months of war, methods were in place to try to protect merchant shipping – including giving approximate routes from departure to arrival, dispersing them over wide tracts of water, not using the same consistent routes, and zig-zagging rather than taking direct routes.' [7]

At the end of August the Germans halted the Russian attack in East Prussia at the Battle of Tannenberg. In the West, the Germans continued to advance, with the British incurring many losses at Le Cateau.

On August 29th John wrote:

'Things are in an 'anxious state' especially with regard to our field force at Maubeuge. The Germans have a concentrated ferocity of feeling and would fair destroy our force, for the intervention. I do not trust the French will be able to bring supports to enable our forces to withdraw to the next stand.

There is the sensational news of Russian troops that have been brought over and shipped from Liverpool, and by train from Leith to the south. I at once said, "From Archangel." It is possible that the French and English Government had a secret agreement with Russia that such troops would be available.

Our Government must have had an idea of what the Germans were up to – to account for this and other depositions of theirs. Browns Nautical Almanac gives 1870 miles from the Tyne to Archangel: this gives for 20 knot boat, less than 4 days. The Russians have a route from Moscow to Archangel: about 700 miles. This mobility would result in a large crowd of troops available for direct transport, and the northern seas are open. Mr Lansborough told me that he had heard of 30,000 as the number in transit, with 160,000 available.'

The newspapers did not mention troop movements, but Mr Williamson on the island told John that his son-in-law had seen 16 troop trains with Colonial troops passing from Holyhead into England at the end of August. John wrote:

'...If the reports are true, these reinforcements should now be well on the way to the French-British Front... There is no doubt but that the British have acted well and given the Germans a stopping.

The whole plan of campaign I have from the first clearly seen to be the one adopted: to fight, no action, but a defensive check action repeated again and again! Anything else would be a mistake.

I am a little surprised at the apparent want of adequate numbers planted down by the French, but my maps give no altitudes to enable me to see the Country as it is.'

On the island, one morning early in September, John just missed seeing a cruiser passing close to the coast, going towards Douglas; Alfred Tonkin told John that the cruiser was Russian, possibly on convoy service from the Gulf of Finland. On the subject of ships, John wondered why the British had not created a floating fort, self-propelling with a slow speed – inexpensive and devoted to armour and a few powerful guns. He wrote:

'The great battleship differs from this in having to have speed, and therefore having to be built as it is, as to be capable of travelling in a Biscay gale. But suppose these two were left out, and strength and gunpowder were all that needed to be concentrated on; the builder surely could make a fighting machine more formidable than a Dreadnought for special contingencies.'

...The Dreadnought was a new type of battleship built in the early 20th century – the first, launched by the Royal Navy in 1906, with heavy calibre guns and steam-turbine propulsion.

In pre-war Britain, the military threat of Germany resulted in the writing of espionage spy stories such as *The Riddle of the Sands* by Erskine Chalders. Consequently, on the outbreak of war, there was a great deal of journalistic fantasy in newspapers. John wrote to Dono on September 2nd:

'As every man in the street may in possibility be a spy, so every piece of work you do may be for an informer, giving in a report on your professional thoroughness or want of roughness.

Be severe in accuracy and fearlessly firm.'

John was of the opinion that Germany had:

'...originated, created, and launched this war deliberately; yet with face of brass it also deliberately enters on a campaign of asserting that England or Russia or France or other, caused and created the war! It is a strange phenomenon. It raises the question again of what human nature is in a Jap, Turk, German, etc. There is no common postulate or standard of moral idea. It is a question of whether lion, bear, eagle, or tiger will come out alive or dead after a physical tussle.

The people have lost all liberty and have got instead the privilege of sharing in the arrogant assertions, boastings, threats etc., of the Kaiser & his entourage of titled slaves! But the boastings and threats are the index of the littleness of measure of the autocrat as a man!

There is another thing characteristic of the Germans in contrast to the English – that is their taking to espionage or spy work as naturally as a cat to fish! There may be manufactured or censored statements published by English and by German authorities, but the motives behind these respectively are totally different in kind. The German mode goes on the ground that falsehood is a greater and better thing than truth.'

On the island, Vess was progressing after another slight setback, but John was not able to say how long it would be before he was back in the Territorials, and wrote to Dono:

'This morning we have been much relieved from the anxiety of the past 2 or 3 days. Dr Godson saw Vess yesterday and was not satisfied. He recommended a consultation with Dr Pantin.

They found him improved – the cloud has lifted considerably.'

Vess continued to improve, but he was still not allowed to talk or to get up from his hospital bed.

Lardy had resumed work on the *I.O.M. Steam Packet Company* ships, but was considering joining some force. John wrote on September 10th:

'I do not wish to say to him that he should do so: but as it was spoken of when I was in the room, I told him he ought to join where his special work would be of use and get the right pay, as engineer or in fitter service. There must be a large staff of repair and fitter men required with trained experience. I do not know that what I say receives any attention.'

Dono sent his father a *Daily Telegraph* contour map of N.E. France, which he used along with his atlas to track troop movements.

Regarding troop movements in England, John wrote to Dono:

'You remember my mentioning Russian troops passing through England? The Daily Mail scouts it with humorous ridicule and the other papers the same. An Italian paper had a note yesterday saying 250,000! On Tuesday I was told of Indian troops passing through or

embarking at Liverpool; this seems unlikely. Would they not arrive at Channel ports and trans-ship there – or Marseilles?

I think that considerable reinforcements have reached the Front.

The turning aside of the Germans from Paris was undoubtedly due to the presence of masses of allies, and the offensive now taken by the allies means that they have sufficient troops to make that move.

I felt confident that Kitchener would not have allowed a single English soldier to land in France except on condition of a plan of campaign which provided that the withdrawal should be maintained until enough troops were massed to take the offensive. I expect that the amassing of troops is so slow a business that we do not know what state of advancement it can make in a week, month, etc.

Indian troops are expected – I gather from today's Echo – via Paris, as if from the south!

But while Indian troops and all sorts of reinforcements are needed for the British divisions, I cannot understand why France has not more than seem to be in the Front line.'

...Kitchener was appointed Britain's Secretary of State for War on 5th August 1914.

It was a fact that at the beginning of the war, Germany had a larger ground force than the Allies. John wrote:

'Today's London Times gives a Russian (Petrograd) article in which it is said that the Germans had 7 divisions more than the allies in the heretofore movements.'

In the Isle of Man in early September, John's friend, Rector Kneale, had been at the Point of Ayre (the most northerly point of the I.O.M.). An official told him that they had been signalling to a Langland's boat to be cautious near Dunnet Head as there were mines laid or adrift there! John thought the loss of *R.M.S Oceanic* may have had some connection with this, as mines were being laid by the Germans overnight in shipping lanes, but the liner actually ran aground on September 8th due to poor navigation.

Meanwhile, in the west, the French finally halted the German advance in the First Battle of Marne (6th – 12th Sept.) In the East the Germans continued to gain ground, defeating the Russians at the Masurian Lakes.

On the island, Vess continued to improve satisfactorily, but had a slight set back and Dr Godson went in to see him again.

On September 11 1914, John wrote:

'When I was seeing Vess yesterday he said the Dr had told him that the German intention was not to touch Paris first, but to work on a mathematically calculated plan from Metz as centre, and that this had been so far done to time. But I am not convinced. I think 'showing off' is so much a characteristic of the Kaiser that some such performance with the eyes of the universe fixed on it and on him may be quite possible. The spectacular plan may have been some other geometrical figure, as in the arrow path: Brussels! Paris!! Adequate troops to enforce their plan, if given to the Allies, would be spectacular too, though a spectacle by no means the object.'

The weather had broken in the Isle of Man and was forecast to be just as bad on the Continent in the 'Race to the sea' in the trenches: with gales and heavy rain. John wrote on September 17th:

'It will be bad for the Allies' forces in the field, but worse for the Germans.

It has occurred to me that the present gales will render it difficult for the Fleet to coal at sea: but probably they will arrange to withdraw the sections to quiet waters for that purpose.'

...The British Fleet were situated in the north of the UK in the Firth of Forth to protect northern trade routes and deter German shipping encroaching into British waters.

Regarding troops, John continued:

'Though we hear nothing of it, there must be a steady flow of reinforcements to the British Expedition.

The Laxey Postmaster, an old soldier, whose son has been seven years in the army and has joined again, tells me that he has a letter from his son, from St Nazaire – at the mouth of the Loire near Nantes: consequently I infer that troops are being landed there, which certainly for railway transport to the Front is a good point, and avoids the congestion on other lines, as well as escapes notice.

The papers mention Algerian troops but say nothing of Indian.

One paper absolutely denies the presence of Russians. However there are reasons for such information as we would like to have, not being made public.

In the most recent Belgian activities they have larger artillery – in agreement with your mention of 80 pounder batteries going across.

A report about a considerable surrender of Germans on their extreme right was in one of yesterday's papers: it ought not to be improbable. Till surrenders on a big scale are reported we shall not know how the Germans stand.'

John found the Russian campaign in Poland in mid-September very difficult to follow; his maps did not enable him to determine on what objective their widely extended line was concentrating.

He made the following apt observation:

'A soldier in an army ceases to know anything of the campaign as a whole; so does even a regimental officer. Geographical knowledge becomes like a lost and forgotten thing. Only the sun and the stars to say whether one is facing north, south, east or west, remains to draw inferences from.'

John was sceptical about German Officers:

'I should think it likely that many German officers have been shot by their own men: for notwithstanding the animating feeling against the enemy, the private soldiers in the German army have many humiliations in their memories.

(I knew an ex-soldier who had gone through the war of 1870 in a German regiment. He told me that the first thing they did was to rip open every drawer and cupboard in French country houses and pack any valuables in their knapsacks. No German soldier could resist a clock. They carried away every clock they found.)'

The war had now been in progress for just six weeks. Throughout August and September it was rumoured that the German army advancing through Belgium, had terrorized Belgian civilians, killing thousands, and looting and burning towns – violating the 1907 *Hague Convention* – prohibiting punishment of civilians and destruction of property. Of course some rumours were concocted to persuade men to sign up, but many were bona fide. The German army carried out civilian executions with the purpose of breaking the spirit of resistance and striking terror into the heart of the population.

...It was estimated that Belgium suffered from around 60,000 civilian deaths and 40,000 military by 1918.

The gravity of the war was realised in the Isle of Man. On September 18th 1914 in the first sitting of Manx Parliament since the outbreak of war, the *House of Keys* immediately proposed a motion for £10,000 to be paid to His

Majesty's Government to help with war expenses. The motion read:

> '...Profoundly convinced of the righteousness of Britain's cause, and of the absolute necessity for prosecuting the war to a successful issue, as well as in the interests of civilisation and international freedom as of the British Empire, the Court declares its anxiety to do all in its power and is convinced that Manx people will readily make any sacrifice in aid of the national cause.
>
> The Court rejoices in the fact that numbers of Manxmen are serving in his Majesty's Navy and Army, and particularly desires to record its satisfaction that the patriotism of so many young Manxmen has led them to offer themselves for these services in the present grave crisis in the history of the Empire...' [22]

Regarding the proposal of the grant, Mr Crennel began:

> "We are met today under the shadow of a great war... I am sure we all find it difficult to realize this...
>
> England, and still more, the Isle of Man, seems very far removed from this. We seem to be living in a different world. Why is this? It is because of our fortunate position in being surrounded by the sea... controlled by our incomparable and invincible British Navy...
>
> ...If Germany wins, the terms imposed on France and Belgium will be severe, but the terms imposed on England will be absolutely crushing... Suppose 10,000 or 20,000 Germans should be landed to-day in the Isle of Man... We should see our country devastated; pillage, burning, insult, outrage: rampant – our freedom gone..." [22]

After these grave and very serious statements and more, the motion was seconded. There was also a discussion in the *Keys* of the alarm felt in some quarters regarding German internees coming to the island to Cunningham's Camp. In the Isle of Man it was now common knowledge that an internment Camp had been secured in Douglas, and local people had their views on this. John wrote:

> *'It seems that 2000 or 3000 German prisoners are to be interned at Cunningham's Camp. The place is being wired all round. Most people here think the Calf of Man would be the better place. But they must be sheltered and fed. I expect Cunningham – who is a keen man of business – has made a tender to cater for them. If anybody can do it cheap and make money out of it, it is Cunningham. Doubtless the authorities will place a sufficient guard on them.'*

The first 200 enemy alien prisoners arrived in the Isle of Man by ship on September 22nd, and were escorted by the Isle of Man Volunteer Company to Cunningham's Camp on Victoria Road near Falcon Cliff where they were housed in tents. With internees arriving daily, the Camp became congested and a larger Camp was soon required.

Cunningham's Holiday Camp, Isle of Man M.N.H. [1]

The first place tried for a few prisoners and guards was the empty 'Bungalow Hotel' at the base of Snaefell (the highest peak in the I.O.M.). Despite the remoteness of the Camp, some prisoners, due to lack of security, followed the tram track down the hillside to Laxey, where they visited shops and public houses and were offered drinks; unfortunately some of the guards who followed them became inebriated and had to be carried or helped by the prisoners back up to Camp! [4]

The search for another suitable camp continued.

John constantly advised his sons regarding better work opportunities and prospects. Dono, still working at Laird's, was wondering if his experience would be of benefit elsewhere in the ongoing battle. John told Dono to look at the Navy list in the Sheffield library and advised him:

> *'Keep on the lookout and make enquiries with a view to getting classed in R.N.R....You will find the London Times worth taking; the Gazette information is important (I find its articles as good as anything in any of the papers).*
>
> *Curiously I found in the Liverpool Echo decidedly the most illuminating account of the movement at the beginning of the month, when the Allies from defensive and withdrawal action suddenly assumed the offensive! The Times had the best article on the effect of that offensive and the Marne Battle on the French army, especially on the French right.'*

Towards the end of September, after a fine spell, the weather on the island deteriorated again. Vess was progressing but still in hospital, and Lardy had joined Kitchener's Army.

Lardy in uniform

John wrote:

'Lardy crossed on Friday to go to Monmouth to join the Monmouthshire Regiment.

He finished at the Isle of Man Steam Packet Company on Sep 19th and entered his name for this Regiment on Monday 21st – there were none being taken on for the Reg. Engineers: but I think this is a good regiment to exchange out of into the Reg. Eng.'s.

Lord Raglan (Lt. Governor) *wrote a letter to Col. Lindsay Morgan, who is a friend of his, saying that Lardy had much experience both of railway & marine engineering, and would be useful in the transport, traction and railway section of the regiment, suggesting he should be attached to that section. This to some little extent would start him favourably.'*

...Lord Raglan was previously Colonel of the Monmouthshire Regiment in Wales. His sons were already on the Front line and wounded – one had his arm broken, the other his teeth or jaw.

Lardy soon settled into the Camp at Monmouth: 'Sapper 7019, R.M. Royal Engineers Camp.'

Regarding Russians in Belgium and Indian troops in France, John wrote to Dono:

> *'It appears from Mr Asquith's speech at Dublin of Friday Sep 25, that the first contingent of Indian troops were expected to land at Marseilles that day.*
>
> *This looks as if the artillery man was mistaken on that point. Do you think he was right about the Russian force?*
>
> *It seems strangely obscure...'*

Late in September, John thought that *S.M.S. Emden*, a German light cruiser raiding ships in the Indian Ocean, had been caught by one of the Australian fleet, and he believed Harrison's had lost one British ship in the raid.

...*S.M.S. Emden* was one of the fleet of five German cruisers; she sank a Russian cruiser and French destroyer later in October and met her fate later in November when she was attacked in the Cocos Islands by *H.M.A.S. Sydney*.

John commented:

> *'...It does seem strange that the Government has allowed such freedom in respect of Welsh coal going off to these German cruisers.'*

Fortunately German submarines were rarely seen around British shores during the early days of the war, but they were becoming problematic on trade routes.

...At the outset of war, it was thought that Germany had 28 submarines, but their fast production rates continued to outnumber the number of German submarines destroyed throughout the war years until 1917. [7]

Nets were seen as a possible way of protecting ports and narrow straits from submarine attack. Dono had designed a submarine net and wrote to his father asking his opinion.

John replied on September 29th (his first mention regarding this subject):

> *'Your letter is most interesting. I have thought of this use of a net – rather as a detector than a stopper for submarines.*
>
> *But your question – 'what force is necessary to hold a submarine?' – was the unknown factor in my problem.*
>
> *To know that is to solve the problem – plus the fact that a loose hung cloth will stop a bullet – a fishing rod that bends with a reel that slacks, will hold a heavy salmon on a line as fine as a hair. So that a net, giving somewhat, will hold with a strength far beyond its rigid resistance. On this could be achieved a practical solution of the one menace of the war.*

Would it not be possible to get it to the notice of perhaps someone in high quarters? It is extremely simple: its simplicity sufficient to account for its having been possibly overlooked.

It is necessary to decide on the strength of rope to be employed in the net itself... The experiment should be made in the Firth of Forth – say on the line of the Bass Rock. Could your net prevent the big submarine fish swimming in there? If so – then extend the scheme.

I don't see why – if they can sweep the North Sea of mines – they shouldn't much more drastically net it for submarines. What is £100,000 – if it saved one cruiser? I don't know what to do: but I think I'll write a confidential letter to Lord Raglan. If Churchill caught at an idea of this sort, he could put it through.'

Drawing of submarine and net by John

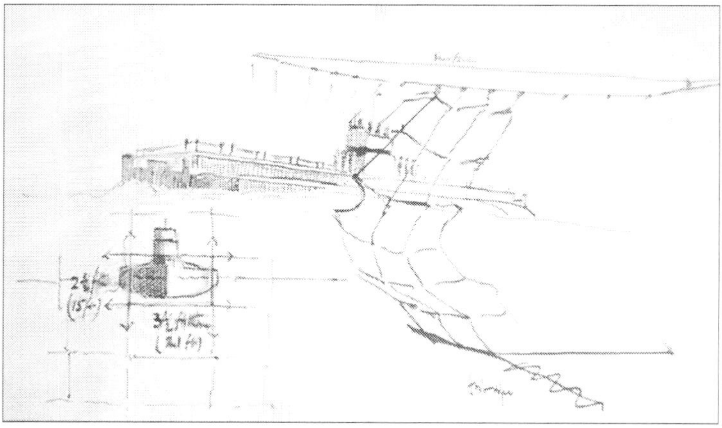

It didn't take John long to make up his mind, and at the beginning of October he wrote to Dono:

'I have sent the substance of your notes on the 'submarine net' to Lord Raglan – with an explanatory note, and have asked him to consider how the idea strikes himself, so that possibly he might convey it direct to an influential personage – who would not hesitate to put it to the test... I recommend you make a careful study of the best size of mesh and the strength of the net rope to be decided on! I advise you to work out by sketches measured to approx. scale, a submarine approaching, and in successive positions in a net. For this reason I think size & shape of mesh important... What about the floats – what size

necessary, what number per mile, to suspend your net? Get approx. size of your fish before you decide on shape & size of mesh, strength etc.

I am absolutely confident that whether it ever reaches testing or not, your idea is a machine that will do its work.'

Submarines were the main subject of John's letters to Dono at this time. Dono and John frequently discussed in detail how submarines functioned, and how to discourage or stop them.

One of the best offensive measures against enemy submarines was the mine, if laid in sufficiently large numbers.

'Unfortunately even by January 1917 the British did not have a mine that was satisfactory against submarines. The Germans were well aware of this fact.' [7]

John wrote on October 3rd:

'This evening the London Times Naval Correspondent – speaking of the new mines laid in North Sea – assumes that submarines are as liable as above-water ships to strike them, and adds:

"But as I said last week, submarines cannot see under water, and their activities may be considerably curtailed by the use of mines."

...I take it that they cannot see, first from want of light, and also because the water outside their ports (if they have ports) is in wavy strata caused by the push of its being parted from the bow, just as a slight ripple on the surface of a deep and still transparent pool blurs the vision for any object at the bottom of the pool. At night and by day, I am sure they could not see a net.'

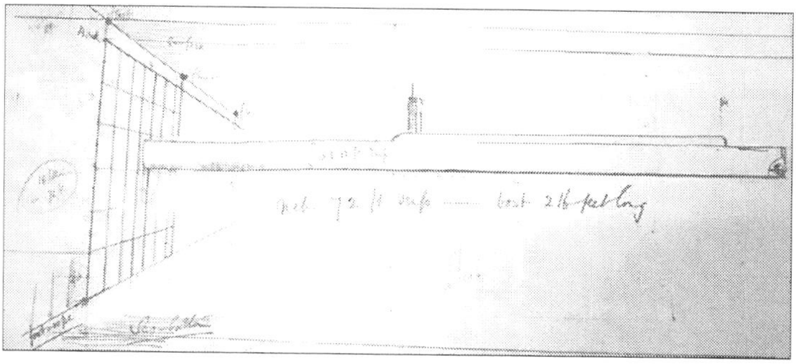

John's idea for a net

One day when John was in Douglas, he met William Knox – Dono's former boss at Knox's engineering firm. Regarding the meeting, John wrote:

'Willy Knox told me that submarines had outlook ports. He told me of his having read in the 'Engineer', accounts of all sorts of experiments at Plymouth in which the submarines failed all attempts to stop them with nets (which means that tests were already being carried out). *They even slid (or leapt he said) over booms, like fish (probably he had mullet in mind) getting over a circling net. His idea was to detect their presence by water telegraphy detectors (Sir William Prices): the noise of their screw etc., being heard by a detector in the side of the ship.*

His thought – that nothing could be done – because everything had been tried for years...

I think your loose and pliant net needs trying – but not to immediately stop the 'fish'.

I see by the Daily Telegraph, that Germany has 2 classes of submarine – 890 tons displacement under water, and 300...

I'm afraid the submarine is a very large bodied fish around the shoulders, and implies a very big mesh... the London Times had an article on the subject.

But your net is far simpler, and I believe far more effective – also less cost!

I see that Mr Horton has accounted for a second German vessel by the active use of the English submarine he commands.

It is not all going to be on one side.'

By October 7th, Vess was progressing gradually from his pneumonia, and allowed to get up for short periods. By the middle of October, he was allowed to sit in an armchair near a window, but was still rather weak.

The new ship orders placed at the beginning of the war by the Admiralty due to shortage of British sea-going war vessels, stimulated more work for manufacturers. John wrote to Dono:

'Very glad to hear that the new cruiser order continues your work at Sheffield.

Glad also that you meet managers of these big firms. Most important experience in meeting men of this class and position...'

During a factory inspection, Dono noticed that all the steel forgings had the 'Three Legs of Man' symbol stamped on them (as on the Isle of Man flag). He asked the management the reason for this; they didn't know... Years later Jonathan Kermode told Dono the reason – he had agreed that the 'three legs' should be stamped on every forging of his in lieu of payment for an oil-fired annealing furnace which he had invented and supplied [*Isle of Man Weekly Times, 6 June 1969*].

Regarding Germans in the U.K., John warned Dono:

> *'...I should not spare any German – and the case of the two revolvers left with the lady in Birkenhead should not be allowed to sleep. Your suggestion to the lady to take the things entrusted to her to the Bank was good enough – either that or to the Police.*
>
> *The Germans have abused the boundless liberty & freedom of this country accorded to them.'*

John felt the situation with regard to espionage, was becoming serious if it involved people who had previously held responsible posts. John reported to Dono:

> *'One of the Lords of (German) Admiralty is under serious suspicion or arrest, I hear, as one of M. of S.* (Ministry of Spies).
>
> *No question the German secret service and spy system is efficient. That is one of the things that England is not good in.'*

...Injury had prevented Carl Hans Lody continuing a career in the German Navy; he became a spy. MI5 knew he was working for German Naval Intelligence. From 27th August 1914, Lody was in the Edinburgh area, noting and reporting British naval movements to Germany, (particularly the British Fleet in the Firth of Forth). MI5 monitored all messages and intercepted his; some misleading messages were allowed to go through to Germany – i.e. that 'a large number of Russian troops had landed in Scotland' (causing concern for the German military).

Lody's arrest was ordered when he wrote an un-coded letter of use to the German Navy. He was captured in Ireland on Oct. 2nd 1914 and convicted of espionage. On 6th November 1914 Lody was shot by firing squad at the Tower of London – the first execution there for 167 years. The details of the case were given to the Press to deter other spies. German archives reveal that 120 spies were sent to Britain during WWI. 65 of them were caught. [15]

John continued:

> *'I am sure the authorities have been blind if it is true that over the Firth of Forth any alien is there, or along the whole east coast, or anywhere from which ships or troops move.*
>
> *The Government agents were mighty serious, solemn and drastic in dismantling our wireless, and to absolute neglect of those that mattered. Not a spot on the east coast should be allowed to escape frequent and constant attention. There are plenty of loyal people that would count it all joy to clear out these aliens: but there's Mr McKen-*

na, or some other, who pronounces that everything has been done, when practically the very keenest aliens remain undealt with. Why? Because the really formidable are the keenest, and will evade detection longest!

There have been rumours in the air, of treason – great English man shot in Paris for pro. German acts – something of the same kind in England etc. The silence of the papers seemed to confirm it. I explained ebullition of anti-alien feeling as due to these and like rumours current in England, not in the papers, and not reaching here.

It is unpleasant if such things are true: but they will not affect the main issues.'

Regarding the laying of a submarine net, John bore in mind the fact that spy trawlers were at sea:

'...To set a net, one must safeguard against all spy trawlers, Dutch etc. The Germans, arguing from their blustering spirit, are people certain to be affected by panic feeling out of all proportion to a disaster experienced by them! Though they may conceal it by a vapour, it will be there.

The loss of a few submarines by a new 'surprise engine', will shift back the line to be netted, nearer & nearer to their own base...'

Thousands of German troops arrived in Ypres, Belgium, on October 7th, but were driven out of the town by the Allies days later. The Battle of Ypres began.

At the end of the 'Race to the Sea' in mid-October, the Germans reached the Belgian coast; both sides dug-in, establishing the stalemate of trench warfare that was to last for the next four long years: two lines of trenches stretched from the North Sea down to the Swiss border – lines that were separated by a tract of land known as 'no-man's land'; this was known as the Western Front. Once this long line of battlefront was fixed, air reconnaissance became a major importance in helping the artillery on the ground.

...The British military air wing was much smaller than that of the French or Germans.

In 1910, Haldane (Secretary of State for War) had said:

'When a new invention like the submarine or the motor, comes to light, the Englishman is usually behind. Give him a few years and he has not only taken care of himself in the meantime, but is generally leading.

As it was with these inventions, so I suspect it will prove to be with aircraft.'

...During the war years, the air service grew rapidly; as did rivalry between countries. Germany had her airships, and France, aeroplanes. Britain was quite unprepared at the outbreak of war; in 1914 a mere 150 aeroplane machines were available for immediate British war service at Netheravon. [24] Some Royal Flying Corps planes were being used for reconnaissance work in conjunction with the British Expeditionary Force, but men on the ground were often baffled by the sight of planes to begin with, and a few were accidentally shot down by their own troops.

The Battle of Ypres continued (19 October to November 22) and the Germans tried to break through. In the Middle-Eastern theatre, Turkey entered the war on the side of Central Powers on October 28th.

Back on the island, at the beginning of November, Vess was finally out of hospital and back at home, and John reported to Dono:

'He gets out every day, morning and afternoon – though yesterday was so bad a November day, raining & foggy, that he only got one short walk. Today he took his gun with him and had a shot at lapwings.'

In November 1914, the newest Manx boat *King Orry*, was commandeered by the British Admiralty and re-fitted as a patrol ship to intercept and challenge any ships in the North Sea thought to be carrying supplies to the enemy: ships flying flags of other nationalities often concealed fuel or goods for use by German ships. Incidentally, Dono had worked on the plans of *King Orry* in the Drawing Office at Laird's prior to the war in 1913; it was one of the first vessels to have geared turbine engines.

Lardy wrote in good spirits from the training Camp at Monmouth. John wrote:

'He got a 1st Certificate in shooting – though he did badly at 500 yards. It was a wet day and the light bad. He has put down his name to try to get into a group that are to go to Longmoor for additional training. He does not know if he will get into that lot.

He thinks it would mean an earlier move to the Front.'

...Longmoor (in Hampshire), and part of Bordon were used for training R.E. (Railway Engineers) and road personnel, using the Instructional Military Railway. The No.2 & No.3 Monmouth Railway Companies embarked on November 11th 1914: 10 Officers and 290 men of other ranks.

There were few designated Railway Construction Companies contributing to the war effort at the beginning of the war. [14]

John went to see Lord Raglan regarding Dono's submarine net ideas, and reported to Dono:

'I had a talk with Lord Raglan on Wednesday about the net. He was more fully interested than before.

He said that he had sent my former brief notes to an Admiralty friend, but had not heard from him. His idea was that they were very much preoccupied with department work.

I see, since Admiral Fisher came in, that Mr Percy Scott is recalled to active service.'

The war at sea began to settle into a pattern. The two main fleets were regarded as too precious to risk in speculative actions and tended to remain at their bases: the British Grand Fleet at Scapa Flow, and the German High Seas Fleet at Kiel. Britain resorted to its traditional tactic and imposed a blockade upon Germany to prevent merchant supplies going into the country. Both sides laid mines, and there were to be a number of minor engagements between smaller ships.

Around Scapa Flow, there was a growing fear of spies. On November 1st the Postmaster and 39 other staff of Lerwick Post Office were arrested on confidential Admiralty orders and their homes searched. John noted:

'...The arrest of the Orkney (Lerwick) post office staff, and your last letter with reference to that region, may not be without connection. Lerwick Harbour, or Lerwick Bay, is very fine I'm told: and the people up there rather alien, resenting being called Scotch, and many of them with foreign names. Mr Quine of Maughold lighthouse told me you would see those ships flying 8 or so foreign flags.'

...The P.O. staff were detained in cramped conditions in Lerwick prison (there were only 11 free cells at the time) until 7th Nov. – but not treated as prisoners. It was initially suspected that secret correspondence for the Grand Fleet had been tampered with, and a spy was in their midst. The assumptions were later proved unfounded. [16]

At the start of the war, German warships at sea used any opportunity to attack British merchant shipping; the Royal Navy tried to intercept them. At the beginning of November, two British ships, *H.M.S. Monmouth* and *H.M.S. Good Hope*, had been sent to seek out the German squadron, but being outnumbered, both British ships were destroyed in the 'Battle of Coronel' – all lives lost. The battle, off the coast of Chile (Valparaiso), involved the German ships *Scharnhorst* and *Gneisenau*, *Dresden* (sister ship to the *Emden*), *Leipzig* & *Nurnberg*. The attacks were viewed with horror by the British Admiralty and revenge was on the cards! John commented:

'This news about the engagement off Valparaiso is fair comment on the necessity of weight of guns, and speed. It was quite out of the question for our ships to do much or even anything; 6" & 4.5" against 8.8". My contention has been to have in home waters, not big ships, but big guns: the monitors have done good service, but they were designed for a foreign Government.

What you want is a machine, a ship only so far as she is a machine for sea going: for the rest a firing machine.'

Later in November, John saw an article in the *London Times* regarding the Fleet, and wrote:

'It is pointed out that the Germans have kept in view 'speed', and 'weight' of gun as the things on which to concentrate attention, not size of ship: i.e. to have the ship stronger – as an effective fighter in proportion to size or tonnage than ours!

I have had this idea in my mind for years – that speed should be got for all vessels where speed really counts – that is, in foreign services; but – that speed may not be always essential in all powerful vessels. Tremendously powerful monitors, where speed was not an object and 15 to 18 knots, nay even less might be enough, has seemed to me a line along which designing might go... Ships for special functions must be designed for their special kind of work...'

Sitting in his study, John realised that in the island, everyday lives were still largely untouched by the war. He commented:

'There is so little difference from the normal state of things here, that if it were not for our reading newspapers, and hearing reference to the war in conversation, a person waking up from a 3 months sleep would not know there was a war. This is not as it should be! I hope there will be conscription.'

As colder weather set in, the cramped tent accommodation of the Douglas Internee Camp caused dissatisfaction among the internees. The Home Office had sent another deputation from London to the Isle of Man to look for a suitable site for a larger camp where more prisoners from the U.K. could be sited. The increase in the number of internees was fuelled by the Press painting all Germans as potential spies. *The Times* reported on October 15th:

'In their eager absorption of the baser sides of militarism, the Germans seem to have almost converted themselves into a race of spies.'

For their safety and that of others, the remaining Germans in the U.K. were to be interned as quickly as possible.

Knockaloe farm site of 22 acres was chosen for the purpose of accommodating more internees, as the area had been previously used for the British Army's summer training camp. New posts at Knockaloe had been filled. John wrote to Dono regarding his artist friend:

> *'Mr Archibald Knox has got his post of a censor of the letters etc. received and sent from the aliens' camp at Knockaloe: he goes there on Monday. We hear there is to be a military camp for soldiers in training somewhere there.'*

> ...A great deal of work was required before men could be sent to the Knockaloe Camp, which was initially intended to accommodate up to 5000 prisoners. With a circumference of 3 miles, 695 miles of barbed wire were eventually used in its fences. Only men, not women, were interned during WWI. The Imperial Government paid the expenses of the Volunteers required to guard the internees. [22]

On November 17th 1914, the Knockaloe Camp received its first 432 internees. [www.knockaloe.im]

Meanwhile, on the same day as Knockaloe opened its doors, complaints were made by prisoners in the Douglas Camp – as weevils were found in the rice. The following day, November 18th, some internees refused to eat their food – meat, potatoes and vegetables. The day after there was a food riot in the Camp which then held 3,307 prisoners.

The soldiers guarding the prisoners fired up in the air to begin with, which made little impact. Guards then began firing towards the men as the situation became more dangerous, resulting in five prisoners being shot dead. [3] The riot and deaths speeded up the necessity of moving some of the internees to the Knockaloe Camp and there was an inquest into the deaths.

John Bull was a U.K. Sunday newspaper/magazine established in 1820, depicting a national personification of Great Britain, England in particular, including political cartoons. John was obviously an avid reader and wrote:

> *'Regarding the 'easy' discipline at the Douglas Camp, John Bull is expected to have something pungent this week. Ladies went to the Camp to teach the 'dear Barons' to knit. J.B is expected to publish their names. It is even said that some of them took shirts etc., intended for our soldiers in France, up there for these 'dear aliens'. This is not business, it is insanity – should it be true... The way in which the Douglas Camp 'row' got out was – I understand – that the I.O.M. Times rushed*

out a special edition of its half-penny paper on the evening of the day the affair occurred. It published nothing about it in the next day's issue: hence I assume the paper was warned, but too late.'

By November, Dono's firm had been taken over by the Admiralty, but he was still wishful to obtain a Surveyor-ship post in the firm of Lloyds, unless his work led to a permanent position in the Service – possibly an Engineering Lieutenancy. He had finalised his 'net' ideas. John replied to Dono on November 18th:

'I'm glad you thought I had firm the essential substance of the 'net' in the notes.

I have since thought most definitely that you ought to apply forthwith for the Engineer Lieutenancy. Your knowledge and experience will be very much greater than a crowd of the younger men who get these Commissions.

I'm glad to know that the staff is now definitely taken over by the Admiralty. Does it not give you a different status?'

German ships seemed to be encroaching nearer to Manx waters in whatever guise they could. John tells the interesting story:

'I was at St Maughold's (Masonic Lodge, of which John was a member) *last evening. Mr Brew told me that they have caught a Grimsby trawler with English Skipper & German crew, and have her at Belfast. The theory is that she was captured by a German vessel, all her crew but the Skipper transferred as prisoners – a German crew put on board, and the Skipper, by price of a pistol put to his head, compelled to accompany them in the service of mine-laying probably. It is not in the newspapers of course. The Malin Head minefield is where she is supposed to have been at work.*

Harrison's have some of their ships in Transport Service, probably over a dozen, some in the N. Atlantic trade. I hope the South Atlantic raiders (Karlsruhe, etc.) will be picked up very soon now.'

...these were German ships responsible for attacking merchant shipping.

By mid-November, Lord Raglan had sent off Dono's net 'memo' to his colleague in London. It is assumed that Dono received a reply from the Admiralty, as John wrote:

'I don't draw any inference from the letter you have received, beyond the fact that through Lord Raglan's interesting himself, it has reached the Admiralty. Whether you ever hear anything further is quite a

question. But the menace is so definite, and the way to deal with it so feasible and inexpensive, it is possible they may try it...

Now much will depend on the preconceived ideas of the official entrusted to report on your memo. I suggest that you reply – to create a presumption in favour of your competence, and also to show that you are in Admiralty service!'

John Suggested that Dono should write the following letter to the Admiralty Whitechapel, S.W.:

'18 Norfolk Road, Sheffield. 24th Nov. 1914...G 22081/14/25369

Sir, I beg to acknowledge the honour of the communication, dated 19th Nov 1914, which my Lord Commissioners of the Admiralty have been pleased to order to be addressed to me, in the matter of suggestions for a submarine net.

I beg leave to enclose the accompanying data with regard to my training and experience in engineering work, and present employment in a department of Admiralty work, in the event of your requiring to make further reference to the matter.

I have the honour to remain, Sir, Your obedient servant – J.L.Q.'

On November 27th 1914, John wrote to tell Dono about Lardy, who was still training at Monmouth:

'Lardy writes in good spirits... he thinks he will be in the no. 5 detachment, to go in the fortnight before Xmas or the fortnight after. He calls it a 'Siege Co'. Of course the outfit has motor carriages, motor cars, motor cycles, common cycles etc.

His shooting is good. If his mathematics had been better – his geometry etc., I fancy he would stand a chance of promotion. I think his arithmetic is sound, but they had trigonometry for advancement. He has been taken notice of by a Mr Bathurst M.P., an officer in the regiment, and has also met an officer in the regiment who was in S. America on Andes Railway work. He found Lardy could speak Spanish, and was very friendly.'

Meanwhile, Vess had been to the doctor for a check-up and finally returned to training in the Camp in Douglas. John reported:

'Vess went back to camp on Monday after seeing Dr Richardson.

He has had a dreadful week in respect of weather – wind, rain, cold the whole week.

...If he gets this week over well, I shall not be so anxious. He is in more comfortable night quarters at least.'

John had heard of a large warship *H.M.S. Bulwark* blown up at Sheerness Harbour early on November 26th 1914 by an explosion in her magazine. Only 12 men were saved out of a crew of 780. [17] He wrote:

'Perhaps this will convince Mr McKenna that there is such a thing as German spies.'

John continued:

'I see our ships have been smashing Zeebrugge. I have thought that the German submarines must have fired a good many torpedoes and missed – in those waters.

Lord Raglan said to me, "The German Generals are too old!"

Apparently the Russian Grand Staff understand strategy. Probably they have young generals who had experience in the Jap war and are now getting their chance in divisional work. Only by the development on the Eastern Front was it possible for us to realize what a large order that campaign was!

The German idea seems to be, to boldly assert the point blank opposite of the facts, as the best way to create an impression of doubt and even complete uncertainty, where they cannot perhaps expect to be believed! It is to treat the world's public opinion, as artillery treats masses of infantry – viz. demoralize by shock, to shake by sheer weight of contradiction!

I hope our Government and the French are creating artillery beyond anything they have had heretofore.'

Towards the end of November, John wrote of the operations on the Eastern Front:

'There seems to be enough evidence to believe that the Russians have broken the Germans a second time in Poland – though particulars have not come to hand. Moreover it is extremely difficult with our maps, to understand the eastern operations – or to understand operations on so large a scale. What was once a battle of the first magnitude is now a subsidiary operation. The Russians have probably a great advantage in far more numerous cavalry.'

...German army corps broke through a section of Russian defence. The Russians in a countering rush, drove them southward and practically surrounded them between Lodz and Lowicz. [17]

Meanwhile, soldiers were being transported from Britain to France, and Dono had seen that a German submarine was in the vicinity of Havre. John replied to Dono:

> *'This is a menace to troop-ships. This is the place where your net – if they had a hundred miles or so of it in operation – would be useful...'*

At the beginning of December 1914, John was also speculating about rifle production:

> *'I think the output of rifles must be more than 10,000 per week – or the work could not be done! Would it be safe to say that 1,000,000 rifles existed on Aug 1? Even then the work could not be done. I read in one of the newspapers that one small arms factory had an output of 800 per day before the war, and had increased its output to 2500 per day. This would give for a year of 365 days 912,500 – not enough. Surely we have several small arms factories. Possibly the gun-smith meant 10,000 per day – which would give 1,000,000 in 14 to 15 weeks. Surely we have been able to turn out this number since Aug 1.'*

On his return to training in Douglas, Vess (shown in his Volunteer uniform, M.N.H. [1]) had a week of very bad weather, but John felt that he was hardening more to his surroundings and reported to Dono:

> *'...Vess was up to see us on Sunday and went back on Tuesday Nov 24. Mother went in yesterday and found him very well. I think his commanding Officer is giving him work in less exposed places till he gets a good grip and toughened a bit. The weather is exceedingly rough and wet. Today we have had a full gale – I should say 70 mph.*
>
> *Fred Brew told me that a Danish or Norwegian trawler, captured off the west or north of Scotland and sent in charge of a prize crew to Fleetwood, had sheltered in Ramsey. There was absolutely nothing discoverable about her at first, but afterwards it was found that she had most ingeniously concealed a quantity of petrol, as if a supply ship for submarines. Whether this was in water ballast tanks or not, he did not know. He says our Manx boats are now on armed patrol service, such as watching for suspicious*

trawlers. If the 'Douglas' was faster she would be a good knockabout boat.'

No Manx passenger boat had suffered from ship or submarine attack yet, but overnight mine-laying was becoming more prevalent in the vicinity of major British ports. Early in December, John advised Dono:

'Considering the old and slow boats, it would not be wise to cross at Xmas.'

John warned Dono:

'Take care of the German agent. Every stranger is a possible spy. Be more discreet regarding your profession, than even as a Mason!

Learn the art of changing the subject of conversation!'

John spoke to Lord Raglan to ask for a Commission for Vess – which he promised to do. John reported:

'Lord Raglan enquired most kindly about Lardy: the 14 officers in the regimental list of Monmouthshire personally unknown to him now, though 3 or 4 years ago he was Colonel of the Regiment.

He also spoke of the net: it was only 'indirectly' that he was able to get it in at the Admiralty: the service such a large order, and his connections with the Army Service! As an outcome of our talk, his intensely strong idea was that 'the present is a grand time for 'young' men!'

There's nothing of news locally. The papers seem to be referring to the 'Audacious' affair as a mistake in not having been made public. The naval and military authorities are the people in whose hands these things are, and must remain!'

...*H.M.S. Audacious* was one of the ships Dono worked on before the war at Cammell Laird – she became one of the 2nd Battle Squadron of the Grand Fleet, stationed (unbeknown to the Germans) at a base at Loch Swilly off the north Irish coast whilst submarine defences were put in place at Scapa. *H.M.S. Audacious* sank after striking one of 200 German mines laid by the German liner *Berlin*, near Loch Swilly on October 27th 1914. The *Berlin* was heading for Scapa to lay mines, but decided it was too risky and deposited the mines in a 'v' shape near Swilly.

[www.worldwar1.co.uk/audacious]

Regarding the progress of the war on the Western Front, John wrote:

'I should like to see Strasbourg and Metz beset by the French! I should like to see the French get astride the Rhone, high up, or a movement made on Coblentz. But doubtless Luxembourg must be cleared of Germans, and the railways out there got hold of – before

there can be a movement on the lower Moselle, which joins the Rhine at Coblentz.

The necessity for men is so urgent, that I don't see that our Government can put off conscription very long.'

John was pleased that Dono's manager at Laird's, Captain Rees, had suggested that Dono should apply for a Commission. John wrote to Dono:

'It would be quite out of the question for you to think of, or consent to any idea of military service other than that service to the Country, which you are now fulfilling – or some commissioned post and rank in Admiralty Service.'

Regarding the Battle of the Falkland Islands on December 8th 1914, in which the British ships there took the German squadron unawares – John reported on December 10th:

'We hear today that a squadron which went out a month or five weeks ago to deal with the German squadron off Chile, has found them off the Falkland Islands, and without English loss, sunk the Scharnhorst, Gneisenau and Dresden: the Leipzig & Nurnberg escaping; also 2 colliers captured.

The Bremen is still at large: with that exception our small vessels ought to account for the rest... At any rate the menace is removed by destruction of S. & G.

This rapid result means either very good luck, or on the part of Vice-Admiral Sturdee, excellent capacity.'

...*Scharnhorst, Gneisenau, Nurnberg, Leipzig* & *Dresden* were sighted near the Falkland Islands by British Vice-Admiral Sturdee. In the course of action they were all sunk except for *Dresden*, and 2 Colliers captured. [5] This was seen as some retribution for their earlier destruction of British ships.

John was speculating on troop numbers and wrote:

'We know little of the French numbers. It always seems to me that they ought to have more than they appear to have. Possibly they are steadily arming and training their ultimate numbers.

But whether they have 2, 3, or 4 million to come forward, we ought to have nearly as many. I should say there must be some 1500 young men on this island who ought to be enrolled, and sections taken for training as soon as they can deal with them.'

Regarding Dono's net memo sent, and to illustrate how 'red-tape' could hamper a military or naval idea being used quickly, John enclosed a newspaper cutting in a letter to Dono in December:

Daily Telegraph:

> 'PROTECTION FROM SHRAPNEL ...Nowadays the infantry soldier fires from a lying position, thus his vulnerable points to shrapnel bullets, given the slanting direction of their fall, are the head, the nape of the neck, and the shoulders. The rest of his body is sufficiently protected by the overcoat and the haversack.'

John wrote to Dono regarding this:

> *'...He (Maurice Barres) suggests that the infantryman's kepi should be lined with a metallic disc, and that the collar and shoulders of the overcoat should be stiffened or padded with strips of metal. Naturally, he says, if his suggestion is brought before the authorities in the ordinary way it will get entangled in meshes of red tape, and made the solemn subject of technical commissions. He believes, however, his idea can be carried out without such 'official intervention...'*
>
> *That is, any suggestion, however valuable, is liable to delays and hindrance through official procedure...*
>
> *Thus your net might possibly be appreciated and approved by some of those whose opinion is valuable, yet get held up by procedure.*
>
> *I cannot help thinking from some of the expressions used in the letter from the Engineer-in-Chiefs' department, that the idea has arrested attention at least!*
>
> *No use counting on anything, nor inviting suspense to distract you.'*

Vess had been sent to Tilbury on a mission, and sent a postcard home saying they had an 8 hours passage in the *Douglas*, and he was dreadfully sick. John reported to Dono:

> *'They left Liverpool by the 11pm train, and had not had breakfast at Tilbury 8am Saturday when sending the card.*
>
> *He did not know where they were going, but from the Daily Mail this evening I think they were taking prisoners to the Batavier boats, which sail from Tilbury to Rotterdam. It is an exchange of interned aliens: the Daily Mail, having incidentally a column about a prisoner who tried to smuggle himself off those boats.'*

John also read in the *Daily Mail* that the Germans were making Ostend a submarine base. Netting submarine bases would stop them from leaving their bases, but so would mine laying or a blockade. He wrote to Dono:

> *'Their activities may increase the chance of your 'idea' taking shape.'*

Birkenhead shipbuilders turned out a light cruiser in a very short time to add to the Admiralty's list, but ships were generally still not being built fast enough, and due to insufficient vessels for the defence of the whole of the U.K. coast, some areas were vulnerable to attack. On December 15th there was a raid on the Yorkshire coast by German cruisers. Scarborough was an undefended town, but the Germans believed it to be defended by a gun battery, hence a target. Two German cruisers opened fire on various points in this locality, causing an outrage in Britain. Eighteen people were killed in Scarborough; Hartlepool further north was much harder hit. [18]

John wrote:

> *'The raid on the Yorkshire coast implies surely some information of the absence of English squadrons supplied to the enemy.'*

In the run up to Christmas, Vess had returned from Tilbury, and Lardy was expected home from Monmouth for a few days; John was concerned about him and reported to Dono on December 18th:

> *'Lardy has had a cold and is troubled with his teeth – he had to get seven taken out. I hope with a few days rest at home and a change of food he will get set up again.'*

Dono had applied for a Commission in the Royal Navy and was called to London for an interview. John wrote on December 20th:

> *'I have written to Mary* (Dono's sister) *to tell her you will be calling at the Engineer Department, Whitehall – and that she might see you either before going in or after coming out!*
>
> *If you get your commission you must get uniform. In this it is well to ask someone for the address of a good tailor who will not ask those extravagant prices that some tailors in that line charge rich young men...'*

Regarding the submarine net, John wrote:

> *'The idea of a line with self-signalling floats would be a good thing – to detect vessels crossing a certain line of sea at night. Misty weather is a difficulty.*
>
> *I still think it quite possible that the net may come to something.*
>
> *Having your Commission will give you a 'locus standi' I believe they would insist on before engaging you in any special service...'*

Dono sent a wire from London later, saying his interview there was 'satisfactory', but that he would not be home for Christmas.

As the war approached its first Christmas there was the portent of things to come with the first German air raid on Britain, and in the Isle of Man, permission was granted by the Home Office to raise a third company of the Isle of Man Volunteers.

...Eventually the 1st Manx Service Company was formed from the Volunteer Companies.

John wrote:

'It is not going to be an era of peace, hereafter! That is out of the question!'

On Christmas Day 1914 in the trenches on the Western Front there was an unofficial Christmas truce; the men played football and exchanged chocolate and gifts from home; the cessation however was short-lived.

Vess, still training on the island, was promoted to Lance-corporal and home for Christmas, and Lardy arrived home in much better spirit and health than anticipated, but the mood was sombre.

John reported:

'Last evening Lardy came home. He had not time to send a wire. In fact it was a rush at Monmouth and at Liverpool. I was very glad to see him so well. He looks very fit and strong. He has gained over a stone in weight and looks remarkably well. He is in good spirits and likes the life and work of the regiment. He has some idea his company may go to Egypt. He has to return on Monday – viz. 3 days at home.

Vess also got home today; so there were Margaret, Nan, Lardy and Vess at home. Vess had to go back to Douglas 4pm.

Have you seen any clear accounts of riots in Berlin? Lardy says he saw a report that 4000 had been shot down, and that the military refused to obey orders to fire any more on the crowd.

If the riot reached such dimensions, then a most serious state of things exists there, and the German nation seems within possibility of a revolt against its military government.'

...Riots in Berlin later in 1915 were mainly due to food supplies being blockaded.

John continued:

'It is becoming clear that the movement against Russia, which they proclaimed as a great victory, is not so much so after all. The report of troops coming west again is not quite intelligible in view of other reports from the east. But what is certain is that they have nearly

2,000,000 troops in the west already – a very large order to hold them contained, and gradually forced back.'

John received a letter from Dono referring to his interview, and replied on December 26th:

'I think it satisfactory. I don't think the refusal to be vaccinated for typhoid will matter. It might be obligatory in a regiment for trench work, but hardly in a Service where the same conditions do not exist.

You are offering them more than they are offering you. I think not to have asked for a Commission might have been a serious mistake!

The fact that after 25 minutes they sent you for a medical test would seem the matter is going forward. What promotion could you expect in your present inspector work without this Commission status?

I don't suppose they want you for sea-service: what they want I should think are men in connection with their building programmes, and in the production of material for contractors and ship builders firms...'

...The end of 1914 was the beginning of the great British building programme of destroyers and submarines. It was hoped that construction times of both vessels would take around 12 months. Germans were taking an estimated 12 months to build U type submarines and 18 months for submarine cruisers. They were ahead in terms of numbers of ships and submarines already built. [7]

John seemed perhaps disappointed by Dono's appointment to *H.M.S. Victory* as a Lieutenant-Engineer, as he commented on December 28th:

'I see it is not a sea-going ship, but is Nelson's old ship at Portsmouth. I infer that it is for some special service – probably not going to sea at all...

I do not know of anything here worth mentioning: it was a very quiet Xmas.'

By the end of 1914 hundreds of thousands of men and civilians had been killed or wounded, and thousands taken prisoner in fighting on land and sea as the war intensified. Worst affected were the infantry slogging it out in trench warfare around Europe, but especially on the Western Front.

For the brothers, Dono, Lardy and Vess, this was just the beginning, as they were yet to become directly involved...

1915

With the German occupation of the Belgian coast at Ostend and Zeebrugge, a constant sea patrol of the Dover Straits and Belgian coast was necessary as a defensive measure, preventing the Germans invading France from the sea, and allowing merchant supplies safely into the U.K. The Dover Patrol was formed to patrol the Belgian coast, and also bombarded the German batteries and other important works when necessary.

The Grand Fleet was stationed at Scapa Flow throughout the war, patrolling the northern seas for protection, and there were further sea patrols at Harwich for reconnaissance and support of the other fleets when required.

German ships were causing problems in British waters in 1914, laying mines and attacking ships, but now, the submarine menace was becoming ever more troublesome.

Men at sea faced the daily threat of destruction by mine, torpedo or gunfire. Dono was about to enter into this melee. John wrote:

'I saw your Commission in the London Times Gazette on Wednesday.'

As Dono moved to Portsmouth for training, his house in Liverpool was superfluous. John and his wife were quite happy for Dono's wife, Daisy, to stay with them on the island, but John suggested to Dono:

'...as lodgings are hard to get in Birkenhead, you ought to sub-let or let your house for the remaining term.'

There was speculation about Dono's Commission and what it might entail. John suggested:

'I think it likely that you may be at Portsmouth for some time – with introduction to rules of the Service. Fred Brew thinks you might be needed for some turbine ship on hospital or patrol service.

I mention that army and naval officers affect a 'superiority' to Board of Trade, and such like services – I heard at the beginning of war that requisitioned officers were not admitted to the 'Commissioned' mess. There was a protest raised among Liverpool officers treated thus.'

Whilst in Portsmouth in January, Dono attended lectures, bought his uniform and eventually found the obligatory sword for his new work. John was sceptical as to whether the turbine lectures would teach Dono anything he did not already know, and wrote:

'...You have had something to do with teaching juniors in the heat engine classes at Liverpool... I should expect that you probably would be competent to act as instructor in the classes you are attending. Do not allow any false impression to exist with regard to yourself, where you are master of the subject!

Odd that you could not get a sword! Still more wondrous – because they were heretofore made in Germany! As to the divinity of uniform – respect it, and yet respect yourself more! You are a Mason.

Get used to your uniform, your sword, your salutes, Commission rank, and relation to higher & lower ranks, and to going into the places you are expected to go.'

On the island, Vess was temporarily stationed at Cornaa, guarding the Cable Station along with a Sergeant and 16 other men. John reported:

'Mother heard that they have good quarters. They will need them today – as it is blowing a hurricane from the S.E. with rain – glass down to 28.1".'

A few days later John wrote:

'Vess came home from Cornaa this afternoon very tired. He has to be at Belmont 9.30am, so – to give him a good night's sleep, I got Willy Kermode to promise to drive him in tomorrow morning.'

In early January, John asked Lord Raglan again regarding a Commission for Vess. A Manx Company was going across for training – 250 men, and the Lt. Governor had asked for three Commissions for its officers, and said he would ask for a Commission for Vess.

The first British pre-Dreadnought battleship to be sunk in WWI was *H.M.S. Formidable*, reported as torpedoed on New Year's Day 1915 off the Devon coast by German submarine, U-24. Out of around 750 men, only 199 were saved. The bodies were brought ashore, and surprisingly a local collie dog began licking the face of one of the men and settled down next to him, keeping him warm. To everyone's astonishment the man was alive, and survived, inspiring the well-known story: *Lassie*.

John was sceptical at the time as to how *H.M.S. Formidable* met her fate:

'...I have a suspicion that the Formidable could hardly have been torpedoed, considering it was off Start Point – far away down Channel, and also in such very bad weather that a submarine could hardly succeed in attacking even if were there. It was possibly a mine adrift –

had she been struck only once. But that there should have been two mines adrift so close together – is improbable: the chances 10000 to 1 against it. Could it be anchored mines? Or – could it be explosions caused by some treacherous person within the ship. The Bulwark Case is not above suspicion.'

John later received a letter from Dono regarding *H.M.S. Formidable* and wrote back:

'...I never believed that a German submarine had any part in the 'Formidable' affair. There is a limit to German seamanship: and that limit falls far short of what the abominably ignorant newspapers have credited to it! Nor did I think it two drifting mines... There should be a merciless scrutiny of all the ship's company. Of course if English mines are laid off the coast in the Channel, running into them would be a tenable theory.

It would be interesting to draw up a list of the possible ways in which a traitor enemy on board might destroy a ship, and draft a list of directions as to what parts of the ship should be regularly gone through in order to detect anything suspicious. I think the first explosion was in one of the bunkers of the Formidable, the other seemingly in the bunkers on the opposite side; this points to the coaling as the time when it was done. I consider the man who poo-poohs the presence and activity and opportunities of German agents in the Country, not only a fool, but an accursed scoundrel!'

John had heard rumours of Holland negotiating with the British Government; whether this was through fear of German war aims, or belief that Germany would ultimately be defeated, he did not know. He wrote:

'Had we 2 million men ready instead of 1 million – an army in Holland operating on the German right flank and line of communications would effect the business.'

The weather on the island was so unspeakably wet in January that John thought the whole atmosphere must be affected by the artillery in Belgium. He told Dono:

'Mother and I went to Peel on Thursday, an unpleasant damp day, and time limited, so we did not go out to Knockaloe Camp; we saw it from the railway line. Mrs Kelly told us there are 500 reservists there as guards – their general habits dreadfully intemperate.

The Peel Public Houses are having a time of splendid trade.'

Vess had also been to Knockaloe, followed by a couple of hours at home; he told his parents of his new status. John reported:

'Vess transferred about 100 aliens from Cunningham's Camp to Knockaloe. He said there are 460 Reservists there.

He has got his Lance-Corporal's N.C.O grade, and has to drill and train the raw recruits in Douglas. Every five days he has a 24 hour guard duty – viz. to replace the sentries every 2 hours, and to generally have charge of the guard room. I hope the Governor's promise to recommend him for a sub-Lieutenancy will result in his getting it.

General McKinnon (of W. Command) is on the island this week to see the Volunteers: he is no-ways military, an old professor – an expert – probably knowing his business thoroughly Vess thought.

They have only done platoon drill since a week or so ago; they had been kept to the old-fashioned section-drill: so it is a review of their work in platoon drill – hard times. As Lance-Corporal he is in a N.C.O.'s mess and gets better food. But in effect, on the island he has no chance to get that regular training got in a right camp.'

By 1915, Lardy had undergone three months of training at Monmouth. His records show that he was regarded as a skilled engine driver (field). [26] He had settled into a routine at Monmouth and John reported to Dono:

'Lardy thinks his new home has done him good. After getting to work again for a few days he feels quite all right. A young fellow from Lardy's regiment in Monmouth, also named Quine – home for a week's furlough – called here yesterday. He was (formerly) *a conductor and driver of the Douglas cable cars. He said that Lardy was a sort of boss, erecting sheds for the camp, and he generally succeeded in getting the Sergeant-major to do the work in the way he suggested! He thought the Welsh members of the regiment quite a decent lot of young men. This young fellow had been six weeks in the Regiment, but had not handled a rifle.'*

Having travelled the seas for a number of years in the Merchant Navy, Dono was something of an expert on the engineering aspects of ships. John knew the subject held great interest for him, and advised:

'What is said about a 'spy' on a new ship, verifies my words as to the necessity of a merciless scrutiny of the personnel of all ships, and of all outfit operations – coaling – and all other things in the interior of a ship. Nothing can be taken for granted with regard to a German!

There is nothing much in the way of news here. A report was about that the Snaefell had met with an accident, but there is no further confirmation of it!'

...*Snaefell* was a Manx Steam Packet cargo/passenger ship requisitioned for war work in December 1914 and was not sunk until summer 1918.

Dono remained in Portsmouth, training on *H.M.S. Victory* until January 22nd; on January 26th he joined the ship *H.M.S. Achilles* as Engineer Lieutenant (temp).

Dono wrote in his memoirs:

'I was one of the first Engineer Lieutenants to wear the 'executive curl' on the sleeve of my uniform, which created a stir on my arrival.'

...The Board of Admiralty issued the first uniform regulations in 1748 to distinguish between ranks of naval officers. From 1856 the curl or loop on the sleeve (in yellow lace) was only used for executive officers, but was extended to engineer officers in 1915, and other officers in 1918.

Dono in military uniform with his sword, 1915

Dono explained his new work in his memoirs:

'Before Xmas 1914 there was an urgent demand by the Admiralty for engineer officers to man new ships, and as my qualifications were of the highest, I was commissioned as an Engineer Lieutenant R.N. and appointed to H.M.S Achilles at Cromarty Firth. It was here that I found they had W/T with a range of only 30 miles, and aerials that glowed. Most signalling at sea was done by flags or search light. Here I was at home and could read the Morse for practice.

I should mention here that my wife (Daisy) *had learnt Morse with me; we used it during the war for our private information. There are numerous ways of sending Morse signals: by winking the eyelid, by touch of finger or toe, by writing an account: the length of the lines can send a Morse signal – a short line for a dot and a long line for a dash, a comma and a full stop, and countless other ways, but it demands skill and practice...' [2]*

Of course John did his homework too on what might be expected of Dono and the ship he was to join, and wrote on January 28th:

'We have a small book 'All about the Navy', which gives some figures for the Achilles – displacement – speed – armament! I trust you will gain valuable experience on the Achilles.

Master the rules of service, and rely on your work well done for the confidence of your Chief.'

John assumed that all letters to and from Dono would be censored. Letters written home were generally censored first by Officers and then again at the bases by an official censor. [20]

Meanwhile, John was still pondering the enlistment problem on the island:

'A circular has come round to house-holders from the 'Parliament Recruiting Committee' – viz. including the Isle of Man in the same ideas already made in England. In the space for remarks I wrote that there were many young men 19-38 in this Parish that ought to enlist or be obliged to enlist!'

John visited Archibald Knox at the Knockaloe Camp where the first internees were now settled, and related his visit to Dono:

'I was shown into an office where Colonel Carpendale, the Commandant met me, and was good enough to conduct me to another office where I found Mr Knox with half-a-dozen others including Major Cholmondsley. By & bye he took me round to the office of another –

Master Lieut. Cubbon, who directed Mr Knox to take me round – suggesting a compound which contained the kitchen.

The camp is on the plan of an American City – square blocks, each outlined by a barbed wire curtain say 10' high – the top with about 2' inward slope. The huts are in the middle of the compound, with open space within the curtain – say 250 accommodations.

The huts are of course one storied and with a partition midway under the line of the ridge, but six feet or so short of the ridge. This gives two long and narrow rooms.

The rooms have 3 tiers of bunks against the partition; 2 tiers along the window side. Between the lines of bunks are tables with sufficient room on each side for passage when the tables are occupied. The tables are separate, enough to accommodate say 6.

Whether all the aliens were men of military training or not, they all saluted or raised their hats, or rose to their feet. As it was the Kaiser's birthday and they had had a celebration of it just before I arrived, they may have been in a higher state of animation than the normal. Mr Knox suggested that they took me for the Bishop. Again the man who was with me was under the impression that he was not saluted, and that they took me for an official visitor. My general impression is that they had very good quarters indeed. The kitchen was absolutely clean, and that food being dished was all right: but possibly it was a Kaiser birthday dinner!'

...There were many German and Austrian men in the two Camps of high standing from a diverse British civilian background. The internees were allowed visitors; there were many official visits from representatives of the American Embassy who were responsible for the interests of the prisoners, as well as visits from the Home Office. Visits were also made by the Red-Cross to report on the welfare of the camps (a visit was made to both camps later in December 1915).

There were strict rules for Camp visitors as to the length of stay on the island (a permit was required to visit the island for 7 days with 3 visits to the Camps. British born and non-enemy born wives were able to stay on the island with 3 Camp visits per month.) Internees were encouraged to carry out useful work in the Camp, whether it was artistic, making items for general use, or employment by the Camp for which a small wage was paid. [3]

By the end of January, the men in Lardy's Company in Monmouth had received basic training and were ready to go and support their country, but frustration quickly replaced excitement and apprehension. John reported:

'Lardy, after being under orders, and actually leaving his Monmouth

Camp, found the orders countermanded. They returned and were inoculated for typhoid. The temporary effects were very disagreeable, though in his case not so upsetting as in the case of some of the others. We do not know yet whether they have moved again.

Vess was home on Sunday evening. He was very well – I think gaining in fibre. He had practically got rid of his cold and light cough of recent weeks.

I understand that Germany has commandeered all food stuffs in their own country – which ipso facto makes foodstuffs from abroad to be contraband! The Dacia with cotton from Galveston has not yet sailed: it seems like a bluff.

Today's papers report the loss of German light cruiser – Kolberg. The papers contain a minimum of news: and I infer that the authorities have decided so. It is the best way.'

Kolberg was involved in the action at the Battle of Dogger Bank on January 24th, and survived despite being hit a couple of times. At the end of January, John wrote:

'The engagement of Jan 24 is not mentioned now. The last I saw was a Dutch report that the Seydlitz and Moltke are at Heligoland: which I took to mean that they have not reached home and are at the bottom of the sea! To say they are at Heligoland will satisfy the German public and sound all right: but it can hardly mean anything but their total loss. I think the English silence is to throw on the Germans the onus of a statement, which they are not likely to make – as to where those ships are!'

...*Seydlitz* was damaged badly, but both she and the *Moltke* escaped to fight another day. *Blucher* was the only warship lost during the battle. The German destroyers withdrew when a German Zeppelin began bombing them, mistaking *Blucher* for a British battlecruiser. The German ships had all been involved in the raids on the east coast of Britain in December 1914.

January saw an Allied offensive on the Western Front in Artois & Champagne, and the first German Zeppelin airship attack on England – on Great Yarmouth and King's Lynn.

Submarine U-21 was fired at from Walney Island (U.K.) on January 29th. She surfaced and opened fire on the 'German designed' airship sheds that had been constructed on Airship Shed Road (West Shore Road). Eyewitnesses reported that U-21 had been sunk. John wrote:

'We hear that a German submarine was sunk in shoal (shallow) *water off Walney Island, and has been raised and brought into Barrow. A Barrow newspaper reported it and the issue was suppressed. Little Kinrade told me he had seen the Barrow newspaper – as all copies could not be called in. She is a U-21 or U-17, according to versions.'*

...In fact, U-21 was not destroyed. The following day January 30th, U-21 sank the collier *S.S. Ben Cruachan* 15 miles off Morecambe Light on route to Scapa Flow. According to *Ben Cruachan's* quartermaster, the Germans placed a bomb on board with a long fuse which they lit when everyone was off the boat. It was reported in the New York Times – February 1st 1915 that the Germans were not particularly hostile in carrying out the task of destroying the ships or unfriendly to the crew. Interestingly, on board the collier, the Germans also found Churchill's inflammatory orders, including those to disobey the Cruiser Rules: to ram and fly a neutral flag.

[www.thenewamerican.com]

More ships were sunk in the same locality, including steamers *Linda Blanche*, and *Kilcoan*. John related the submarine affair as follows:

'On Saturday Jan 30th about midday, an enemy submarine sank 3 vessels – two small colliers and a tramp of about 1500 tons – some 15 or 20 miles from the Liverpool Bar. The Manx boats in and out passed there about an hour or so afterwards. The Belfast to Liverpool Graphic was nearly held up (chased by U-boat), but changed course and raced to Holyhead.'

War was encroaching on Manx life. With submarine activity nearer to the Island, the 'Extinction of Lights Order' came into force in Manx towns and villages, and the showing of seaward lights in houses or streets during hours of darkness was prohibited. [3]

John noted other happenings in the Irish Sea and could see an urgent requirement for Dono's submarine net. He wrote:

'On Tuesday I saw 4 destroyers manoeuvring off Ramsey Bay near Maughold Head. It seems to me, 100 destroyers might race to & fro in the Irish Sea and miss 100 submarines. There is no device but one to deal with the 'tin fish'. I cannot understand why the authorities have not adopted it in some form. All these closed seas could be made perfectly safe, and the 'fish' caught. There was nothing of the nature of panic or fright in consequence of the raid, but while one takes a gun for food of the air, of what use for 'fish of the sea'.

I hope Sir J Fisher, who is said to have a device for submarines up his sleeve, will use, condescend to use, that which is simplest and best.

As I speak with the greatest respect for the great experts and naval authorities, I hope the Censor will not object to a loyal person holding a strong opinion on the merits of a method against this particular method of the enemy.'

...John Fisher, persuaded out of retirement by Churchill at the outset of war, became First Sea Lord, and was responsible for despatching the powerful squadron in December 1914 to deal with Spee's German squadron in the Falkland's Battle.

John had done more 'homework' regarding the ship which Dono had joined:

'Mr Cooper has a navy list, and tells me the Achilles has an Engineer Commander, Engineer Lieutenant Commander, and Engineer Lieutenant – whom he calls Lieutenant Minhimnick – a Cornish name I should say. The Gazette *called your appointment 'additional' – which I take it, would mean a period of service with the regular staff to give you proper acquaintance with the actual service on a ship of that class – or to relieve an officer during a furlough. At any rate, actual experience of this routine is valuable.*

Here there is a proposal to raise a half-battalion of 500 to join a Scotch regiment.

Old Mr Kelly, Balachrink (Tom Kelly's father) told me in the tram on Tuesday, that he saw a submarine a fortnight ago in Laxey Bay, and looked at it through a 'glass'. He reported it to Mr Wales, Harbour-Master of Laxey, who told him it was all imagination and laughed at him.

But Caley, a Douglas man, heard old Mr Kelly tell this in the tram, and went next morning and reported it to Mr Sargeaunt at the Governor's Office: so possibly the Harbour-Master of Laxey may be called on to explain.

The fact that a submarine, or several were actually here ten days or a fortnight later, seems to show that the old man was right.'

In February Dono sailed as one of the crew of the ship, *H.M.S. Achilles*, from Invergordon at dawn, and witnessed the grand spectacle of the battle ships and submarines of the British Grand Fleet in formation. On February 7th 1915, John wrote to Dono:

'I found your letter on my return from Ballaugh, where I had gone to give a lecture. We took it for granted that your letters in active service would be very short: but none the less we are glad to hear from you,

if only a line or two.'

H.M.S. Achilles [1]

John offered some advice to Dono on *H.M.S. Achilles*:

> *'It is most important to grasp the whole spirit & system of the navy... Adopt the system in its utmost rigidity, giving it your whole-hearted acceptance. But your work, your individual experience and intelligence as developed in engineering, is that service which the Country now requires of you. Bring to it all the code, conscientiousness and thoroughness which you devoted to taking the old 'Workman' through the Suez Canal on your first voyage to India, when she broke her main shaft in the Bay of Biscay. Remember the saying of Lord Beaconsfield: "It is the unexpected that happens!"'*

Following the submarine assaults in the vicinity of the island, lookouts were stepped up around the Isle of Man coasts. John reported:

> *'There is a small guard at Garwick, Old Laxey, etc., and all round the coast... Since Thursday Jan 28, Vess has been at the war Signal Station at Spanish Head* (southerly point of the Isle of Man)*: a Sergeant – Corporal (himself), and seven men.*
>
> *They have to patrol the coast daily. Their quarters are in an old hut, brought from Castletown with a stove: but he does not say what sort of reports they have to give, whether to note passing vessels or merely to look out for submarines. They have sou'westers and oilskins supplied, and a good supply of cartridges.*
>
> *There is a coastguard station, but whether at the Head or where, he does not say. He reports himself fit and well, but the weather there*

must be very bad. The weather is so bad here, in rain & wind, it matches the worst spells in Nov and Dec...

At Spanish Head, about 50 or 60 ships passed daily; some signalled. Vess could read all their Morse code. In one case he had a full message which the Coastguard had not been able to get in full...

I think that the necessity of guarding the coast points has involved an alteration of the arrangements of the Manx Co. going to a depot to train, and the question of a Commission for Vess is for the same reason no doubt, held over. That he should get hardened by the outdoor and active life he is leading, is what I am most wishful about: for it needs some time to get clear away from the effects of his illness in the autumn...

Things here have become insignificant in contrast to the larger interests.

Lord Raglan has sent round a Circular advising economy of coal etc. (As a result of the submarine – perhaps more than one – round here). But it is possibly the miners' threat of a strike which has led to the Governor's Circular.

I hear that troops are crossing to France steadily now – as was generally expected. Of course we only gather what we can from the newspapers – which have very little to offer to their readers, but have acquired a great skill in the display of the new, along with much older news.'

John was at a meeting in Douglas at the Town Hall and heard that Vess had got his Commission. John wrote on February 12th:

'...after the meeting I stayed, as the Mayor had provided tea. Vicar General Hughes-Games came up and told me that Vess had got his Commission. Vess had been there ten minutes before (unaware of my being at the meeting) to get the Vicar General and Mr Kneale to sign a form – in addition to which there was the certification as to health by Major Dr Richardson – and the signature of Lord Raglan.

Afterwards Mr Kneale and I walked out to the Camp and met Vess – who explained that Major Mackenzie had told him this morning about the Commission. Till it is 'Gazetted' of course, he has to wait in suspense. He is very fit and well. (Major T. Mackenzie was in charge of the Isle of Man Volunteer Corps.) *200 go off next week to join a Battalion of the Liverpool Regiment with 5 Commissions issued to accompanying Officers: Vess will go as a Sub-Lieutenant. This is all right. I told Lord Raglan that he will make a good officer. Vicar General – Hughes-Games thinks the same.*

Here in the Isle of Man, Lord Raglan has ordered all oil to be removed inland from stores and shops. His wireless – Roman Catholic Church tower to Government Office – is now in working order.'

...The wireless (W/T) was set up to communicate with the mainland in case communication was lost by means of the under-sea cable. W/T was a valuable asset for locating submarine activity in Manx waters during the early part of the war, as well as airships; the Government Office W/T was manned by naval authorities for a while: Commander Sims R.N. in charge. [3]

Lardy had got over the typhoid inoculation – making him unwell for several days, and was still in Monmouth expecting orders to move to France; but this, kept up for weeks, was trying to the Company. John wrote:

'We got two wires from Lardy on Saturday, one that he was leaving Monmouth that morning; the later one that he was going to Longmoor and crossing (they supposed) to France on Monday, i.e. today.'

Vess was also preparing to leave the Isle of Man for further training, and John reported:

'...Vess was instructed by Major Mackenzie on Friday morning to get certain forms filled up regarding his Commission, and on Saturday was told to order his kit.

When Vess saw his friend Mr. Dickinson, he very promptly handed him a cheque for £25 (for his uniform), *and told him to come and get another according to immediate requirements, when he had ascertained them. He said he could not go himself to fight, but he could show his spirit. Vess came up* (to the Vicarage) *on Sunday evening.*

The outfitter said there was a difficulty in getting revolvers, but Vess has hope of getting a Browning automatic: rather small calibre, but possibly may pass as sufficient.

They had a Church Parade on Sunday, and a little problem arose through the full Company getting rather jammed in a street near the Church. It is interesting that Vess saw it as a problem for which there was a simple and direct solution; it was solved by three movements which would be seen only by an officer accustomed to handle tangled masses of men!'

...The Sunday Parade was a farewell Service in St. Thomas's Church, Douglas, I.O.M., for Volunteers about to leave for military duty.

Meanwhile, John was hearing some tales of concealment of goods on ships from men working on the vessels assigned to this business:

'...A man named O'Connor has been home on short leave from the 'Snaefell'. Of course such men have a budget of first hand experiences: interesting because they come fresh from the sea; I heard some of them from J. Cannell.

They stopped a vessel under a Danish flag carrying oats on top and petrol underneath; this was found out when they for good reasons sent her into port for examination.

O'Connor says the 'Ben' (Manx ship – Ben-My-Chree) *is being prepared for water-plane service. The 'Queen Victoria' & 'Prince' are on another Service for which I thought trawlers would serve: but not so well probably, e.g. they are altered. The 'Empress Queen' is also requisitioned, but for what service I do not know.'*

...Gradually, more of the Manx boats were requisitioned for war service. Sea-planes were assigned to the naval authorities for reconnaissance work.

During the long February nights, John had seen some suspicious lights on the hillside behind the Vicarage and reported to Dono:

'I have a sort of suspicion that there is possibly a 'German spy' on this country side, and that night signalling has taken place.

Vess thinks that some of the 'Adler' car party that stayed at the 'Keppel turn' (Creg-Ny-Baa) *at the time of the motor-races, were military officers. They called themselves Austrians. He went out a lot to see the car trials and spoke to these men. They could not speak English and he could speak French: so they talked in French.*

I reported the camp signallings which we have seen above the house at night to Mr Sargeaunt at the Government Office, and mentioned these 'Austrians' of the Adler group as having been there at the time of the motor trials. Having motor-cars they could easily make enquiries about every ship supplying petrol etc., on the island.

Quite recently it appears that Ronan and another equally brilliant genius came into the reading-room at the tram station one evening, where half a dozen lads were assembled.

Ronan explained that it was reported that there was a German spy somewhere between Laxey and Garwick: so they searched the room, carefully looking into the coal box. That done, they went on their way southwards!

I told Mr Sargeaunt that inland a little might be the sort of place an enemy spy might chose for communication with the sea. It has a hinterland of moorland, yet near enough for lamp-flashing, and less likely to betray itself.

He said he would act on the hint.'

In February 1915, as the war continued and German submarine production increased, the Germans countered the 'British blockade' with their own blockade imposed by U-boats, known as the 'Blockade of Britain', to try to starve Britain into submission by cutting off vital supplies; merchant ships in a specified zone around Britain were now legitimate targets.

America had so far been neutral regarding the war, but warned that Germany would be held to account if any American ships were sunk. American passenger ships were frequent visitors to British waters.

During February there were ongoing Eastern Front attacks by Austro-Hungarian forces on Russian Poland (Galicia), and the Russians suffered heavy losses during the 2nd battle of the Masurian Lakes.

Lardy had finally moved, but not to France, and wrote home giving his address; Sapper L.L. Quine, 7019, Royal Monmouth, Roy. Engineers (R.S.), (Railway Co.), Longmoor Camp, Hants. John wrote:

'Going down to Longmoor they had to march by highroad from the railway terminus to the Camp – which was several miles. Later he found there was a railway to the Camp, and he was ordered to take a train down to the main line. He asked for someone in the engine cab that knew the curves & gradients, but was told that it was a test and important that he should find his own way and run as near as possible to a given time for the journey without having seen any part of the line beforehand – with no one to accompany him.

He was only a few minutes behind on the run out, but did the run back on time. This is the only explanation he gives of what being in a 'Railway Co.' means. He may be given driving – as competent drivers are not likely to be available in great numbers.'

Regarding Vess, John told Dono:

'Vess was here yesterday. Mr Sargeaunt saw him and pressed his getting of kit. He has most of it already. The Manx Company, as soon as arrangements are complete, will cross to an English Depot, where he will begin his officer's training... Vess considers his experience – not

to call it training – in these past months, of great value to him – being that of actual work, and contact with men such as he will find in the 'material' of the 'King's Liverpool'. His point of view is that he will start his training as an officer from the ABC of it, and this is right.

At College they leave an O.T.C. – Officers' Training Corps – from which two of the new subalterns are chosen. A certain hard attitude which Vess acquired in his Law training will stand him in good stead; and he thinks the recent experience added to this, are better assets than the O.T.C. experience will be to them.'

...By 1915 it was evident that the short war-time training course of three months just wasn't sufficient to prepare officers for the Front. Some of the junior officers were just 17 years old. [20]

John was doing his bit for the community in trying to encourage the young men of Laxey to go and join the fight for their country, and told Dono:

'Last evening I went to a recruiting meeting in Laxey – open-air – in the entrance to the Laxey gardens. Major Hamilton, the Officer in charge here, had asked me to come down and speak.

I found the Major and Lt. Hampson (in charge of 2 doz. Reservists at Old Laxey), Hulme the recruiting agent, Captain Roberts, & Dr Godson.

R.T. Corlett (Captain of the Parish) was not there. They said Corlett shirked lest someone should cry out: "Why isn't your own son Neil enlisted?"

So far as addressing a meeting – they were helpless. They asked me to be 'Chairman'. I said: "I'll do anything." There was the top of the hotel steps and a crowd in front. I opened the meeting – spoke 25 to 30 minutes – all the men very quiet and rather interested considering. Dr Godson spoke – very brief and very nice – only hardly drawing blood! I was hoping I had done some good; at the end of it there were 21 names: for Laxey this was surprising.'

The recruiting meeting in Laxey had gone relatively well and John felt he had done his duty, but there was still reluctance on the part of some men to enlist. He later reported:

'The meeting in Laxey resulted in 24 giving names: but these were from the Parish parts more proportionately than from Laxey.

The farmers strongly object to being deprived of their hands. Laxey is the difficulty: for the young men will neither enlist, nor would they go out on farms to relieve any shortage there.

Major Hamilton – Recruiting Officer – acknowledged it the best meeting he had had on the island.'

Things on the island were very quiet, with the exception of a few incidents at sea, which John noted:

'I saw two small trawlers pass this afternoon – flag and foremast lowered.

'S.S. Graphic' – Belfast to Liverpool – reported a submarine off Copeland Island (mouth of Belfast, Lough) *on Friday morning.*

This sea from this coast is very quiet. We see nothing.'

However a submarine had been active in Manx waters; John wrote:

'A submarine sank a Spanish ore boat off Point Lynas, and afterwards a Dundrum Collier (300 foot) light, off the Calf of Man.

It is said this submarine came to grief off Glen Meay at the hands of a destroyer; one story – that she is ashore, but we have no means of disproving what would be good if true. In the case of the 'Downshire' (300 tons, light) – it appears that half a dozen destroyers were on the spot a few minutes too late.'

...On Feb 20th 1915 the *S.S. Downshire*, with crew of eleven, was sunk by U-30, 8 miles from the Isle of Man. Port Erin lifeboat was launched. A Colby man was one of those rescued [22]. On the same date the *Cambank* heading for Liverpool or Galveston with copper ingots & sulphur ore was also sunk by U-30. No mention has been found of a submarine coming to grief off Glen Maye.

As Dono was now with the Grand Fleet up in the north of the U.K., his wife, Daisy, had let their house in Liverpool as suggested, and found lodgings in the north of Scotland. John reported:

'Daisy wrote to Margaret from a northern town. She has an Orkney or Shetland landlady – just arrived from those islands I gathered. These days everybody must be treated as masons treat non-masons: for a German spy is a possibility in female as well as in male guise. Daisy will I hope, take care not to speak to anyone about things English, lest she be speaking to a spy in the most plausible disguise.'

John later reported:

'I was glad to see that Daisy was aware that in such a place as she is, there are certain to be enemy agents. Remember the nasty report in a few of the papers about the Orcadian's or Shetlander's three or four months ago. To Kirkwall & Lerwick in the great fishing season used to come crowds of vessels of many nationalities – buying fish, and in all

sorts of other trade stirred by the fish industry. There must have been long preparatory arrangements for espionage. Sometimes I fancied that a summer in those Islands with a small launch would have been a fine thing, with a roving Commission to collect data for the secret service...

English people have far too little given attention to the acquisition of foreign languages...'

Vess, still on the island, had some difficulty getting a revolver. John wrote:

'A Laxey man from S. Africa has lent me a Browning automatic .320, which he can have till he is able to get another to suit. Of course he can take it off the island with him. It is the best sort of pistol I have seen – American idea, Belgian make.'

When John was in Douglas, he took note of any unusual vessels in the harbour, and reported to Dono:

'In Douglas on Tuesday I saw four N.E. Scotland trawlers with the government flag coaling by the pier. I could not see from anything on deck what their work is, but I judge it is naval service.

A big east coast type of trawler came to anchor in the outer harbour, and to have a look at her coming in, I went to Battery Pier. Her name, number, port, etc., were painted out, but I made out the name under the paint. She seemed the sort that probably goes to an Iceland fishery. Some of her crew had naval caps, and one man wore a naval uniform. There was nothing on deck to indicate fishing – white flag with small jack in the corner: the others – blue flags with small jack.

Mr Pult, a share-holder in Douglas, spoke to me on Tuesday regarding the navy. He had a terrible idea of its discipline, and quoted somebody's saying that 'it would crush the heart of aliens!' In the very nature of such an institution, discipline must be intense, and in the higher ranks – not less but more...'

Regarding naval activities at sea – after the German threat to merchant vessels, a net barrage was established in February across the North Sea Channel between Ireland and Scotland to impede submarines. Another barrage was started in the Dover Straits, but this was not completed until April. John wrote:

'I know very little of what the navy is doing. In aggregate it is doing much, or everything. From Mr Broadbent on Thursday – his source Mrs Lay, a Lawyer, just returned from London – her source, a Solicitor,

her husband's London agent: two submarines have been netted at Dover! Our view here – was to make every ship going up or down the Channel, pass through Dover harbour, and outside that – trap the whole straits.

The newspapers say the Admiralty have made a closed area. Thus every ship coming through from west or east must pass south of Rathlin Island.

I assume the rectangle is severely mined: but what device is cased in the 6 or 7 miles of channel between Rathlin & the Irish coast, I don't know.

The St. Georges' Channel is peculiar – between Ireland and S. Wales – i.e. there is no rise or fall of tide at Arklow on the Irish side, the tidal rise and fall very large on Welsh side. This should enable that comparatively narrow channel to be dealt with.'

Lookouts had been stepped up on the coasts around the Isle of Man due to possible submarine threat, but were some of the men on duty taking this seriously? John reported:

'We have two dozen Reservists at Old Laxey.

A submarine was solemnly sworn to have been off Laxey at 9.30 one morning. I asked a farmer whose house overlooks the bay – "Did you see this submarine?"

His answer: "Do you believe there was a submarine?"

"Well I want information!" I said.

He said, "Well – the Reservists are having a good time at Laxey – hot cakes & coffee all hours – and I daresay there will be a lot of wonders seen off here – they're not going away in a hurry!"'

John gave a lecture in February on the idea of 'swank' amongst Germans. This was published in a local newspaper – quite a lengthy piece; John informed Dono:

'If you have read the inadequate report of my Ballaugh lecture, there were several aspects of the 'swank' question omitted. I did not really lose sight of them; for example 'style' and 'swank' are to be clearly distinguished...

Vess's description of General McKinnon, who came over to inspect their company was a case illustrating the distinction. He did not seem at all like a soldier, but he soon created a deeper impression, by making everybody discover that he was a soldier: an expert, a specialist.

He had measured, weighed, sized & summed up the whole company and put it into its proper category in a very short time...'

On the war Fronts, the need for more planes and pilots was urgent, as their usefulness was increasingly realised for defence, and military and naval reconnaissance, although the aircraft for the two forces were still operated separately. John reported to Dono:

'I see some arm-chair strategist has advised to have an air-fleet of 5000 aero-planes – at a cost of nearly £10,000,000; and by one swoop, destroy the whole of Essen for Herr Krupp.

A good many others have been designing equally wonderful things. They have designed in idea, a mine-brush carried ahead of a number of vessels – through the Dardanelles etc.'

...Krupp produced most of the artillery for the German Army. Essen was the Headquarters of the Company.

Finally Lardy's training for railway work was complete and he and his Company were to leave for France. He visited his sister Mary in London and sent a card home from Southampton on the eve of sailing to France.

John told Dono on February 21st:

'We infer that he is in a Company for railway work – which I suppose will be in the rear of, and up to the fighting line. I think in railway work he will do well.'

After months of waiting, Lardy was in France: Sapper L.L.Q. 7019 No.3 Monmouth Railway Co... with the British Expeditionary Force – but what lay ahead? John wrote:

'Lardy writes Feb 25th from Rouen, where he is under canvas, but leaving Feb 26th for Front: weather there pretty cold.'

...The two main army base depots in France were at Le Havre and Rouen. Here, the men, equipment and supplies were sorted before despatch to the Front. Boulogne was also used as a subsidiary base. [19]

Vess had spoken to Lord Raglan regarding the delay in the issue of his Commission through incorrect papers being given to him, instead of 'Regular Army' papers. On February 28th 1915 Vess wrote to his brother:

'Dear Dono, I'm just scribbling this line to put in paters letter. I'm waiting anxiously to be Gazetted.

I have got a commission in the King's Liverpool Regt. I don't know what Battalion but it's one of the Kitchener's Army Battalions.

We are waiting orders to cross to England any day now. I hope to get to France before May. I'm glad you're having a fairly decent time. I had a note from Daisy.

I'll let you know where we get to. As yet I've no idea where we're to go.

Well good luck old man.

Your loving brother, S. L. Quine (Lonan Vicarage, Laxey)'

At the beginning of March, John wrote with some excitement:

'...I've just heard that 2 submarines have been trapped in Scapa Flow, and 2 others near Dover; if so, the Admiralty are dealing with them fairly well.'

John was also still pondering enlistment:

'The London Times for many days past has columns devoted to letters – 'Ought Clergymen to enlist or fight?' The class of men that have become Clergymen in the island for a good many years past would be no use at that.

The farm lads have gone to enlist for the most part and not Laxey young men. The farmers are backward with their work through a wet season and it is the most important time of the year getting crops in: so they are full of grumbling. Not a man or man's son of them has enlisted. They enquire, "How long do you think the war will last?" meaning that they hope it will last a long time; they are doing well, and their only idea: to make a bit out of the war!

My taking part in the recruiting meeting was unpopular with the farmers: where are they to get men to do the work?

Young miners have told me they have tried to enlist but been rejected for bad teeth, etc.; however true of a few, the generality have held back.

We are having decidedly bad weather: wet, considerable wind – raw & cold.

The Dardanelles work is a large order, but is making good progress. The Dardanelles is about 30 miles. The fleet have cleared about 10 miles of it.'

...The Allied forces In the Dardanelles expected to bombard the passage of the Straits through to Constantinople, knocking Turkey out of the war and providing a supply path to and from Russia, but the defences of the Germans and Turks in the Straits were formidable, with well hidden batteries and forts, as well as the danger from mines, despite mine-sweeping. Allied ships attempted to bombard the Dardanelles, resulting in failure and loss of many British men and ships. This led to the development of an invasion plan.

John continued:

'We hear so little of Fleet movements; the definite reports of the Dardanelles work takes up all attention: other work being unreported. But now with a blockade declared, one may assume additional work in holding up German bound ships.

I enclose some newspaper cuttings – about that that attack on the Suez Canal. As you know the Canal – it will interest you.'

...Dono had travelled through the Canal during his earlier Merchant Navy work. The raid on the 100-mile-long Canal took place between 26th Jan and 4th Feb 1915 by a German-led Ottoman Army Force. It was unsuccessful due to the strong defences in place. The Suez Canal was an important supply route, particularly for oil, and the British forces defended the Canal for this reason.

Regarding Dono and his work on *H.M.S. Achilles*, John continued:

'I hope you have a comfortable cabin, and that all your meal arrangements are good. You need to pay the greatest respect to – sleep – food – warmth, and maintain the highest state of physical efficiency.'

Dono expected to remain on *H.M.S. Achilles* for some time, but he was taken somewhat by surprise in March, as he was ordered to join a new ship, *H.M.S. Prince Rupert* – a monitor being built in the stocks at Glasgow.

Unfortunately when Dono arrived at the ship-yard, the engines were in the process of being moved to couplings on the propeller shaft, and as a result of some mismanagement prior to his arrival, the shaft was bent. Dono tried to rectify it, but the want of alignment had to be put up with. He had many problems to deal with whilst this ship was in building, and on trials.

At sea, the 24 different categories of British ships had their place in the defence of the English coast to deter German raids on vulnerable areas; some were involved in mine-sweeping, others assisted convoys or were on submarine alert. The British Navy felt it was a necessity to oust Germany from the ports of Ostend and Zeebrugge, near to the U.K., and ordered the building of more monitors to use in the bombardment of the Belgian coast. *H.M.S. Prince Rupert* was one of these monitors of the *Lord Clive* class. [23] Dono was head of the engineering department of *H.M.S. Prince Rupert* and supervised the installation of her W/T power: all electrical work came under his charge, there being no separate electrical department in the

Royal Navy at that time... But it was to be a long wait until the monitor was complete, trialled and fit for action in August 1915.

Meanwhile Vess, who was still on the island, unexpectedly found himself in 'hot water'! Major Mackenzie had a message from Col. Madoc for Vess to call at the G.P.O. Regent St. Douglas, where two officials interviewed him. John explained to Dono:

> *'Vess came up yesterday (Sunday) and gave me a fuller account of this interview.*
>
> *It seems that a packet of letters – mine, and one from Vess to you – was found sometime in February in a carriage of the overhead Railway, Liverpool! The professed finder was a Steward on a Cruiser, resident at New Ferry, Liverpool (your house – 10 River View, New Ferry). He handed the packet to the Police, the Police to the P.O. authorities – and then to the Admiralty! Vess's letter referred to wireless, and some of mine referred to submarine traps: so consequently explained interest of Officials from both G.P.O. wireless and Admiralty.'*
>
> ...The officials came over from Liverpool to see Vess to verify his identity. They asked questions about his original Feb 1914 wireless letter [Appendix b]. They also had type-written copies of John's letters: the latest dated Jan 22 1915 – the day Dono left Portsmouth to join his ship. Once they knew that Vess had enlisted and was in active service (or in hospital), there was no further doubt or suspicion...

John continued:

> *'They expressed themselves as fully satisfied, saying the letters would be returned, wished him success in the service, congratulated him on his Commission, etc...!*
>
> *Vess asked them if they had seen me; they implied that there was no occasion for that.'*

John was confused as to how the letters may have been lost. His first idea was that Dono had given the letters to Daisy, and that she had lost them when she and her mother returned to the house in New Ferry in February. John wrote:

> *'I should think something very stupid has taken place – unless one adopts quite another theory – viz. burglary of your house. A steward of a liner might conceal any kind of adventurer – quite the guise for a German spy. Did he hand in all the letters he found? Of course I have no objection to any of my letters to you being copied by the Admiralty. What I do object to is that they should get into the hands of anyone but the Admiralty or Government authorities.*

How did a letter of Feb 1914 get to be along with the very latest of my letters? The official representing the Admiralty would not tell Vess when the letters were found. But he asked, "Where was your brother last week?" This would mean Feb 14 – Feb 21.

As you were on sea-service since Jan 24, Vess could only say that. The official thought you were on Swiftsure – one of the Brazilian boats taken over, and now at the Dardanelles... They professed to know that you had been in Laird's and at Sheffield.

I still think the official ought to have come to me! I should certainly have given him information to guide him...'

Vess was finally ready to leave the island for further training at Hoylake, Liverpool.

John wrote:

'Vess was here this evening in Lieutenant Uniform for the first time. They cross tomorrow to Seaforth Barracks, and afterwards to the Camp at Hoylake.'

Vess: G.H. Evans, Douglas & Port Erin, Isle of Man.

Regarding this, John wrote:

'We saw the Manx Volunteer Co. off on March 9 (the same morning a Langland boat was sunk by a submarine, 9.15 off the Liverpool Bar: so clearly the sub had no intention of having a shot at the Manx boat.)

The Co. had 150 men in 5 sections; a Lieut. in charge of each section. Vess looked very fit. All the men wore their great-coats, and Vess his. But the other four Lieutenants did not wear their great-coats – too evidently in order to show off their smart uniforms. I was glad that Vess had the common sense to do nothing of that sort: I think he sized up their motive. He identifies himself with the 'regulation' code, and has the rule for himself that an officer's duty is to take care of his men.'

...The Manx Company transferred to the 16th Battalion Kings Liverpool Regiment.

John continued:

'The Admiralty man who interviewed Vess on Friday March 5th was on the boat – effusively pleasant. Vess noted as rather peculiar the indisposition of the two men who interviewed him at Douglas... I still ask the question – were they bona fide?

What I think you had better do is to ask Daisy to recall every step she went with her mother when at New Ferry – the house – was anything disturbed there? Were they on the overhead? Had they anything with them? Have you and Daisy been shadowed by German spies?'

Late in February, Lardy sent word home from the Base at Rouen. He had heard his Co. was going to the Front somewhere near La Bassée, where the No.2 Monmouth Railway Company were constructing a 'barrage' across the canal near Givenchy, but in fact Lardy's Company was sent north of this to Ypres in Belgium.

According to the No.3 Monmouth Railway War Diary, Lardy and his consignment of men joined the Company in Ypres on 3rd March, working on rivetting (wiring) the trenches already dug, which were opposite a portion of the Western Front where firing was very heavy with many bullets coming over. It had rained incessantly from October 1914, and continued until 10th March 1915: the trenches were waterlogged. The job of the sappers was to erect a double apron barbed wire obstacle in front of the line of trenches. [13] John reported on March 19th to Dono:

'Lardy has been sappering on the firing line for some time, and has got through his first experience of that. They are now at railway work in a different part of the Country.

I gathered that they were at Ypres in Belgium, and are now in France.

The sapper work was at night, in water to the knees; German shells falling over and behind him; star shells (Roman candles) lighting up the place for German snipers to get a chance at them. It reminded him of his trying to get a shot at lapwings. Bullets passed between the sappers, and he often felt the wind of one on his face. Also shots from the German trenches fell about them.

The first night he was a bit nervous, but not afterwards.

I think the purpose is to give the engineers an immediate experience of being under fire, to harden them and steady them before employing them on other work, rather than set them to work with the suspense of inexperience as to danger zones, keeping them more or less anxious – as they would be until after being under fire.

Lardy implies that just now their work is not close to the firing line.'

Regarding Lardy's work, notes in the March 1915 No.3 Monmouth Railway Company War Diary revealed:

> 'On 12th March, the No.3 Monmouth Railway Company was replaced by the Cornwall and Wiltshire fortress Companies and the No.3 Company left Ypres and marched to Abeele, Poperinghe, where they entrained for Abbeville.
>
> There the men were billeted in a large loft of the rope works near the town with the No.2 Company; hence they were rather crowded'. [29]

It is interesting to note that possibly whilst in the Ypres area, Lardy made the acquaintance of a young Belgian mademoiselle called Yvonne Armand and their relationship flourished. Later, he became engaged to Yvonne, and intended to marry her when the war ended; no mention was made of the fact in John's letters to Dono, but Lardy kept his thoughts to himself.

Major battles had taken place in Belgium around Ypres from October 1914, although the Germans were unable to capture Ypres itself. Having said that, many buildings were destroyed and the people were eventually forced to evacuate the town, moving towards Poperinghe.

The build-up of the British Army was underway, involving extensions to lines of communication and many new miles of railway; engineers were required in various places from Calais to Rouen.

John later reported:

'Lardy has moved to railway construction in France.

I think they get a certain excitement at the actual Front: for he seems to miss it. His three weeks or so at the Front was a wise system – so it will not concern them if their work brings them into the danger zone.

The Railway Engineers are quartered in railway carriages so as to move along the line as their work requires.'

...Towards the end of March, the No.3 Monmouth Railway Company moved into trains from the billets and worked on moving ballast in the vicinity of Abbeville. [29]

Lardy was in the thick of the ongoing operations in France, but Vess's adventure was only just beginning with his training at Hoylake in Liverpool. John reported to Dono in March:

'Vess is now hard at work, and I think in his element. They have a long day of field work, trenching, etc., with lectures on trenching and topography. He has notebooks for field-work, and lectures.'

John was also intrigued by Dono's new work, but frustrated that he couldn't relate his experiences in his letters home due to censorship. He wrote:

'...I quite understand that more and more you are unable to discuss anything, in which I should be ever so deeply interested.

I see William Quine of Manchester, your cousin, was 'Gazetted' to the Collingwood (as Surgeon R.N.R) on Mar 6; also a J Quine 'Sen. Engineer' R.N.R. – from the Birkenhead employ? I think you mentioned there was a man of that name there.

I was in Ramsey this week at St. Maughold's (Masonic Lodge). *I stayed at Fred Brew's. He said that the Admiralty had directly made enquiry at the Harrison Line department regarding your credentials – Edward Brew was much pleased with your entering Admiralty Service.'*

...Edward Brew was Dono's employer when he was in the Merchant Navy.

The lost letters were still causing John some concern, and he wrote on March 25th:

'Thanks for the clear list of letters – showing that mine of Jan 22 never reached you when you joined Achilles. I do not find on your list the letter I wrote, about Mar 7th. I can understand the letter of Jan 22 1915 being in the hands of the P.O. authorities, but still cannot understand their having a letter of Vess's dated Feb 1914.

Assuming the two gents bona-fide – they might tell a little yarn about where the letters were found, merely to see what answer would be given.

Thanks for your photos, which we are exceedingly glad to have. I rather like the more front face one better. Mother thinks a full length would have been nice – showing the uniform completely. I notice you have nothing on the shoulders... I chanced to be in Douglas today to meet Mr Kneale on business and went down to see the boat in. A Naval officer came across with her and I noticed on his shoulders, I think – three small bars of gold lace and a wreath.'

By mid-March 1915, the enemy appeared to be closing in on the island as *H.M.S. Bayano* was torpedoed between the Isle of Man and Mull on March 11th. There were only 26 survivors; 197 men lost their lives. One of her dead crew was brought into Ramsey by boat. Other bodies later washed up around the Manx coast.

A patrol of the Manx sea coast was developed after this: the auxiliary yacht *Dolores* was used until August 1915 when she was destroyed by fire in Douglas harbour. [3]

John noted a greater presence of war type ships in Douglas harbour, and wrote:

'When leaving Douglas by 6pm tram – two mine-sweepers (as they call them here) came in with after mast only; later there were seven boats which I took to be seven destroyers astern, head on, coming up from the south for Douglas Bay. Perhaps the official who came ashore from the Douglas *was a Paymaster to meet these boats. We were round Banks Howe before they rounded into the bay. The foam which I could make out at the bows made me think they must be destroyers. We have not seen any about for some time.*

Since the operations in the Dardanelles began I have wondered what provision was made against mines sent adrift from above the Narrows. I imagined submarines a more serious nuisance to the ships than the fire of the forts. To 'sweep' the lower area from time to time is all right: but what about the current from above constantly, every hour, bearing down into this area a score of submerged mines? A net could be used (submerged a fathom or so) to deflect mines to be scooped aground. A device to encourage slipping of a mine along the net could be thought out...'

...Mines were a constant problem in the Straits in 1915.

At this point in the Dardanelles, repairs were being made to ships, and daily mine-sweeping patrols of the Straits.

The decision was made to reinforce operations with military forces and some air machines. Nets were used when necessary to protect the ships when in bays, or at least to give some warning of the presence of the enemy.

Regarding Vess, John reported:

'Vess was in a big march past of 12,000 before Earl Kitchener at St George's Hall, Liverpool on Sunday. He seems well and cheerful: but as they are not yet formally gazetted, he seems impatient about that. He said that other lieutenants there were receiving their lieutenants' pay. He likes his Captain – Capt. Harston, a Canadian, who is an expert, and gives them lectures, etc.'

On the island, things were quiet on the surface, but underneath there was a hive of activity – women were now playing their part in this war. John reported:

'Here we see nothing of any part of the great activities!

In Laxey I am told there is a seething whirlpool of feminine jealousies and rivalries over 'efforts' – for Belgians, Serbians, Red Cross, etc. Mrs Bob Corlett can find no milliner to make a hat quite large enough for her present state of head... the others resent her monopoly of lead and want their innings – well to be out of sight, out of hearing of this feminine war!

I see the Kaiser's Court Preacher – Faulhaber says – "If a man smites thee on one cheek, turn to him the other also! Does not mean, if the Russians take East Prussia, immediately give them West Prussia also!"

It's another example of my frequently stated theorems that, because a man occupies a great place, we must not necessarily accept that he is a man of great gifts, merits or capabilities. Yet by virtue of this utterance, the whole of Europe and America hear of Faulhaber as somebody!

Lace, who sails on the S.S. Tynwald told me the Ben (Manx ship – Ben-My-Chree)*, being prepared for water-planes, is still in Birkenhead; also the Campania. I thought the Ben was away weeks ago.'*

Lardy wrote home – April 5th 1915 (British Expeditionary Force. No.7019):

'Dear Mother and Papa,

I am very well and getting on all right. I am shunting in the siding we are making here. Bridson is on the same job. The weather here is very wet now and as the place was a swamp once it is very muddy now. I hope you are all well again. You can send me a cake occasionally as it is a change from bread, and for every night. I had a parcel from Aunt Wilson on Saturday. We don't get any days off. We had half a day on Easter Sunday and today they have another, but I am on nights so it doesn't make any difference to me. Tell Nan I would like a letter from her. With best love I remain your loving son, Lawrence Lindsay Quine.'

John wrote:

'Lardy's work involving shunting at a new siding in course of construction on lines of communication is important enough: for a great deal depends on a responsible hand for that work. He will feel at home – as he once had to do shunting and other driving in the I.O.M. Co. at Douglas...'

...There was plenty of ballast to be moved by train for making new rail lines on the Abbeville 'Triage'. [29]

On the island, John's wife had become involved in the war effort, helping to boost funds:

'Mother was out a good deal, getting subscriptions for the 'Serbian Relief Fund', preparatory to the tea at Glen Gardens, Laxey, on Easter Monday.

We had a wet Good Friday; Easter Sunday moderately bright; yesterday, a fine day. After the Easter Monday Vestry – a mere quiet business affair – mother and I went to the American Tea for Serbian Relief: the Governor Lord & Lady Raglan down, Bob Corlett & Mrs; and Walton & Mrs, having tea with them. Lady Raglan made conspicuously a lot of Mother: placed her on her right, myself on her left. Lord Raglan enquired particularly about you: much interested in your moves, though I could tell him nothing of your work. He was glad to hear of Lardy too, and Vess.'

Early in April 1915 the Dover Straits net barrage was completed – minefields across the Channel from Dover to Belgium were replaced with steel indicator netting anchored to the sea-bed, a deterrent to vessels entering the Channel, and giving some protection to the ships crossing daily (carrying troops from England to France without loss of a single ship throughout the war). [23]

Mine-laying was becoming more prolific in the Irish Sea in April 1915, the idea being – if German boats laid mines in shipping lanes overnight – important supplies could be stopped from reaching their destination. The shipping lanes therefore needed to be swept regularly for mines.

John reported:

'Two patrol trawlers – or minesweepers – have been working for nearly a week past off Laxey Bay. I could only explain some of their movements by supposing they have a quarter-mile wire dredge out. Whatever they are doing it is continued work.

I have since heard that an explosion took place about a fortnight ago at Maughold Head – a supposed mine drifted ashore. Possibly the sweeping resumed to find any other mines that were about.

Regarding the Ben – Kelly's brother told me yesterday that Kelly had gone away in the Ben, and was an 'Eng. Lieut. Commander (temp) R.N.R.' Probably the importance of the vessel implies that rank for her Chief Engineer. He could not say her destination.

Have since heard that Kelly of the Ben is a 'Warrant Lt.' – whatever that may mean.'

...The *Ben-My-Chree* was sent to the Dardanelles in July.

Regarding submarines, John continued:

'I think as the submarines have had three hunting grounds – lower Bristol Channel towards Scilly Isles, Beachy Head, and Maar Light off Holland – some device might have been employed to entangle them there. But possibly we do not hear of the actual successes...

The submarine does seem to be in process of evolution from submarine with torpedoes, to submersible light cruiser.

I infer that their torpedo shooting has been to miss for the most part, and lose the torpedo, and that small guns are resorted to in order to stop the vessel! The recentest case shows two torpedoes missing, and the third hitting at about 50 yards range!'

As many of the Manx steamers had been requisitioned by the Admiralty (11 out of the 15 in service), fewer holiday visitors were expected from Lancashire, although the Manx people were still hopeful of plenty of visitors.

On April 9th 1915, John wrote:

'The people here are anxious about there being no prospect of boats to convey people here for the season.

The Lancashire and Wales coast places will benefit accordingly.'

In April, Dono was still stationed up at Glasgow working on the construction of *H.M.S. Prince Rupert*, and Daisy was lodging in the locality. John's wife was considering visiting them, and John told Dono:

'Mother has decided, I think, to come out to see you. I may also do so – possibly later. I'm not certain whether we can come together.

I do not know that the Manx boats have any special protection (e.g. destroyer convoy) against submarines. There does not seem to be much concern felt generally about it: I heard the Manx boat had been intercepted or chased? The newspapers would not say so, as they do not wish to frighten visitors thinking of coming across.

At present the passages are decidedly rough. Yesterday the Douglas crossing was 6.5 hours; the Fenella took 13 hours from Glasgow.

Mother favours the boat direct to Glasgow. I said, "The Fenella took 13 hours!"

She says, "I don't care if it was 60 hours – so long as I get to my destination, and back."

She is evidently a better sailor than I am!'

The question was – why did the Manx Boats seem immune to attack? Was their immunity due to the Germans and Austrians being transported across to the internment Camps on the island?

John continued:

'Yesterday Moses Lace, a Victoria Pier Official, told me of a good coup regarding submarines: the source I believe, some patrol boat sea-man home for a holiday.

According to his story, the patrol fleet captured an oil-supply vessel and got possession of her papers. They removed the crew, put a naval crew with gun or guns on board, and went off to the rendezvous to await the submarines for which she had oil. In due course, at a succession of rendezvous, they sank four submarines!

Unfortunately I had heard the story previously from another source, but with two submarines – one for certain, and the other supposed to be sunk also! I thought four submarines rather a big bag.'

Regarding Vess, John reported:

'Sydney Corlett, son of Tom Corlett, and nephew of Capt. Bob Corlett C.P., is in the 16th Battalion King's Liverpool where Vess is a Sub-Lt. Sydney was over at Easter and I had a talk with him. He is going in for quarter-master work and has done no drill work. He said Vess looked very well and was working hard, enjoying his work, and generally was a success as an officer.

Vess has to work a platoon or field-unit of about 60 men; Sydney thought the officers were working harder than the men – field work plus lectures, etc. He said that Capt. Harston, who has this Company, was a Barrister.

I think the legal training is good preparation for Vess's duties.'

Vess was finally *Gazetted* in the *Times*, on Sat April 10th. John wrote:

'Vess is 'Temp 2nd Lt.' The other 5 Lieut.'s of the Manx Co. are J.C. Cunningham, P. Gell, T.S. Handley, A.P. Lace, & P.D. Kissack...'

John wrote to Dono regarding naval action:

'I suspect the Germans view with chagrin the fact that their commerce destroyers on the high seas are gone. Newspapers seem to think they have last week attempted to rush the cordon, and get some new ones away, and that a reported affair off the Norwegian coast was of this nature. I see Captain Kelly R.N. – H.M.S. Gloucester, has got C.B. for hanging on to the Goeben so pluckily. I cannot help thinking that the Goeben was seriously hit. For such a ship, if sound and whole, ought to have done far better in the Black Sea than anything achieved by her.'

...*H.M.S. Gloucester* patrolled the Central Atlantic seas, and was one of the ships responsible for chasing the Goeben at the beginning of the war.

John reported the loss of another ship, *H.M.S Wayfarer*:

'...You may have seen that Harrison's Wayfarer was torpedoed or mined off the Scilly Isles, and towed to Queenstown. The explosion was at the stern, and damaged the rudder.

On Saturday coming up from Laxey I saw a yacht near an armed trawler. Afterwards the yacht went in as far as Garwick Bay and round Clay Head. A woman at South Cape, seeing me looking at this trawler and yacht, said that the yacht had been stopped and made to come alongside the trawler. Afterwards I was told that the trawler had fired three shots before the yacht rounded up and came to her. Someone told me that they had watched with a glass and had seen the yacht's crew go on board, and some of them go back. This yacht was a stranger, and would be 50 tons or so...

There was firing practice – three big ships off the Dhoon on Saturday, but I did not see them.'

For some young Manx men involved in the war, the prospect of travelling to different countries and meeting people outside the island was seen as a great opportunity. Vess was enjoying meeting people as well as concentrating on his training. John reported:

'Vess tells me that he has met a son of Mr Walker, the liquidator of Dumbell's Bank, a subaltern in the Battalion at Hoylake. Finding who Vess was, he came and introduced himself, and asked him to go with him to his home near Chester. Mr Walker was decidedly cordial; Vess stayed to dinner.

When they first went to Hoylake, the Colonel said he wished two of the Manx Officers to join his mess. The three who by volunteer seniority got first choice did not want to go: so Vess immediately accepted, and Lace ditto. They dine with the Col. & senior officers – subs from other Companies also – at 8pm: this mess is at a big house lent by Cain the Brewer. The other mess is at the Club House – where Vess etc., have breakfast & lunch.

They expect to move at an early date to Rhyl or Whitchurch.'

On April 20th 1915, John wrote:

'Vess crossed home on Saturday. We met him at the boat. He looks well and seems more energetic and fit than when he went out...

He describes his field work. He has got a good grasp of it – for example, to advance a Co. of four platoons across Country to attack a position. It is very interesting.

I understood it or worked it out before, but did not divulge details. The repeated training of the men to perform such a movement like a machine is all important.

If things had been rightly managed we ought to have had two battalions of Manx – with officers.

When the war gets to be taken more seriously, able men will be at a premium. I think the combatants should be more highly paid. Beggars here can get to be motor and transport hands with £2 a week and allowances, whereas the combatant soldier has 7/- a week. There is something wrong about this. The skilled worker on ships and armaments ought to get well paid: but not the labourer. I hope that the war may evolve a sounder standard in the matters of promotion etc...'

John was not impressed by the reports in newspapers:

'I think our newspapers need squeezing down by the authorities. Note the premature jubilation and childish rantings over incompleted operations – Dardanelles, Neuve Chapelle etc. I hope Earl Kitchener

will do more in respect of stopping the press from this foolish and noisy kicking up of dust...

I should be sorry if the war could not have the effect of discrediting the liar in this Country. My conviction that Germany was doomed, was long ago based not on military preparations or numbers, but on the fact that they were manifesting themselves indubitably to be swanks & liars, insolent, and resorting to trying to frighten!'

In France, with spring in the air, the British held their ground from Ypres down to Armentières and La Bassée. The 2nd Battle of Ypres ensued and poison gas was first used on the Western Front in the German attack on Canadian troops there.

Lardy had discovered an activity to distract from his work on the railways. John reported on April 22nd:

'...Lardy writes asking for Stuart tackle and line – as there are perch in the river near them, and he would like to catch some. They have had an engine derailed into a very muddy place.

He reports he is well and weather very fine out there. His work is mainly night work – shunting, so I expect he will have some hours off during the day.

It seems odd his fishing in a French river.'

Vess returned to Hoylake to continue his training after his brief leave at home.

Regarding the effects of the war in the Island, John commented:

'...The most we can see of activities are the patrol trawlers passing here.

One's inexperienced beforehand impressions of the war are like one's distant view of a range of hills or mountains: as one travels towards them, they increase in magnitude, and the separate ridges, slopes and valleys assume larger proportions.

Here in this island and Parish and neighbourhood, one's sense of magnitude gets dwarfed. Yet it is sitting in a little room like this study of mine that the mind can think out what may have an effect as far reaching as to baffle the Berlin staff.'

Towards the end of April 1915 an Allied ground assault (amphibian landing) began in Gallipoli. The Dardanelles Strait provided a sea route through to the Russian Empire. British and French naval forces therefore intended to secure the Strait, and launched an attack. Hamilton commanded the Mediterranean Expeditionary Force.

With the object of visiting Dono, John and his wife crossed from the Isle of Man by the 8.30 Douglas to Glasgow boat on Mon April 26th, arriving in Greenock around 6.30. John had arranged for Mr Kneale to take his Church duty on the following Sunday. After visiting Dono and Daisy, John and his wife took the train south to Manchester.

The great tragedy of May 7th was the sinking of *R.M.S. Lusitania*, a passenger/cargo ship with 1,959 passengers on board, torpedoed off the Irish coast near Kinsdale Head by German submarine. She sank within 20 minutes; 1,198 people went down with her, including a great number of British and many Americans. It was hoped that this would prise America out of her neutrality. The I.O.M. Peel fishing boat *Wanderer* rescued 160 of the few survivors.

> ...At the news of the sinking of *R.M.S. Lusitania*, jubilation broke out amongst the men at the Douglas internment Camp. Formerly the prisoners were allowed to go out of the Camp with guards in groups for walks along the prom, but after this their liberty was curbed. [3]
>
> Anti-German Riots in UK towns led to the Government stepping up the operation to move Germans to internment camps, partly for their own safety. Although the Knockaloe Camp was only initially supposed to house 5000, the numbers there increased dramatically after this.

John wrote the following to Dono from Manchester:

> *'...We got here about 4.30pm Friday. Yesterday we saw the Cathedral etc.; today, the Church in morning. In the afternoon we went to Heston Park.*
>
> *The loss of the Lusitania, and Harrison's two big vessels off the south of Ireland indicates I think that the 'pirates', more than one probably, have come round from north & west.*
>
> *It renders necessary a most drastic movement to deal with their craft, and no doubt this will be done beyond anything heretofore attempted!*
>
> *I hope you are well, and that your work is progressing to your satisfaction. We hope to see Vess of course, and will go to Liverpool the day before crossing to see him in the evening.'*

John and his wife visited Vess at Hoylake and had returned home to the Vicarage, crossing to the Isle of Man from Liverpool on *S.S. Tynwald*. John reported to Dono:

'We had a delightful passage back on Saturday May 15th, so far as regards weather. The passage was 4 hours 10 minutes! Unfortunately Mother got a speck of smoke dust from the funnel in her eye going down the Mersey and she was in great pain all the way.

Approaching the harbour, off Douglas Head we saw some floating stuff, such as is sometimes thrown overboard from a vessel.

Today there is a report about that the Tynwald passed a floating mine; one version is that she had to make a wide detour to escape it...'

John wrote later:

'It turns out that on Sat May 15th, the Tynwald passed a 'floating mine' about 10 miles off the Liverpool Bar. But I am sure none of the passengers saw it. There never was a move on the part of anyone on deck to show that anyone had seen anything: and though I was in conversation with several persons, none of them had evidently any idea of our having passed anything suspicious.'

...Floating mines were a constant danger to boats, and on one occasion, *S.S. Tynwald* came close. When about mid channel a small object was sighted and the crew just had time to alter course. The wash from the propellers of the ship turned it over so that they could see the mine and its horns. If the mine had exploded, the ship would have been destroyed. [21 – Manx Fleet pp56/59]

Lord Raglan was once again offering help regarding obtaining Commissions for John's sons. John wrote:

'He will do anything he can in backing up an application for a Commission (Eng. Lieut.) for Lardy for transferring from land to sea-service. He was profoundly interested in the data to confirm that we had all done an important service to our country. "My dear Canon," was the cordial way in which he spoke to me.

He was very glad indeed to hear of your present service.

The universal wail in Douglas is 'no season – poverty – misery – ruin'. The authorities say we are to have no extra boats at Whitsuntide and no visitor traffic this summer. Douglas will suffer. The agricultural interest on the island is prosperous. Ramsey for example, as the town of the northern district, will manage to get on in spite of the loss of a visitor season. Peel is much better of late on account of the big camp at Knockaloe giving them some business: and the town but small.

Douglas and Port Erin will suffer most. Fred Brew says the solution would be a sum of money found by the Imperial Government. If the House of Keys was a sufficiently intelligent body it might formulate a scheme: but it is too weak as a whole to attempt such a thing. Of course 'the Government' ought to do 'this' and 'that', and a good many other things: but the Palace, the Cinema, etc., are advertising as usual, and all the various 'religious' bodies are after money. Till they stop, I don't intend to sympathize.'

...According to a later Manx newspaper report, the Palace opened for Whit week, the attendance much higher than expected. Given a programme of dancing, the majority were young and mainly local people. The paper reported:

'It was surprising to see so many Douglas men of a military age dancing, who would have been better employed fighting at the Front... or training...'

John continued:

'...I saw William Knox, and told him about your idea of turning his lathes to account. As usual he flew off in contradiction. 'There was no want of machines to turn shells; but his difficulty was lack of firms that could cast the particular sort of steel! There were concentration camps, but no orders for the firm of W. Knox' (where Dono served his apprenticeship).

However he was genuinely interested in your job...'

Dono's ship *H.M.S. Prince Rupert* was launched on May 20th. Regarding the launch of the monitor, John wrote to Dono:

'Thanks for the photos & sketch of your voyage down the Clyde. I think that in steam trials, very careful experiments should be made, to discover which set of engines gives best results – port or starboard: for the chances are that one may develop greater efficiency...'

John was longing to hear more about Dono's ship, but he had other matters on his mind. John was sure that the individual 'representing the Admiralty' who interviewed Vess in March was bogus and wrote to Dono on May 25th:

'The enclosed cutting refers to the man, the first time he is said to have come to the island. I believe the beggar is a German spy.

You should carry your revolver for it is possible that you might be watched! If he was in Portsmouth in January, then I take it he got my letter dated Jan 22nd, and it is for that reason missing. The original, even if copied, ought to have been forwarded to you, but it never was!

The impression left on Vess by the interview on Mar 5 – was that Wardle evaded all questions as to why he had not come to see me –

he was eager to know your whereabouts. He is now in gaol. I am trying to get at him – per Government Office.'

I.O.M. Daily Times May 24 1915 (Résumé):

'Bogus Naval Officer – Well deserved sentence – The mysterious Captain Wardle: Case heard at Douglas Police Court... Charles Francis Wardle, 50, from Huddersfield, supposedly not in the employ of the Admiralty from April, but wore a naval uniform on 21st May 1915 in Douglas – calculated to deceive... Charge made under Defence of the Realm Act...

He came to island for first time on Mar 5; had taken a residence in the south of the island... Sentenced to three months imprisonment...'

John continued:

'An enquiry is being made as to the antecedents of 'Capt.' Wardle; they are trying to trace his movements. I gave Mr Sargeaunt the list of dates of letters which you had received from me – showing the letter dated Jan 22 not reaching you.'

At the end of May, Lardy was still hopeful of a transfer to Naval Service. John wrote:

'Lardy's Commanding Officer has sanctioned his transfer to Naval Service, if appointed. I wrote to enquire, and had a note from Admiral Austey – who knows you! I filled up the application...

I now have a reply from Whitehall to say they have decided not to issue a Commission (Eng. Lieut. R.N.) to Lardy.

Lardy does not wish the matter to go further, as he says he is all right in his present work.'

Life on the island continued with fund raising and the normal meetings for John in Douglas:

'Mother and I went to Government House this week to a tea on the lawn. Not many men were present, but a good crowd of local people, as there was a contribution of 1/- for Red Cross.

There is a very quiet aspect of things here, through the total absence of Whitsuntide visitors. Today in Douglas I saw Callister, Schoolmaster of Onchan, who showed me a letter from his son dated Wed 26th I think – relating particulars of the Wayfarer etc.; incidentally it mentioned that 'T-28, German latest type has been caught intact with all the crew outside the Bar and taken to Barrow'...

Also... two others were 'taken between Liverpool and the Clyde'. I also met a Dalby farmer in Douglas, who showed me a cheque for £147 received from the caterer for the Camp at Knockaloe. I expect it would be for meat supplied. He implied that farmers were not losing money.

Cannan of Kirk Michael told me his son, an engineer in the navy, was at Athens, sent out by the Admiralty for service in the Greek Navy – on shore I gathered.

It seems that Lord Fisher has left the Admiralty, and Sir Jackson moved to the vacant place as successor.

I gather some real progress is being made at Dardanelles; but Mr Churchill's acceptance of a back-seat in the Cabinet seems to imply that his policy in these operations was thought unsatisfactory.

Of course at Lord Fisher's age, ill health may account for his retirement.'

Early in June, Lardy had written from Abbeville, where his railway work had been ongoing, but said they were leaving for Ypres again shortly. On the railways:

> 'The work was hard and hours were long, but on the whole living conditions were fair. At times the Companies were housed in railway wagons fitted with wooden bunks'. [13]

John wanted a revolver. He wrote:

'...Lardy lent one to Fred Kermode, but Sam Kermode seems to have taken it, supposing naturally it was Fred's own. If you are sending yours home when you go to sea, perhaps I might have the use and loan of it.'

There had been some unrest in the Knockaloe Camp. John reported:

'They had some Indian soldiers here at the Knockaloe Camp. A German insulted one of them and the Indian nearly killed him. I have had different versions of the story. The Indians were removed, but I think a hundred or so would have been a very useful reserve to have kept as guards.

We have too many rather worn out reservists who are always drinking. I have no idea what sort of officers are in charge of them. Half the number of vigorous men would have been better. Mr Sargeaunt told me that there were 10 guards to every 100 prisoners at one camp, and 12 to 100 at the other.

Of course there are the I.O.M. Volunteers, a more vigorous lot; the motor carriages are retained so that the Volunteers could be conveyed rapidly to any point at short notice.

We are having rather good weather. Mother is wondering if a box of magazines would be of any use for your engine room crew. If so she will send them via steamer to Greenock (Glasgow). *I think, as Greenock is full of German spies it would be well to keep an extra look out – so no unauthorised person gets on board the ship!*

It is a strange thing that our people, if in Germany, would not attempt what these Germans will attempt... they are not to be trusted. For my part the cause is everything: but then I am one of those that have for years lived in a state of pain and regret over the 'individualism' rotting England.'

The submarine menace was now a real threat to the British and Manx economy, as ships carrying food and supplies were increasingly targeted. John wrote on June 8th:

'I enclose a cutting from London Times; also Churchill's speech at Dundee. It would seem that both writer of the article and Mr Churchill, speak with a sort of confidence that submarine warfare is confined to definite limits. The further extension of those limits in the direction of the enemy's base is a matter of time, no doubt.'

London Times June 7 1915:

'...50 ships sunk during 3 months since inauguration of the German 'blockade' – 1 for every 600 arriving or leaving ports of U.K. Since May 19, 12 more steamers sunk. Many trawlers sunk in last month – war upon fishermen... No suggestion that Germans intend to abate the virulence of destroying the merchantmen...

"England wishes to starve us," said Grand Admiral von Tirpitz in Dec 1914: "We might play the same game and encircle England, torpedoing every British ship & those of the Allies – cutting off the greater part of England's food supply."'

Part of Mr Churchill's speech – Dundee June 5:

'...Those years have comprised the most important period in our naval history, a period of preparation for war, a period of vigilance & mobilisation, and a period of war under conditions of which no man had any experience... I look also to the general naval situation. The terrible dangers of the beginning of the war are over. The seas have been swept clean. The submarine menace has been fixed within definite limits... The superior quality of our ships on the high seas, have been established beyond doubt or question. Our strength has greatly increased actually and relatively from what it was in the beginning of the war, and it grows continually every day... You have taken the measure of your foe. You have only to go forward with confidence...'

On the island on June 8th there was another military meeting in Laxey. John wrote:

'Mother and I went. I had to sit on the platform.

Willy Kerruish and Ramsey Moore came down to move the feelings of the community to join the Manx Loyal Volunteer force, of which they are members in Douglas; Fox, of the theatre management, came with them in his motor.

It had its amusing sides: for those two were anti-all-militarism before the war... Jas Corkill asked Kerruish if he had not been against all militarism before the war; Kerruish said, "Absolutely not!" A point blank lie, of course!

It appears that a now extinct organization, the Loyal Manx Association, were in the position that if one of the men had fired a shot and hit anybody, he would have been open to a legal charge of manslaughter. The new Manx Loyal Volunteers will now be able to fire a shot without being open to such a legal charge.

What they want, is all men over 40 excused from the obligation to enlist. They are going to drill and march etc., but not likely to have any firearms given to them. One of the arguments was to organize 'in view of the large number of alien enemies in our Camps'; but on the other hand it was asserted that these were so safely guarded that the chances were 10,000 to one against any escaping.

'A raid on our shores' was also trolled out, but this was not convincing.

The Dr made a speech, showing that those that did not join would, in event of a raid, be made to go indoors – or be called out by the enemy to dig their trenches etc. – altogether, the matter overdone. On the other hand, all rejoiced over utterances by members of the Government that there was to be 'no conscription' and the inference – that we had already sufficient forces enlisted etc.

To have taken the thing too seriously would have been a mistake. It seemed all too ludicrous – W.M. Kerruish and Ramsey Moore, two ant-militarists, trying to catch at popularity as heroic hearts ready to lead, when it was certain that no actual contingency would arise of risk to their own skins.'

...There were several escape attempts from Knockaloe Camp. The Governor convened military Courts on the island, which was where any prisoners of war were tried. There were 345 convictions over the period of the war Camp years, of which at least 98 were for escaping or attempting to escape from the Camps. [3]

In mid-June, Lardy was sceptical about getting a furlough (leave). John told Dono:

'I heard from a Douglas man, whose son is out there (in France/Belgium), that Lardy was driving an armoured train. Lardy wrote to Mary for four respirators but he has not mentioned to us anything of that. He says he is quite well.'

The regulations were tightening regarding Manx sea-vessels and John reported:

'Small boats are not allowed to go out from Laxey or Garwick without permits: I do not know the reason of this regulation. But it gives a control, which the patrol boats ought to have. After the case reported in the paper of the Glasgow firm supplying the enemy with iron ore, it is no surprise to find any and everybody open to suspicion.

Yesterday morning I heard of the accident to Lt. Warneford V.C. I mentioned it to a Lonan farmer with several sons in his house, but he had not heard of Warneford's Zeppelin feat. There are lots of these people that don't care a straw for anything but the inflated prices of farm produce. They deprive brave men of one important part of what is due to them: viz. that their names should be known and associated with their brave and daring acts.'

...Reginald Warneford was the first man to destroy a Zeppelin in combat over Belgium on 7th June 1915.

The German airship, adopted and improved by Zeppelin, was the pride of Germany, although the idea was initially designed by the French. The Zeppelin was an impressive engine of terror and destructive action, yet frail – a pencil shaped rigid structure with aluminium framework. There had been many airship catastrophes in preceding years; hence Germany was turning increasingly to the idea of aeroplanes.

The German Emperor is reported to have said that he never willed the war. If war with England had been any part of the German plan, German airships would have been more numerous – ready for immediate action. The initial German theory was that England was not prepared for war and therefore would not go to war. [24]

After the launch of *H.M.S. Prince Rupert*, Dono was Engineer Officer on board the ship, where he worked from 22nd June 1915 until March 1917, under Captain H. Reinhold. The ship had to undergo trials at sea before going into action. John wrote to Dono advising:

'You might possibly give Daisy a small code by which to indicate where you are, if that is permissible.

I should like to know how you get on with the steam trials, and if in general the machinery turns out satisfactory.

I know you are too busy to write; things must be in a state of confusion till you get them into shape. I assume you have a service rule book, which must decide absolutely everything, and simplify your work in one sense.

Remember the words of the Admiral – 'an opportunity to distinguish yourself!' You have done that in engineering; now it is to be as a sea officer.

There is no doubt that a big ship like the Achilles was grand experience.

'No friends at sea,' was a saying of your own, and a good one. It applies on land too.'

John considered the German submarine blockade:

'...From certain expressions quoted from German papers it would seem that they have found their submarine blockade considerably a failure. One quotation was an admission by a German of 11 submarines lost: but whether it included all those sunk by ramming etc., I don't know.

Perhaps the German in question knew no particulars more than any other man in the street. I gather from similar quotations that the enemy has an idea of submarines to attack ships in the N. Atlantic, out on the ocean – a larger type of submarine no doubt.'

John wrote on June 23rd to Dono:

'It is interesting to have an idea of your destination.

We have heard nothing of any submarines off the island, or anywhere in the Irish Sea of late. But in the few mentions in papers, a writer asks if some device could be found to deal with the airship menace, 'such as the Admiralty have applied so successfully to the submarine menace'! '

Regarding the suspicious Admiralty man, John reported:

'...I have heard nothing of Capt. Wardle since, but if I hear I will let you know. Apparently a few German spies are being dealt with: and the detention of this man may mean that he is being enquired about!

We have almost nothing to tell you of home news: everything is extremely quiet.

There are of course no visitors on the island! We heard that one day only three passengers crossed.'

At the height of summer, John's wife was helping with a Soldiers & Sailors Help Society function at the Nunnery in Douglas.

The charitable organization was dormant in autumn 1914, but revived in 1915. Lady Raglan, wife of the I.O.M. Governor was President.

John wrote to Dono:

'...Mother rather enjoyed it. She heard a good story there of the Knockaloe Camp. A guard raised a midnight alarm, and raised the Officers.

Dialogue as follows:

Guard: "Aeroplane!"

Officer: "Did you see it?"

Guard: "No – heard it... there it is again!"

Officer: "Why, you blooming idiot... that, an aeroplane? Why... it's a corncrake!"

It seems the guard had never heard the sound before in his life.

I believe the Camp at Knockaloe has now an immense crowd in it, but I have not been over on that side of the island for a good while.'

...Corncrakes are related to the moorhen and coot family, but differ in that they live on dry land. They have bright chestnut coloured wings in flight, brown streaks on their body, and a rasping call.

John wrote to Dono on board his ship on June 27th:

'I am hoping that in spite of delays you are getting on satisfactorily with the ship.

We have a note from Lardy; he implies that men have overstayed their leaves and that there is a chance of leaves being stopped. '

In the summer of 1915, the Manx Company and the Kings Liverpool's were sent from Hoylake to Kinmel Park Camp Rhyl, N. Wales – to join a Brigade of 9000, and also for training at St Asaph Camp.

On June 29th, John wrote:

'Vess has gone to camp near St Asaph, three miles from Kinmel Park Camp. They are under canvas and have had wet weather.'

...The Kinmel Camp was established in 1914 for the training of Lord Kitchener's Army.

A young man named Bridson in the Royal Monmouth Co. visited his brother (in the Manx Co.) at Vess's Camp in Wales. Vess asked him about Lardy. John reported:

'He seemed to Vess a decent sort of fellow. He had been a good lot with Lardy – in the same Co. – and lodged in the same train or railway

carriage quarters. He said Lardy was very fit and might get a furlough possibly next week.

Vess gave him a note to give to Lardy, asking to wire him if he got home, so that he might meet him in Liverpool.

Vess seems as usual. He calls some of the seniors 'asses' – with no motive but arbitrary alteration of his plans. The case of point seemed to be the 'course' to go through at the Officers Training Depot!

The others are taking machine-gun courses: he thinks signalling his forte.

I have advised him of the absolute importance of machine-gun training and I am only too glad to hear that it is receiving attention!'

On July 5th (Tynwald Day in the I.O.M.) the Manx Company in North Wales treated the rest of the Battalion to an imitation of the ancient Tynwald ceremony. The Battalion returned to Kinmel and later moved to Preese Heath in Shropshire. [4]

Meanwhile on the island, John, being Chaplain to the *House of Keys* had attended the Tynwald Church Service at St John's. On the journey, John learnt of defects in soldiery which could be easily avoided: some points to be considered by his sons. He wrote to Dono:

'...Mr Robinson provided a motor car to go to Tynwald on July 5, taking Mr Aylen & children, Mother and myself. Commander Sims R.N. was at Tynwald. I met him some weeks ago. He has charge of wireless etc.

After Tynwald we went to Peel, then to Port Erin via Foxdale – the object purely to eat a lunch in one place and have tea in the other.

I rode beside the chauffeur, whom I found was an ex-soldier, disabled by a foot wound – he was in a West Yorkshire Regiment last August – and by October, in France. He was intelligent. He had two points only – the delicacy of the service rifle and ability to jam – through dust, mud, or any kind of dirt getting about the breech-action.

He said that an enormous number of men in the trenches were helpless through jammed rifles, with no means of clearing them. For 'Bisley' and clean green fields and fine weather he thought the rifle perfect, but not among picks, spades, mud or sand or dust scattered by shell fire, and when men were dirty with trenching.

His second point was machine-guns. He said, 'two to a battalion was nothing, versus the Germans' twelve. Germans, a dozen or so, with 4 machine guns could hold a whole trench and offer no target, but spaces of blank ground for our artillery; whereas a whole platoon of ours with rifles had to hold a trench with far greater risk of casualties from German artillery'. These were the main topic of his 'experience'!

I have mentioned these points to Vess. I grasp the man's point about the dirt jamming – because I have thought it out before...

A small shield could be made and supplied to men going into a trench, that might be far more useful than at first the apparent trouble of it; something to protect the breech and muzzle. The sights would have to be visible, but these hoods would rather help to concentrate the eye along the sighting line. Perhaps you could design such a thing: the material need only be light and cheap, so that if a few million were made they would not cost much. I assume you have service rifles on board – to get exact size and shape of parts to which such device might be accurately designed. For a winter campaign the advantage would be enormous. Papier mâché or cardboard would almost be enough if it resisted rain. It might be kept in view that a man wishes to lay down his rifle while trenching, and it ought to be protected from mud when laid on its side on dirty ground.'

John wrote to Dono regarding *H.M.S. Prince Rupert*, during her trials:

'It is a great satisfaction to get your letter this evening. I was quite certain you would have much anxiety and worry over the trials period. It is interesting how true your calculation, that 7.5 knots would be the limit of speed.

I have been recalling your experience in the trials of a destroyer built by Lairds for Argentina, afterwards sold to the Greeks – how the thrust block and other bearings heated at the turning tests.

I am glad that your ship has at least done what you conjectured, and is as fast as any turned out yet. I hope the further trials, and remedy of any short comings will be satisfactorily got over.

You will overcome greater difficulties than these, but it is provoking when the things to be overcome are due to other people!

Yes: but it would be more provoking if they were due to oneself...

The defects in the condensers, I understand to be the main short coming of the job... I omitted to ask what time the ship took to build, and if that time was too short for the work to be rightly done? – Or if the fault lay with the outside firm?

Vess mentioned having heard of your possibly coming to the Mersey – which I thought might mean getting another firm to complete the job! I recognize the place described in Daisy's letter, where you got your launch aground. I don't mean the exact point, but the bar that exists there.

We hear from newspapers that Admiral Sir John Fisher has been visiting the Clyde. I was wondering if he had paid a visit to your part of it. I see that he resumes active work as Chairman of the Investing Board, a new department of the Admiralty. I think it was under him that one invention, which I hear is highly successful, was tried. Mary has heard that the results are a big thing. A gentleman from Dover, visiting a neighbour of theirs, was debating on the wonders of Dover harbour in war-time; among other things – six captured vessels which he had seen there.'

Nets and mines were a deterrent to submarines. Later, John wrote:

'How little thought is given to the fact that spite the existence of submarines, the English Channel in that area is clear of the menace. I consider that your net is one of the great things, as great by itself as any other single achievement of the war. I trust that due recognition of the simple and direct thought which created it, will come in due course...'

At the Vicarage, John was watching for unusual vessels or activity at sea and spotted what he at first thought was a submarine. He told Dono:

'I saw what I took to be a possible submarine on Tuesday evening about 10 miles off here: weather bright with hazy visibility, sea – flat, no breeze; position of craft – on line Douglas to Barrow or Douglas to Heysham; time 3.45 – 4.45. Craft was moving and manoeuvring, sometimes head on. White foam was distinct – consequently a motor-boat. No other craft in sight – except S.S. Tynwald five or six miles south on passage Liverpool to Douglas. About 4.45 the craft turned and moved rapidly off towards Barrow – disappeared suddenly after 5 minutes. If to cause the impression of a white yacht by small mast & sails – the effect was successfully obtained. Of course I do not know if there is anything in Irish Sea of enemy craft, but two hours after I saw this craft disappear, a flotilla of 8 patrol trawlers emerged from behind Clay Head halfway between that and St Bees Head. I had not seen any for a fortnight. I concluded there might be something in my

conjecture. I reported to Sargeaunt next morning and I think he wired my report to the proper quarter.'

John wrote a few days later:

'Patrol boats are still about here. I saw five this morning – including a fine yacht, which seems the mother ship of the flotilla. I was told their station is at Holyhead.

I saw this yacht beside Douglas pier. They were all R.N.R officers, but I thought some of the men might be navy trained from their look. They have a gun-platform amidships forward of the bridge, and the trawlers have now the gun on a platform on the forecastle deck – instead of near the bulwark amidships, as when I first saw them some months ago.'

Dono's ship, *H.M.S. Prince Rupert*, had arrived at Plymouth. On July 18th, John wrote to Dono:

'From Daisy's letter last evening, I was glad to see the good result of your steaming! 440k in 70 hours, or 6+ k average.

I assume you had good weather throughout – weather not so good here.

The Governor is very wishful to see Lardy if he gets home; I gather that he has the idea of getting him a Commission. No word of his furlough yet – I don't know what principles are given: I heard one man who has been in France since August last without getting leave home.

Vess writes from No.8 Camp, Kinmel Park – very well and keen on work. He is detached for Officer's training course.'

Regarding the role of women in the war, this era was one which opened up new opportunities for women – they were given jobs which they had never done before. On the island, the woman's place had been strictly in the home, but many were now in poverty, suffering lack of boarding house income with loss of holiday trade.

To benefit these women, Rev. Copeland Smith with other investors, founded the Manx Industries Association and helped set up a small factory with knitting machines in the Isle of Man in July 1915. Women were instructed how to use and maintain the machines.

Eventually, due to expansion, the business moved to an unused entertainment pavilion on Douglas promenade. In the Derby Castle Theatre, items such as socks, coats, stockings and overcoats were manufactured.

The Palace Ballroom in Douglas was used for the production of airship components including silk balloons which were sent to Vickers in Barrow for airships. [3]

Derby Castle Theatre knitting machines M.N.H. [1]

After the 'Munitions of War Act' which came into force on July 2nd 1915, manufacturing companies in Britain and on the island were increasingly being turned over to the manufacture of war materials.

John had seen from the newspapers that some factories in Britain were turning out standard munitions in great quantity and wrote:

> *'I saw William Knox a few days ago. He was exceedingly angry because he had not been asked to meet when a sort of Committee was summoned to discuss and offer opinion as to whether any munitions work could be carried out on the island.*
>
> *Robby Knox, Ashburner, Blackburn, the Foundry man, etc. were summoned – but W. Knox overlooked. Certainly he had a grievance. Possibly his utterances on the Town Council have accounted for this.*
>
> *There are a new lot of troops, about 700, now camped at Ramsey – recruits in training I think – as a sort of reserve group and stand-by in case of trouble at the aliens' Camp.*
>
> *I have not had any opportunity of seeing the great camp at Knockaloe since the autumn. I hope to get a day over on that side of the island before long to see what it is now like.'*

Lardy's Company moved from Abbeville on July 7th to the Calais district (Beau-Marais) where they cleared an area of ground of gorse, and levelled it for the site of a canvas hospital – the groundwork was completed by the end of the month. [29]

Lardy finally got home for a few days leave, and John reported on July 22nd:

'Lardy is just the very same as he was, quite cheerful and quite well. He is stationed a few miles from Calais just now – his Co. has been there for about a fortnight. Today we went out to the Lhergy and he fired some shots from the .380 revolver: very good shooting, though at short range.

He had an interview with Lord Raglan who suggested that he should try for a Commission. Lord Raglan will recommend him all he can – suggested I make an application. Yesterday after seeing the Governor, Lardy went to see Aunt Mary Ann, and in the afternoon to Silverdale – saw Uncle Thomas & Aunt Eva. He came back to Douglas and took Nan to see a picture show.

Mother and I hope to go in to see him off by boat tomorrow. It is the S.S. Tynwald: so I hope he will get the early train to London, to report at Victoria Station about 5.30 on Saturday, and get the train for the Channel boat.

I'm not sure whether Vess will get to Liverpool to meet Lardy tomorrow evening – it is a good distance from Rhyl. He hoped to see Margaret and Mary & Graham in London on the route back.'

In the height of summer the streets of the Isle of Man were usually bustling with visitors, but in the summer of 1915, John wrote:

'Things are more and more quiet here. I passed through Laxey street today – as far as the tram station and back. It was the half holiday. Scarce a person was visible in the street.

The trams, much curtailed in their time-tables, are said to be losing £40 a week – viz. about 10/- on every single journey they run. Yet every time I have been in the trams the seats seem all occupied, or well occupied.

The people on their part find money to travel. But mortgage interest and a big plant, absorb several times more than they earn.'

...By the end of the summer season of 1915, the number of holiday makers had dropped significantly to just 33,786 from the 404,000 of 1914. The latter figure included soldiers on furlough but not aliens or soldiers on the island [16.10.1915: I.O.M. Examiner]. The drop in visitors was due to lack of boats to convey them as well as the added danger of crossing.

...Regarding some Manx vessels employed by the Admiralty, the Manx sea-plane ship, *Ben-My-Chree*, was working off the Greek coast near Smyrna in July. *H.M.S. Ramsey* was on patrol in the North Sea. Early in August, *H.M.S. Ramsey* was attacked by the German mine-layer ship, *S.M.S. Meteor*, masquerading as a Russian ship, and sank in 4 minutes; out of 98 crew, 52 were killed, the majority below deck. Four officers and 39 men were picked up by *S.M.S. Meteor*. [21]

Once the trials of Dono's ship, *H.M.S. Prince Rupert,* were over in August, the new ship came into the action for which she had been built – patrolling and bombarding German batteries along the Belgian coast.

In his memoirs, Dono wrote about the Dover Patrol on which he was engaged:

'It should not be forgotten that from the beginning of the war to the end, the normal Front line occupied by the naval forces of the Dover Patrol was never more than twelve miles from the enemy coast. Monitors and destroyers were within sight of the Germans from Zeebrugge and Nieuport practically every day, and the big guns of the shore batteries frequently fired at the ships. Mines did not stay in position very long after being laid. For a lengthy period the whole coast from Dutch Territorial waters to Dunkerque was ringed in with our mined nets. The nets were constantly renewed and inspected by our destroyers.

It would have been no surprise to the enemy to see a force of monitors accompanied by an escort of destroyers, monitors, smoke-boats etc. cruising about in daylight any day, as it was normal routine.

To this extent, the ground was prepared for the Zeebrugge blocking operation.

Special bombardments were carried out by the monitors both by day and night from time to time in addition to the daily patrol.' [2]

...On 9th August *H.M.S. Prince Rupert* lay in the Thames Estuary practicing bombardment techniques along with the ships *H.M.S. Lord Clive* and *H.M.S. Sir John Moore*, in preparation for a bombardment of the Belgian coast later in August.

Vess had now had around ten months of training and crossed home for a week's leave. John wrote on August 10th:

'This morning Vess went in to call on the Governor and on Major Mackenzie. He seems very well, slightly less robust than three months ago, which he attributes to marches, carrying kit of 90lb – which the officers do as well as the men. He has had a musketry course at Conway; this completes the training requirements so that he can now be drafted for active service.

I think he has got a thorough grasp of handling men, a platoon of 60, or a Company of 4 platoons. He says that all the different Companies are alike to him; he could take charge of a platoon or Company of any regiment of infantry without it making any difference...

It appears that when they went to Hoylake, the Colonel promised that the Manx Co. should retain its identity, remain as a unit and go to the Front – officers and men as a unit. Vess discovered that this was probably unlikely by the arrangements Headquarters make, and drafts will be sent as Headquarters decide.

Already a draft of 60 from the Co. is ordered to Salisbury to join the 12th Battalion of the Regiment, a Service Battalion – the 16th remaining a reserve or training Battalion. He thinks that this will be repeated and that he may be sent to Salisbury or elsewhere to fill gaps in Service formations – as a 2nd Lt. preparing for active service.

Yesterday he met on the boat a young Manxman named Kermode from New Zealand, who had been at Gallipoli and been wounded. Young Kermode was going to Peel to his Uncle Thomas' house.

Today Thos. Kermode, his brother and this young soldier motored over and called here, but only for a few minutes. His impressions as quoted by Vess are interesting, and not too optimistic.

He returns to the N. Zealand contingent at Gallipoli.'

The impact of the 'Munitions Act' was beginning to kick in; John wrote:

'I heard yesterday that Gelling's Foundry have signed an agreement to manufacture munitions, at least to turn shells; they have nine lathes for the work (which eventually worked day and night).

The Governor has a scheme to turn Douglas into a 'turning factory', getting its power from the engines of the Manx Elec. Railway Co.'

Some thought was still being given to net design. John wrote:

'...I have not thought much about the torpedo net around anchored ships.

The following is a device that in anchorage conditions might work; rigidity must be avoided.

I take the ship to be 100 to 200 yards long: -Net to drop from a set of floats, the resistance to submersion to be the decelerating resistance.

-Size of mesh sufficiently small to prevent the hemispherical head of a torpedo going through, but as large as possible.

-Booms or gaffs from ship to line of floats, to hinge freely, to keep the line of floats at a distance from the ship's side ...to act as lever arms; when float is pulled down, its path to be a circle.

-The net is arranged with a 'pocket' at the bottom on the principle of a salmon net – continuous along foot of net on the outer side.

-Torpedo strikes net – the net fires, resistance only that of the floats, which are submerged a little, the lever arm not causing any rigidity. The torpedo presses the yielding net, which sweeps back towards the ship; meanwhile the torpedo tends to slip along the surface of the net till it heads into the pocket or trough.

-After meeting the pocket, the torpedo pulls on the floats, and decelerates it gradually – so it cannot reach the ship's side...

I need not work this out too closely at present – I merely give the idea.'

John's brother Thomas, and his wife Eva, ran the tea-rooms and the amenities at Silverdale, which included boat swings and a Victorian water-powered roundabout, as well as a boating lake. During summer months it was common for Eva to prepare large numbers of picnics for visitors, as well as the annual Sunday School picnic; John's wife often went over to help. John wrote on August 14th:

'This week we all went to Silverdale on Thursday to a tea organized by Uncle Thomas and Aunt Eva, with the Committee of the Red Cross fund. Lady Raglan and her two daughters came and stayed till nearly 6pm. There was a great crowd of people: about £150 realized.'

Silverdale Garden Party 1915 M.N.H. [1]

In the photo, Lady Raglan is seated at the front with a feather in her hat and is wearing a very elegant gown. The gentleman seated to the front-right is Thomas Quine, John's brother.

The 1915 garden party, opened by Lady Raglan (photo: M.N.H. [1]), was a very dressy affair. The summer of 1915 had been relatively busy at Silverdale despite the lack of visitors on the island.

Obviously John was aware that Dono's ship may be engaged in battle at any time, and wrote:

> *'The Daily Mail this evening reports considerable gunfire heard off the Kent coast, making us conjecture that you may be in that neighbourhood.*
>
> *I hope that the defects, which the severe strain of sea-service and with the mercantile standard machinery, may be within your power to cope with. Leastways I hope that you may have opportunities of recuperation and sleep after spells of work and worry.*
>
> *The Daily Telegraph of Thursday Aug 12th had lengthened extracts from an article in a German review by Capt. Pertius, a well-known German Naval critic, headed in large type 'Confessions of Failure' referring mainly to their submarine campaign. Certainly the tone was such as to justify that title.*
>
> *Things are unspeakably quiet here on the island. Our weather has been rather moist and warm. It is apparently Zeppelin weather. The newspapers give only a brief account of the recent raids, and as everything is simply 'E. Coast' we have little clue to exact locality.'*

...There were failed attempts of Zeppelins to reach London on 9th & 12th of August, but the latter raid killed 6 people.

Vess crossed back to Rhyl at the end of his week's leave, and John and his wife went to Douglas to see him off. He wired to say he had a good passage of 5 hours on the *Douglas*, and John wrote on August 16th to Dono:

> *'His battalion is moving to Whitchurch in Shropshire, and so are all the English battalions.*
>
> *The Camp at Rhyl is to be solely Welsh. Vess seems to have got a dislike to the Welsh. N.C.O.'s, and men of the Welsh battalion drink together in pubs: hence no discipline. There is much of the same thing in the case of officers and no control. Some drafts of officers have gone from the 16th Kings Battalion, so he thinks movement to active service is nearer than heretofore.'*

On clear cold days – the coast from Whitehaven down to Barrow, approximately 50 miles from the Isle of Man, is faintly visible. Around 1910, a plant was installed in the vicinity of Lowca by a German manufacturer to extract chemicals from coal – the plant was designated 'top secret' by the Germans during WWI. On 16th August 1915 a U-boat surfaced off Harrington and began bombardment of the Lowca area. The report appeared in the Whitehaven news on 19th Aug. There was also an airship factory in the vicinity which may also have been a target. John reported:

> *'This morning 4.30 – 5.20 a submarine shelled Whitehaven, Parton & Harrington a stretch about 6 or 7 miles of the Cumberland shore: no casualties, and little damage. Of course the Admiralty do not tell us if the raider was intercepted: in these matters, much secrecy observed.'*

John later reported:

> *'The German submarine which fired on Whitehaven is reported or said to have been captured and taken to Birkenhead the same day, Aug 16th.'*

John recounted an incident which occurred about the same time in the north of the Isle of Man (told later on a brief excursion to visit Jas Martin in 1917):

> *'Jas Martin told us of an incident which was visible from his house windows – the ramming of an enemy submarine by a new vessel on her engine trials, called the Kempenfeldt (I think): when the submarines were in these waters and fired shots ashore at Whitehaven or Workington. The Kempenfeldt came round the Point of Ayre at a very high speed, and seemingly the submarine was in the track with no idea of the rate at which the 'K' was travelling.*

Jas Martin was absent that day at Ramsey, but his son and daughter both saw quite plainly the collision and its effects. This would be a unique experience I should say, to witness this from the land.'

Regarding spies, John wrote telling Dono:

'I think there is still place for a great deal of activity on part of our secret & detective service, in respect of spies about. The register may be all right for a purpose, but every man in the street should have his identity established and his presence in any locality accounted for.

Our universal licence to move to & fro has been such a matter of course thing, that today in this island we might have had ten spies living in this open parish for months, and never asked a question.

You will see that the White Star Arabic was sunk off Fastnet about 9am by a submarine. The German excuse, that she had munitions on board will not hold in this case (as in Lusitania) – as Arabic was outward bound (to the U.S.A.).'

...A diplomatic incident ensued as a result – it was thought that if the attack was made on purpose, the U.S.A. might sever relations with Germany.

Orders were given to German submarine Commanders that passenger ships could now only be sunk after warning and the saving of passengers and crews. America was informed of this.

Dono was finding difficulty in coping with the men in the engine-room of his ship.

John advised:

'...I was sorry to find from Daisy that your work makes such a demand on your personal supervision of everything, and that you have so little rest. But it is a good thing to be a hard driver of men.

I think you have got so firm on your feet that you can afford to get to be ruthless in making your engine-room crowd work.'

On August 23rd 1915, *H.M.S. Prince Rupert* was involved in the first bombardment of the harbour and docks at Zeebrugge, together with the other monitors *H.M.S. Lord Clive*, and *H.M.S. Sir John Moore*.

Dono wrote in his memoirs:

'During the bombardment, some problems were identified by the crew on board H.M.S. Prince Rupert, including that the gun rams needed lining. Fortunately the guns did not explode as was the case in H.M.S. Achilles – where a 9" gun was blown in half due to the same problem...

Plans to bombard Ostend were cancelled as H.M.S. Prince Rupert and H.M.S. Sir John Moore suffered problems with their turrets – these having been salvaged from much older ships.'

On returning from the bombardment, Dono was called upon to sort out the problems with the engines of another ship, for which he received much praise. [2]

John wrote to Dono on August 23rd:

'I infer from Daisy that you are engaged on some active operation, but not very distant from the S.E. bases.'

And later, John wrote...

'We heard of the bombardment of the Belgian coast. Papers say very little. One report – '40 ships engaged'.

The Germans deny any damage sustained, but the Amsterdam papers say that correspondents at Flushing, Sluis, etc. – report considerable damage done. We can only conjecture that you were on this Service.

I hope you are trying to get all the sleep you can... the concern you must have for effective working of machinery, makes it ridiculous for me to advise rest...

Mr Lansborough told me yesterday a new destroyer just out of Cammell Laird's had cut through a German submarine in the Irish Sea, and had come in on Sat 21st with her forefoot much broken with the collision.'

Regarding submarines, John continued:

'Head Postmaster of Cheetham Hill, Mr Robinson, cousin to Frank Sherriff, was here last evening; he told me a friend of his (who has access to correct information), told him that there are 4 German subs 'in the black hole' at Cammell Laird's – some side dock at their works.

Callow, member of a great bakery firm, whose head partner is an M.P., told Mr Craine of Laxey on Friday that there are 40 German subs sunk in various known and now charted spots, to be eventually raised. He also told Mr Craine that the orders now were 'to sink at once and not bother to capture'.

Mr Robinson told me that recently he was at Ainsley near Southport and saw several 'bottles' which had come ashore – nine in all he heard – but he saw only one or two – supposed to be floats of submarine apparatus. He described them as spheres of about 9" diam. – with a sort of handle but no neck. They had drifted ashore on the Lancashire coast sands.'

Mr Robinson, post-master, argued against the 'lost' letters from John and Vess being intercepted at Portsmouth. John reported:

'...He gave his theory that they had been intercepted on the island, and possibly not even reached the Douglas Post Office. He suggested the box at our own tram station as that possibly opened. He also said that there was the maximum of safety in registering a letter; it implied the certainty of its getting into the care of the P.O. at least...

He gave some interesting instances known to him of Germans in England, 2 or 3 years ago, aware of their own parts to take up in a far extending programme, whenever war would be declared or brought about by Germany!

He also told me of an ex-naval man whom he knows, who told him that he is stationed at Canterbury in a motor service for the purpose of rapid transport of naval officials to any point from Dover round to the Thames; he had accompanied officers to Thames side places among others to works where steel-wire nets were made; from this man he learnt that there was a (submarine) *mesh of 12 feet long, or square.'*

The seas were becoming even more perilous for the Manx fishing fleet and trawlers with submarines in the area and masquerading German boats. Fuel supplies were limited and Manx fishing vessels were now restricted to a 2-mile range of the island. John wrote:

'There have been some persistent rumours here of Manx fishermen – I think on the west side of the island – detected in securing or having quantities of petrol – and a suspicion of their meeting subs in the Channel to supply them. Something has taken place, but possibly the real facts have not transpired. Fishermen's licences have been recently curtailed to a 2 mile limit.

J. Kelly of Baldrine, when he got this ultimation, was so maddened that he smashed furniture in his own house and then went up to Ben's and started an insane display of rage there!'

In early August, John reported news of the Battle in the Gulf of Riga:

'We have news today of a success of Russia in the Gulf of Riga, which seems as if it was in part, submarine defence of that gulf. The papers say the Germans have lost a Dreadnought, 3 cruisers, and 7 destroyers

in the Gulf. Other paragraphs say it is the Moltke, a fast ship or battle cruiser, sister to the Goeben. English subs are understood to be out there. The Daily Mail does not quite support this news; says it is unconfirmed.'

...The German and Russian Fleets were involved in the Battle. The Germans failed to take Riga and lost more of their Fleet.

John continued regarding operations in the Gallipoli area:

'The Daily Mail has a sensational American correspondent's account of the landing in the Gulf of Saros, at the top end of Gallipoli peninsula: it says the Turks' communications are cut, and that the landing was effected by a surprise so there was practically no resistance.'

On August 26th 1915, John wrote:

'Lardy writes saying that from his part of coast, Calais to Dunkirk, some English ships have been seen.

He is well, and a large order of work before them.'

...Lardy's Company continued in the Calais area, working on the construction of a depot: including roadmaking, and construction of a water supply for the camp near Peuplingues. Sappers were assigned to a construction train, of which there were eight in operation in mid-1915.

Each train had up to two complete Railway Companies with a Captain commanding the train. This allowed them to carry tools & equipment to where work was required.

They pitched tents for accommodation as required. [14]

Meanwhile, Vess had moved to no. 11 Camp – Preese Heath, Salop. He was uncertain how soon any of them would be sent to a Service Battalion at Salisbury or elsewhere, but the monotony in the camps was understood to be very irksome. John reported:

'He seems to find the change agreeable. It is generally speaking a level country, though a heath and probably at some considerable elevation.

He seems cheerful.'

On the island, John and his wife had gone to a performance hosted by Lady Goldie-Taubman for a war fund in the Strand Cinema. John continued:

'It was a rather monotonous sequence of American melodrama unrelieved. I came away before the end of the performance.

I thought they were going to give navy pictures. There was one view – it seemed in the Suez Canal with part of a Dutch cruiser to right of picture – then the King, and the flag. I expect they do not allow anything interesting for this sort of entertainment... Today I spent an hour watching two so called 'mine-sweepers' off here, towards Black Combe direction, say 10 miles out. I could make nothing of their movements – if they were doing anything more than putting the time in. They came alongside and seemed to drift, then eventually moved slowly off to sea.'

Early in September 1915 there was an unfortunate incident regarding the patrol yacht in Douglas in the outer harbour towards the base of the battery pier. John wrote:

'The 'Manx Navy' is the sarcastic soubriquet for a motor boat or yacht in charge of a Mylechreest who had a mates' certificate, and a young assistant harbour-engineer, who have R.N.R. Commissions.

On Saturday night last, with both these officers ashore, the yacht was burnt. There were two men left on board. They got her to the battery pier – and what is left of her is sunk there. Captain Moughtin (House of Keys) has his sarcasms.'

Vess expected a move soon. He had met Capt. Harston, a Canadian, formerly of his company. He went to the Dardanelles and had come back wounded.

Dono continued to work out different ideas for ship defence.

John wrote on September 5th:

'...If I am right, I think I have now your sort of idea of a workable ship-at-anchor defence... I think this idea of a drogue dangling at the bottom – which would help to keep the cotton curtain from sweeping towards the hull under tide influence – is a good and sound idea...

I should like to know if you see in this, an approach to a solution.'

John was still in hope of Dono being recognised for his submarine net submission and sent a newspaper cutting to Dono.

Daily Dispatch Sep 6 1915:

'Germany's Submarine Losses – Mr Balfour – Estimates of subs lost believed to have reached the half-century... When the time comes to disclose the measures taken by Admiralty... the nation will pay tribute to splendid thoroughness and inventiveness of British Admiralty and their naval experts...'

Dono was about to embark on another bombardment of Ostend. John wrote:

'We have no idea where you are, but hope you get back to your base

occasionally, and are getting some sleep.'

On September 7th Dono had his first experience of being bombed from the air whilst on the ship *H.M.S. Prince Rupert* on the Dover Patrol. Dono wrote in his memoirs:

'We had been bombarding the German fortifications on the Belgian coast, and were at anchor 15 miles SW of Ostend. Two attacks were made, the first at 12.25pm, just as we were assembling for lunch in the Wardroom, the second – 40 minutes later. Curiously, the first attack was reported by the Officers of the Watch as gunfire from the coast, and it was only when the second attack was in progress that it was realised that the projectiles were from aircraft.

They did not hit us, but the light cruiser, H.M.S. Attentive, which was anchored nearby, was hit by one bomb from German aircraft, which fell through the deck into the sick bay and killed twelve men. After this, all ships weighed anchor and got moving.

Some weeks later, we were surprised when two German sea planes flew over us in Dover when Prince Rupert was moored in the harbour. Their bombs fell on the town and in the harbour, and fortunately did little damage.

Historically, this was the first time that bombs from German aircraft had landed on Great Britain. I went ashore to see the effect of the bombing for myself.' [2]

Regarding the same air raid witnessed by Dono, John reported on September 12th:

'Margaret wrote an animated account of the raid they saw from their part. Mary adds details, as she went forth on an expedition to visit the scenes affected by bombs.

She went to Worthing on Saturday and met a man from a ship, a General, seemingly from an extreme S.E. port, who said they had 'pulverized' parts about Ostend – 16" guns against them from shore.

Lardy tells us of a German aeroplane which lit in their camp – 'some fun' he calls it. The aeroplane is figured in Daily Mail as captured at the place where Lardy is.'

...A few unarmed men from the No.3 Monmouth Railway Company, based at Frethun railway station, went to the scene of the enemy plane mentioned – B220, which landed voluntarily due to shortage of fuel on September 6th about 400 feet from the Company working at Peuplingues near Calais, and the two occupants were taken as prisoners.

Regarding Lardy's work in September, large-scale work was required in the construction of major stores and ammunition dump, ten miles from Calais – at Audruicq. Here there was great use of Chinese Labour & R.E. Labour Companies to prepare the ground for plate-laying sappers. [14]

Lardy told his daughter later that he met some good Chinese men through his work in these quarters.

Regarding Lardy, John wrote:

'He has seen several large war vessels in the offing – his company being stationed near the coast e.g. Calais. He is well.

I hope you got my letter referring to float etc. I said nothing about the device, which I believe exists, to automatically cut any curtain in a path.

Surely there is a limit to the efficiency of any such instrument; and a mode of neutralizing it...

Is it possible that men have gone out to assist the Russian Fleet?

From their success (apart from submarines operating with them) I should imagine that naval officers and N.C.O.'s have possibly arrived in Russia to strengthen the hands of the Russian Navy personnel.

Perhaps this sort of thing is not done.'

...At the beginning of September 1915 Tsar Nicholas II made himself Russian Commander-in-Chief – therefore putting himself in a position to take the blame for the later failure of the Russian Army.

In Mid-September following another Zeppelin raid on London and Suffolk, and the attack on Ostend by British ships, Germany had taken control of Austro-Hungarian forces.

John continued:

'I hear Lord Derby is coming to the island, to speak at the Villa Marina. Mother says she'll go in, even if she has to walk home.'

...There was a recruiting meeting at the Villa Marina in Douglas. Regarding the meeting, the *Isle of Man Examiner* reported on 25th September 1915:

'PRESSING NEED FOR SOLDIERS. About 2000 persons were present: the majority were ladies or men debarred from military service...

It is appreciated that many men have already gone to do their duty, but there are still many young men in the Isle. Young men are encouraged to go and fight, if only to protect their mothers and sisters from the enemy...'

John sent a photo to Dono and wrote:

'I enclose a little photo, taken by a man at Garwick, when Lord Raglan opened the miniature rifle range in the enclosure at the back of Wood Glen near Ballagawne Mill.'

Wood Glen Rifle Range Opening

John was impressed by some of the Loyal Manx Invalids on the island:

'Mr Kelly has been miniature rifle shooting in the Garwick contingent of the Loyal Manx Invalids, and has developed marvellous workmanship; an average score of say 95 – 10 shots at 10 each, made 99; and in 10 shots in 100 seconds, made 96.

He keeps it up, and nobody approaches him...

You will see the uniforms of the Loyal Manx. The officer on the right is Major Hamilton, Recruiting Officer for the island.'

...John is pictured in the top-hat, and Lord Raglan, front-centre.

The situation of the boarding house owners on the island had worsened with lack of holiday makers. Summer visitor numbers had been much lower than expected. John reported:

'To relieve the clamorous boarding-house people, there is some talk of billeting troops in Douglas @ 2/3 a day – 15/9 a week (to compensate for loss of holiday trade).'

In September the Women's Institute was formed in the Isle of Man, and German born Joseph Pilates, previously a circus performer and boxer, arrived at the Knockaloe internment Camp. He used his time there as an opportunity to develop exercises for the men who had little else to do and needed to retain some control of their bodies – the exercises are known today as 'Pilates'.

Some strange objects were washed up on the shores of the Isle of Man. John reported on September 25th:

'...Last evening at a School Board meeting, Moughtin the Innkeeper at Old Laxey told me of a 'mysterious' machine picked up by a fishing boat – now at Old Laxey – also two glass globes that had drifted ashore. This morning I went down to see them and made notes.

Of course with all the rumours of nets, floats, etc., the folk in Laxey thought them 'floats'.

Moughtin, a 'Loyal Manx', scientific & poses with 'catchwords' – had warned the men not to open the metal boxes as they might contain 'T.N.T.' – 'the most terrific explosive known', etc. 'T.N.T.', which sounds like 'thunder terrific', settled it. I think the boxes were empty.

I made sketches of the machine, and also of the two glass globes – which I asked the corporal to get weighed.'

John's letter showing his sketch of the 'float'

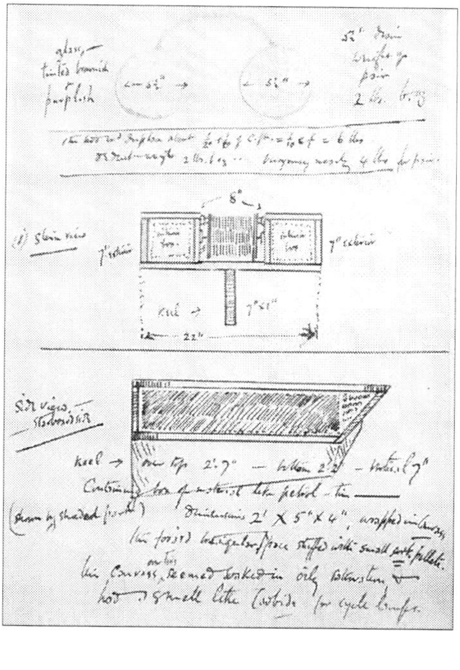

John continued:

'If I meet Commander Sims (in charge of W/T on the Isle of Man) *I'll mention them to him and give him a sketch if he has not already seen them. I think they ought to be guarded even here: as we have a*

chance suspicious person about. I had an idea that this is a float designed to travel – as the 'boat' – with bows like an English river punt – slides over and lifts: the open stern allowing all water shipped to get clear again.

I cannot understand the purpose of the drum and coils of wire, unless to perplex the sea-faring population at villages like Old Laxey. Of course if the wooden boxes, as distinct from the metal tanks inside, were water tight, its buoyancy would be much greater. They had been exposed to the water and seemed to be by no means water tight. As this is a jetsam of the sea, I suppose it is all right describing it to you.'

Later, John met the Laxey Harbour-Master and asked him what he thought the machine was. John wrote:

'...Promptly he told me – "the bed frame of a small motor engine of a small motor launch!" I asked what the purpose of the drum with wire was. "To lessen the vibration," he said. So far as he was concerned this was final. I pursued the enquiry no further. Mr Wales, right or wrong, is delightful: his answer is final on all questions!

Later the Laxey Corporal met me in the road and told me that an official – customs man had called to see the box, and pronounced it a 'float'.

There was no doubt in my mind about the flotsam picked up...'

John heard of an example of poor discipline at the Douglas Camp:

'A 'Loyal Manx', Innkeeper, and great chum of a Corporal who drilled the 'Loyal Manx', was allowed to smoke not only at the stand easy but also whilst doing drill. This 'Loyal Manx' went to the Douglas Camp for night guard. On guard, he was smoking – when a certain Major came on his round. He proceeded to argue with the Major that he had come before the usual hour and that he had come from the wrong direction! Result – an order to the 'Loyal Manx' Commandant not to send this man on guard duty again as he was 'inefficient'!

I see Harrison have lost another boat off the south of Ireland!

Lardy is well. I do not know where he is, but expect somewhere in the same part of France as before. He speaks of a probable move of his section at an early date.

Vess wrote last evening. He is well and working pretty hard. He has been range-finding and supervising musketry at the ranges some miles from their camp (at Preese Heath).'

Meanwhile on the Western Front, an Allied offensive in September led to the Battle of Champagne and the 2nd Battle of Artois & Loos.

Lardy's Company had moved again. John reported on September 29th:

'He does not know much about the locality, except that it is to be the rail-head. I think that means the terminus towards the Front – you may draw the inference that it is nearer to active operations.'

...In October Lardy's Company was sent to join the 4th Army in the vicinity of Albert at Méricourt Ribemont in making trench tramways to move materials and supplies.

Regarding the Loos affair, John continued:

'I read this evening an account, by Special Correspondent at Head-quarters in France, of the affair near La Bassée or Loos. It leaves the impression that he saw a coal-mining landscape, heaps of 'deads', heterogeneous buildings, and heard guns.

It is practically useless for anyone that wants to form a definite idea of anything, but possibly exactly suited to the readers – 99.9% of whom don't want anything definite. Of course the censors may strike out all but this sort of stuff, and the Correspondents might explain that to us as the case...

As I understand you get English papers, it is not necessary to mention recent news.

The newspapers seem to me to obscure everything in a cloud of confetti if it is a successful operation, and to throw a newspaper over it if it is otherwise.

The Mona's Isle has been requisitioned from Douglas by the Admiralty. A stoker in the Mona's Queen, home on leave, living at the foot of our road, told me he had made 20 trips across the Channel in the Queen, carrying 1500 troops per trip. 'Good grub was his general impression of the Service.'

...The *Mona's Isle* and *Mona's Queen* were Manx paddle-steamers.

Another attempt had been made at bombarding Ostend by *H.M.S. Lord Clive* and associated monitors on 17th September and there was a later bombardment on Westende on the 25th.

German coastal batteries were fired on occasionally for the remainder of September into October. Dono recalled seeing the tall lighthouse at Ostend destroyed by a 12" projectile from the monitor *Lord Clive*, with Admiral Bacon on board. It would be two years before another attempt at blockading Ostend was made.

John wrote on October 3rd:

'This week past has had much news, of the affair in Champagne and in Artois – La Bassée – Loos – and Hooge, near Ypres. We have also heard of activities on the Belgian coast.

Yesterday Nan was at the dentist; he told her of the naval engagement, 11 enemy ships, 3 English sunk; also something at Zeebrugge. Later a mason who works at Knockaloe Camp told me of the same thing, with landing of 100,000 British troops in Belgium.

But there is nothing today to confirm it. Mary writes that the rumour in London was that Ostend had been occupied.

Generally we inferred that you might be in action. We can only hope that you have passed safely through whatever actions you have been engaged in.

There is so very little news or variety of topic here. '

Vess had crossed home for a few days – with a slight cold, and Lardy had sent a postcard to say he was well.

John was obviously fearful of Dono's part in any naval conflict. A letter or note home gave immediate relief that all was well.

John wrote on October 4th:

'Most glad to hear from you this evening.

All last week was a time of news and conjecture.

'Wires to neutral countries' notified as subject to 48 hours delay in transit – from which we inferred that important business might be in transaction. A report of Sir John Francis in today's papers mentions acknowledgements to Vice-Admiral Bacon for support to artillery on the Front.'

In September, the Germans announced an end to their first U-boat campaign, begun in February, targeting ships around the British Isles. The U-boats were then sent to the Mediterranean. John wrote:

'I enclose a cutting from today's I.O.M. Daily Times – the source of which I have not found, though probably in some other paper. It mentions: 'between 60 and 70 German submarines – sunk or destroyed'! (October 4 1915)

If one goes upon previous newspaper reports, there must be an average of about 10 per month, and the success in this branch steadily continued.'

Regarding submarine activity: *Manchester Guardian* Sep 21st 1915:

'Herr Von Jagow, Foreign Minister, on Germany's conduct of submarine warfare – 'Germany has hedged the promise made by Von Bernstorff with so many conditions that the 'concession' about not attacking liners without warning has virtually vanished.

Germany proposes to use U.S. to further her own ends. It is considered in this country that the British have fairly 'scotched' the submarine business and that the terror no longer exists...'

Newspaper cutting October 13th 1915:

'Trapping the Submarine – Novel methods by which under-water pirates are destroyed. G.B has discovered and put into effective operation, means of combating the submarine, which already have resulted in a loss estimated at between 50 & 70 German submarines... Reports reaffirm the Dreadnought still is the mainstay of warfare on the sea...

There need be no doubt that an antidote... will teach even the Germans that man has never invented an offensive weapon for which some other man cannot devise an antidote, as their gas policy has recently illustrated.'

...Both sides adopted sophisticated gas masks and clothing to protect them against the chlorine gas in the trenches.

On the island, the Knockaloe Camp was continuing to grow, and to facilitate moving the great quantities of materials required in the camp from the quay, it was decided that a railway should be built.

Knockaloe Camp and railway line, constructed from Peel harbour to the Camp for easy movement of goods and men.

(Photo: September 1915 M.N.H. PG/529/10a)

The *Peel City Guardian* reported:

'With a view to supplying the Camp at Knockaloe with necessaries, the authorities have decided to build a railway from Peel Quay to the Camp. The railway will run along the east quay to Peel Railway Station... The work has already begun at the camp end, and is proceeding satisfactorily. Material for the construction of the railway arrived by the *Tyroconnel* this week, and a cargo of rails was brought to Peel by the *S.S. Carrick Castle.*'

Internees were arriving daily, and John reported:

'A crowd – 180, I heard, aliens arrived by steamer today; a Sergeant: rather loquacious, who leaned on the pier rail near me as the boat came alongside, told me that several hundred more were expected via Peel tomorrow.

He said there are 25,000 now in the Knockaloe Camp.'

With the growing number of internees at Knockaloe, thought was given to building yet another Camp, and John reported later in October:

'A new alien camp is spoken of, somewhere about Douglas – to be in upper Onchan, Pulrose or Hillberry – between the old reservoirs and road from Keppel Gate to Douglas.

It seems to imply a transfer of aliens from English detention camps – perhaps in order that nothing but military camps may require the attention of the authorities there.

Langness and Fort Island would have been the best place for such a common camp, and proximity to the sea easily dealt with. All material could have been landed at Derbyhaven, and the fraction simplified by a light railway – provided that small steamers only were used. As for exposure it is not a bit worse than Knockaloe or the present sites. The cordon there would have been simplicity itself.'

Regarding Lardy, John reported on October 10th:

'He is well and is at, or near a large town – weather cold, and has some unnecessary discomfort from damp in Camp quarters – things damp in the morning etc.

Lardy is at the Front or near it. He is engaged on work similar to that on which he was engaged when he first went out to France. They see aeroplane encounters and are within sound of the machine gun fire! I am sending him a pipe he asks for.'

...The Monmouth Companies were in the vicinity of Albert near Hébuterne (see French map) 'with the 4th Army by the end of the month, enlarging rail-heads and creating tramways to transfer supplies and ammunition by night'. [14]

There was a Zeppelin raid over London on 13th October.

John wrote to Dono:

'Thanks for your letter, which I handed to Daisy also. The censor's penknife had cut part of a sentence out on the second sheet.

We have heard from Margaret of the Zeppelin raid – which came nearer than the former one. Her letter was partly written during the raid. It must have been a strain on her nerves, though I cannot understand how far off the Zeppelins were. Her description is as if they were quite near to her district – yet I think they were 3 or 4 miles off; maybe not!

We have a Letter from Vess this evening; he is in for an exam, and is doing some machine-gun practice, and signalling – the latter I think elementary for him!

You will be interested a little to hear that Johnny Kelly has presented himself for sea-service and has been accepted; also his son that is at home. Another son now at Baldrine is going into the army; I understand his idea is for patrol trawler service...

I see Lord Haldane is in evidence again – political or semi-political missions in France – just returned! This is tactless on part of the Government as he is not a popular man or the most positively loyal and patriotic – if 'popular' means a man on whom Englishmen have confidence. Utterances such as, that Germany was his spiritual home or spiritual birthplace, are flap-doodle. Statesmen should be impersonal!'

...Haldane was Secretary of State for War from 1905 to 1912, and served as Lord Chancellor from 1912. He was forced out of office in 1915 due to suspicions of his alleged German sympathies (re-appointed in 1924).

John continued:

'The Balkan complications are now the chief newspaper handle for diatribes against residents at the Capitals of these states. If they have failed in their diplomacy, this kind of outcry will mend nothing and avail nothing.

The whole nation unitedly convinced of one thing is what we want; with half a dozen or twenty religions in a country, that can with difficulty be.

I suppose that people – like myself – merely standing on one side, want to see what is going on; we have no claim to be gratified in that way. We can actively do nothing, but we at least want to see what others are doing and how, etc. It is not personally a thing I complain of; I rather think the authorities have enough to do, without having to give dress circle tickets to us.'

Early in October, French & British forces were landed at Salonika. On October 21st 1915, John wrote to Dono regarding the Gallipoli Campaign, also known as the Dardanelles Campaign, which lasted from April 1915 until early January 1916:

'Today's papers mention an uncertainty of decision with regard to the Gallipoli expedition being persisted in – viz. in view of the Salonika expeditionary force being augmented. What the papers know about it is the question.

Last evening I was informed of news – that a naval officer in a high post in the east was no longer to serve in any capacity.

I meant to write my views on the whole Dardanelles expedition...'

...British and French confidence in the Gallipoli/Dardanelles operation was failing. Hamilton was responsible for organising armed landings in the Dardanelles, and had requested further reinforcements. However this could not be done in light of more men required for landing at Salonika and the invasion of Serbia.

Hamilton was recalled to London on 16th October 1915, ending his military career. Kitchener replaced Hamilton and Brathwaite, and Monro was put in command of the Mediterranean Expeditionary Force.

John continued:

'What I thought likely a year ago, was that Earl Kitchener had up his sleeve the grand plan of campaign – to hold Germany on the west, on the east (by Russia) on N. Sea, and to organize a grand offensive at the heart of Austria.

I have the idea that he was hampered by the politicians and diplomatic obstacles, and that his plan – assuming this was his plan – was made impossible, for that sort of reason.

The German scheme was – suppress Serbia, get possession of a through route to Salonika, link up with Bagdad railway, strike at the Suez line of communications and Egypt, and open a freeway to the Indian Ocean – whether by getting Egypt and the Suez line or not!

Therefore my idea was that an offensive, point blank counter to this, via Salonika and Serbia, was the great offensive we ought not to hesitate about. Incidentally we should then isolate Turkey, and deal with Turkey in concert with Russia. Such a movement, had it been carried out with great energy when Russia (under the Grand Duke Nicholas) penetrated into Hungary, might have rendered Austria helpless south of the Danube, and reached Vienna long before any offensive could hope to reach Berlin.

The only argument for the Dardanelles affair now is to bottle up 1 million Turks in the Gallipoli area. That expedition from first to last was I believe the self-wish of one manikin – who got his own way in the crazy intoxication of our country by 'talk', words, verbiage, platform speeches, etc. To conscript 3 million more men, lick them into shape as soldiers, and begin this plan of campaign would still be the best course for this nation... But we are governed by lawyers.

The scope and limit of the work of ships against land defences is known to naval experts. I assume the naval men have been set aside in the Dardanelles operations, viz. in the decisions first taken.

They were told to batter down front doors with stones. They did so to the limit of the possible. But to afterwards enter the house, with owner concealed and armed, is another pair of gloves. The ships did their part as far as ships can. I don't think you should land men anywhere without being at any time able to take them off again, even in a hurricane of wind! But this was done at the Dardanelles.'

John wrote the following advice to Dono:

'It occurs to me to note, that such a time as the present is a great strain, which tests one's staying power. You may feel it: though what I refer to is not the 'active service' strain, so much as that of the austere and waiting life! I am hoping that your work will so fully occupy you, that you do not feel anything of this... Others must take their cue from us, rather than we from them – 'He would do, what he could do, what he should do, in a way quite new'!

Recently I was given a nice chart – on one side the Isle of Man and on other side, the British Island including Shetlands, and part of France. It has at various parts a sort of compass. I have hung it in the dining room.'

At the Vicarage on October 27th 1915, the excitement over seeing an airship nearby was tangible. John reported:

'As the censorship applies to letters from you, but not in the same sense to you – I suppose there is no objection to my telling you of the air-ship we saw passing here this morning about 9am.

Daisy heard and saw it first and called to Mother; we had a look at it and watched its flight. Daisy saw the ship before hearing the propeller, only faintly – I had to listen, as did Mother. It was passing off Garwick Bay towards Barrow: I afterwards ascertained that it had gone the opposite way a short while before and above Baroose (Lonan plantation) – *in line with Douglas, as from here it had risen somewhat and turned! So we saw it only on its return journey. It could not have gone much beyond Douglas.*

At first glance from our window, as it was not seemingly above the horizon, I thought Daisy had been mistaken, and that it was an immense ship: though it was not so far away as a ship on that level would be.'

'The shape was not that pictured of Zeppelins. This was more a fish shape, with a tail end, long & round, tapering. It continued its flight, rather more towards Whitehaven. My last glimpse of it was through the trees: and when I went down the road a little later, it was out of sight.

I considered it would reach Barrow or Whitehaven comfortably in an hour: say 60 miles or so an hour. What struck me was the good target it made. For assuming it was 600 feet etc., the hitting of this by a charge of large shrapnel, bursting at 3, 4, or 5 miles seemed to me no great feat of gunnery from a land gun! If shrapnel on bursting, continues its flight, I don't see how a large case of it could fail to hit. I have not much idea of the strength of a Zeppelin envelope; but surely, thin!

Of course I should mention – morning very quiet, calm, still air, ship was grey (navy grey). It moved very steadily, but occasionally it seemed to have a slight list (may have been wind or from steering, to maintain direct course.) I thought underneath, the projection 3/4 way towards tail was the propeller, and the fin on the back above a rudder-fin. The carriage was the other projection, not clear in detail. What this vessel would do in half a gale I cannot imagine...

Of course we suppose it an English vessel on trial cruise! For observation this vessel would be a fine friend to a squadron in good weather...

I cannot get out of my mind the effect of wind force on such a large surface, and so light a body... Some nice problems to solve for the man who designed it!

A small steamer say 500 tons said to have a cargo of dynamite lay in Laxey Bay last evening.

We have not seen any war vessel or even patrol trawler in these waters for many weeks, almost months!'

...The airship seen near the Vicarage was probably built at Vickers in Walney Island, Barrow-in-Furness on the Cumbrian coast and was perhaps on a trial flight.

Generally British airships (S.S. airships) of that period were around 143 feet in length, far short of John's estimate, and were used for naval reconnaissance.

Dono had to solve many problems whilst at sea. The monitors on the Dover Patrol had 17 days at sea followed by a refit. Dono had a well-equipped workshop on board *H.M.S. Prince Rupert*, enabling him to solve mechanical issues whilst at sea.

Towards the end of October, John wrote to Dono:

'I just send a note tonight, as you seem a bit tired with the worry of machinery anxieties. Not that it is possible to say anything helpful, with so little notion as I can have of the weight on your shoulders.

But remember that you had things to bear and put up with in the Harrison period, that in their way seemed then fairly heart-breaking: yet you weathered them all finely...

There is an American expression much in use in recent years, viz. 'it is up to you, to go through!' I prefer the view of saying 'it is in you to do so'...

The skill is not to let the imaginary augment the actual...'

H.M.S. Prince Rupert had 'two lucky escapes': one near La Panne from horned mines strategically placed just below the water's surface, laid off the Belgian coast by the enemy overnight; the other from a salvo of heavy shells from shore batteries, having gone too near to shore, which gave the ship a pretty good shaking. [2] *H.M.S. Prince Rupert* had 12" guns and a range of around ten miles, but the shore battery guns were increasing in range.

At the beginning of November, John reported regarding Lardy:

'Lardy is working within say 200 yards of the German line, their billets about a mile back from it, maxims and big guns all the time he says. I think it must be in sapping or tunnelling under their line.'

...According to the War Diary, the No.3 Monmouth Railway Co. was working on a proposed rail line from Hébuterne to Foncquevillers and the main camp billets were at Sailly – beds of straw for the men. Men were working under dangerous conditions at night, and were shelled. The German trenches were between 500 to 800 yards away from the men; guns overlooked several positions of the work, and shells were fired towards Sailly.

Work north of Hébuterne ceased on 5th November as it was too dangerous to continue. [29]

John continued:

'Mary writes that a soldier they know was seeing them on Friday. He said that he had been in France, and quotes – "I was in a certain place and saw your brother (Lardy). I stood only a few feet away from him, but was unable to speak to him. He is a splendid soldier and very well and busy."

Mary also says she has information that the (submarine net) *'idea' has been standardized and now constitutes our permanent defences, and was the main factor in the capture while things were busy.*

Graham (husband of Mary) – *under Lord Derby's scheme is compelled to volunteer if medically fit; the latter I should doubt. His only suitable service would be in office work.*

Frank Sherriff (Fiancé of Marge – John's 2nd daughter) has passed as medically fit. He contemplates offering himself for Army Service Corps. His idea in view of this, is to be married to Marge at the beginning of January.'

There was some confusion regarding where Vess might be sent next; John wrote on November 4th:

'...This week we have been kept in expectation regarding his move. We heard they were going to Birkenhead to join the 3rd Cheshire's for Salonika. His Sunday letter confirmed that.

I heard they had sailed yesterday.

Today I heard they sailed this morning...

Now I have Vess's letter of Wednesday, saying they are still at Whitchurch ready to leave – that a draft of their battalion is for the Mediterranean, but so far as is known, the Manx Co. are for France to reinforce the 2nd Cheshire's. In any case it seems they are to go to Birkenhead for equipment and rifles, and to embark there.

Vess says that Preese Heath Camp is to be wholly vacated by Xmas in order that it may be occupied by the New Army.

The formation of the New Army is something definite: for it is precisely what will be required, in order that it may be in being when terms of peace come to be discussed.'

Lord Derby was appointed Director-General of British Recruiting on 11th October 1915.

As numbers of volunteer recruits were dwindling, the 'Lord Derby Scheme' (also known as the 'Group Scheme') was launched to raise numbers of men – men aged 18 to 40 (raised from 38).

Under the scheme they could enlist voluntarily as in the past, or attest with an obligation to come if called upon later. Voluntary enlistment would cease on 15th Dec 1915. Regarding this, John told Dono:

'I do not know if Lord Derby's Scheme will apply to the island, but it ought to...'

John continued in a later letter:

'...Here I think Lord Derby's system is to come into force by definite canvass of the men of military age, by a personal call – and asking for their reason if they decline to enter the Service.

I am to go on this business; we shall be supplied with a list of persons to go to, and their own statement in their registration form; it will give us a definite line to go on.

I'm told there are 5000 men of military age still on the island – a large estimate I think: but I have no doubt about 3000 for whom there is the plain duty to serve.'

Vess and the rest of the Manx Company, now fully trained, were transferred to the 3rd Battalion Cheshire Regiment based at Birkenhead. John wrote on November 7th:

'Yesterday we had a wire from Vess from Birkenhead, to say the Manx Co. had arrived there to embark.

This morning I went to Laxey and sent a wire about my idea of crossing out to Birkenhead, but we think he must have already embarked.

Fred Sanderson, who was at Whitchurch, came across home yesterday. I saw him this morning: he says that they were for Egypt and were embarking today on the Olympic...

Vess wrote during the week to say he had heard they were for Serbia, and later that they were for France: so it may be that they are for Egypt en-route for Serbia...

We hear that Lord Kitchener has gone to Egypt, or the near East. There is need out there of a man who can definitely control all the operations, both the Gallipoli and Serbian expeditions. Egypt itself is just now very important: it will be necessary to have a really large force in Egypt to meet all contingencies. Probably Marshall Joffre, when he visited England, discussed this question and urged the necessity of a directing mind in the S.E. of Europe. I think I mentioned – more than a year ago – that Kitchener must have up his sleeve, the main offensive from the south via Serbia or Vienna. I stated this so often as my view, that I could only explain its not materializing as consequence of our Government's not raising (by conscription) the forces required.'

On November 8th John wrote:

'The papers this evening mention an English – Italian expedition via Valona on the Adriatic to penetrate into Serbia that way: these troops may be for that Service... If we had had a force of 3/4 million landed at Salonika 6 months ago, what would now have been the situation?

I see that German submarines are doing mischief in the Mediterranean. They have advantages, unless their bases can be hit on. Of course the Italians ought to equip a good lot of police vessels, viz. destroyers for anything emerging from the Adriatic.

The Germans no doubt, through their advantage in Greece, can get bases in the Aegean. Yet again will come in the necessity of the only device that can cope with this menace!

We hear this evening of an air raid on Dunkirk – possibly your neighbourhood?

A Manchester gentleman, whom we met when we were in Manchester in May, was here yesterday. He said that in England, men who have lost relatives were now having their eyes opened to the truth that 'inefficiency must be scrapped'.

Unfortunately England has suffered terribly from the ignoring of this honourable truth; 'efficiency' not 'influence' should be the mode of preferment in the public services. There has been such a terrible concession made to 'influence', that the enthusiasm and zeal of the country has been paralysed...'

Meanwhile Vess was still at Birkenhead and as he was busy, he thought that it was not worthwhile his father crossing from the Isle of Man to see him.

John wrote on November 12th:

'Marge saw Vess at Crewe on his way to Liverpool; he was very well and in the best of spirits. His Company is now definitely of the 3rd Battalion, Cheshire Regiment; the new badges of the Cheshire's assumed. He does not know when they will sail, but the idea is to Egypt.

All the others are well by last letters; Mary however rather nervy I think, perhaps at the idea that Graham may have to volunteer, and her consideration that he is not strong enough for anything but office work or the like.'

On November 19th, John reported that Vess had moved to another Camp at Bidston:

'They shifted a week ago from the Laird St Depot – where they had got equipment. It is not a good camp – bad huts etc. He has a billet in a farm house; passably good. He says this delay has had a curious effect on the men, making them require delicate handling.'

Summary of newspaper cuttings regarding submarine destruction enclosed in letters to Dono by John:

Nov 19 1915 – 'Queen of the Seas – British Fleet through Russian Eyes – 67 German Submarines Destroyed:

'On the occasion of the sinking of the Undine by a British submarine, the Press devoted lengthy articles of praise to the British Fleet...British subs have made their appearance in the Baltic and totally cut off German supplies from the Scandinavian peninsula...

Fifty-Eight 'U' Boats Gone since Feb 18 – The splendid work of our Navy: Statements made proving that Germany admits failure of her 'U' boat campaign. ...British public little realises what part in the sudden reversal of the submarine situation has been played by British Admiralty...'

Later in November, Lardy was well but reported much delay in parcels. John wrote:

'...He is at the point where the trench line intersects the Belgian & French frontier.

Weather there is not so cold as it has been here, but very wet.'

...Lardy's Company was north of Albert at Sailly where they had been working throughout November.

There had been quite a few very wet days which impeded work and caused problems moving vehicles around. Fog was an advantage to the men as it allowed work to continue unobserved. [29] ...The work on the line around Fonquevillers continued until the end of November, as detailed in the drawing.

The Company moved to billets in Albert at the end of November.

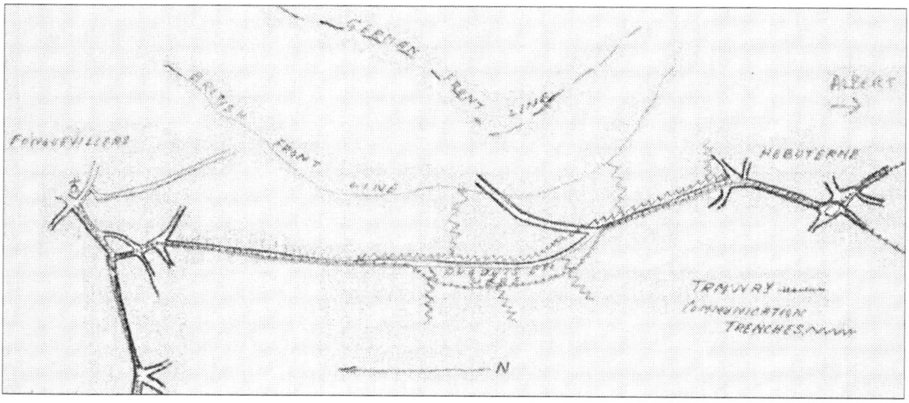

From No.3 Monmouth Railway Company Diary [29]

In the Isle of Man, the Lieutenant Governor was ill. John reported:

'Lord Raglan is in London – ill with influenza. He went away about 5 weeks ago, the day Nan crossed out. Mother thought he looked very ill then. I expect he has allowed himself to get worried. My idea is that the men he sees have no reserve of spirit and hardy firmness of out-look; as he needs the influence of such men, he has not kept himself in good heart.

I hope you are keeping physically fit, and relying on your tenacity of spirit.

I saw a good quote of Lord Fisher's recently – 'Do right and fear no man; do not write, and fear no woman!' It is brilliant.'

Regarding the Lord Derby scheme, John was at a recruiting meeting in Laxey in November and reported:

'We have subdivided the Parish into 5 districts, and Laxey into 4. I am taking (with another) a Parish district and also a Laxey district.

My view is – with all respect to Lord Derby, not knowing how uphill his task may have been – to round up all, and let local committees deal with the district requirements in deciding how many should be exempted.

The Earl's scheme is rather beginning at the other end of the stick.

No local news. Yesterday I heard some very big guns in practice or experiment from Barrow.'

John wrote later on November 26th:

'I have been out on the Lord Derby Canvass for recruits – with Fred Corlett (formerly of the Manx ship King Orry), yesterday and today – till 11pm each evening – had to knock some up at 10.30pm (some men not findable till after half a dozen calls).

We have the Church quarter of the Parish, and the South Cape quarter of Laxey with Old Laxey – 60 cards out of the 140 in the whole parish of Laxey: ten other – 80 divided between 14 canvassers. We have got nearly half of our 60 to go and report at the recruiting office to attest as ready for Service in their class. A few will be medically unfit.

The farmer class are the worst. They have no patriotism: they are exempted totally in their view, in order that they may make money out of the war – under the pretence that they are feeding the country...The merciless selfishness with which they expect that the miner and other working classes should go and do the fighting, while they fill their pockets, is a wonderful thing to discover.

We are adding notes to their cards which will be good reading for somebody.'

On December 2nd, Dono's wife, Daisy, gave birth to their first child, Jack. She was staying at the Vicarage and was looked after by a nursemaid to begin with. Daisy was lucky; many women must have found themselves in this predicament during the war and had to cope without such help or that of their husbands. As she stayed at the Vicarage for short periods, John had much to say about baby Jack in his letters to Dono over the duration of the war, but only a fraction is included here for mere interest.

John reported:

'As you would know by my wire, Daisy had a son, born yesterday, December 2nd about 6.30am As she had kept very well indeed, and was quite cheerful, I had practically no anxiety... Mother says that Daisy may be able to write herself in a very few days. But that in my opinion is a matter not to be harried about...'

Lardy was thinking up ideas to impede aeroplanes. John wrote:

'Lardy is well. He asks, 'would it be possible to make a shell, such that when it burst it would cause an electrical or magnetic wave that would clash with the magnet on an aeroplane, if it burst say within 50 yards or so, something after the style of wireless? It would be the means of making aeroplanes helpless and have to come down, and for Zeppelins, make them at the mercy of the wind'.

I have often been thinking of it after working on a magnet on a motor bike: they are so delicate that it might be possible to do so. I don't know enough about electricity to know. Let me know what he says.'

Dono replied and John later wrote:

'I have sent Lardy your reply regarding magnets being well protected electrically. He thought that if by the explosion of a shell, a high or intense and instantaneous wave could be created, to act with sudden shock, or if of sufficient intensity, it might overcome the normal safeguards, and so clash with the magnets as to put it out of action. I am speaking of things I do not understand.

I see that Mr Churchill is to command a Brigade (4 Battalions or 4000). This is rapid promotion in the Junior Service. I wonder if in the Senior Service any such rapid promotions can take place.

A 'bit of history', as I am assured, is that your cousin Surgeon William Quine has had the honour of dining with the Sailor Prince at Buckingham Palace. They met in H.M.S. Collingwood in the early part of this year. Nan tells us from Aunt Champion (John's sister), that recently he went to London, or being in London the Prince met him, and he was asked to dine with the Prince at Buckingham Palace.

I should rather your recognition, say by His Majesty, should not be thought to being due to the circumstance that this precious cousin was a persona grata with the Sailor Prince.

It has its humorous side: as the Prince is probably about 20 he should find this young surgeon an original sort of fellow!

There is a proverb – Better be born lucky than rich!'

In December, the Dover Patrol was involved in bombing the Belgian coast around Zeebrugge. John wrote to tell Dono about Daisy and the baby. He also said that Lardy was well and spoke of leave. On December 5th 1915, John wrote:

'Daisy and the little boy are both as well as possible...

I see there have been bombardments of the Belgian coast recently; the paragraphs being German news (via Amsterdam).'

John, already involved in canvassing, had been nominated for service on the Lord Derby Recruiting Military Tribunal for Douglas and the Eastern District to decide on appeals for exemption, and had accepted the nomination.

He wrote on December 10th:

'Four such Tribunals are to sit (N.S.E. & W.) associated with the four towns & districts.

There is one representative for Lonan & Laxey. This should have naturally been R.T. Corlett C.P., but I think there has been some idea that my being on the Tribunal would be better; I don't know that his patriotism has shone during the last year or so – in the shadow of his personal interests in this business.

If Laxey mine is producing speller (zinc) *for Government orders, we should have an instruction to that effect, and information as to the minimum number of men required to work there. I intend to work up the agricultural data for the district so as to see what average there is – the number of farms etc., and get an idea of the minimum number of men necessary to be left on the farms for their sufficient working. Doubtless we shall have data supplied to us, instructions, and advice...'*

Vess, still at Bidston near Liverpool, had written home regarding some interesting work, and John reported:

'The Manx Co. and 300 more drafts went out to a point about 10 miles from Bidston on the Dee coast to occupy a position and wait a night attack. Vess had to go out and make a reconnaissance of the positions for General & Company Headquarters: lines of communication, kitchens, telephone stations etc. They were attacked at 7am and beat the force off; very interesting he says. His knowledge of the country is an advantage.

He reports the men restless after weeks of daily expectation of embarking. Vess is very impatient of their being kept at Bidston... I hope he is not forgetful that impatience is a mental phenomenon...

I see that there is considerable submarine activity – Austrian & German in the Mediterranean. Our papers do not give us any hint of the operations against them: but no doubt these are energetic and fairly well advanced.

We are having a rough and very wet December. Our highroads are in a very bad state in patches, cut up by Corlett's big steam grain lorry. We see a few trawlers off here occasionally. I fancy they are patrol boats...

I see in today's I.O.M. Times that Lord Raglan is convalescent at 13 Great Stanhope Street (London), and is able to get up every day.

He must have had a bad bout.'

Serbia had fallen to the German, Austro-Hungarian and Bulgarian forces in November 1915, and in December the Allies began withdrawing from Gallipoli – sanctioned by the British Government. John reported on Dec 15th regarding operations in the Balkans:

'The Balkan Campaign was of course doomed to failure. It was begun 6 months too late, and with only 25% of the men there should have been. An amazing paragraph (to me) is in yesterday's Despatch; it quotes a Major Humbert of the French Artillery Reserve, who said that the German force was no more than 17500, but had guns enough – according to normal standard – to support close on a million men!

It has always seemed to me that there is no normal standard... why our authorities have not multiplied so simple a thing as machine guns amazes me!

Is it that there are no good officers with intelligence and thought in the army? No! – Is it not therefore some obstinacy among the controlling persons in departments, or some entanglement of red tape in our system, that the reports and representation of the intelligent and thoughtful officers are foiled and blocked?'

John continued:

'I have heard nothing further of the Military Tribunal for our district. I suppose the returns are under consideration, and a report based on them – which should result in some declaration as to conscription...

Aunt Mary Maggie was here today and says William Quine (surgeon) *has gone on the Calliope, a light armoured cruiser – launched January 1914 – displacement less than 4000 tons... Aunt M. says she is a 'flag-ship' of course: but so are they all.'*

Regarding family, John reported on December 19th:

'The boy (baby Jack) *has I consider, very fine eyes and is in every way a fine and healthy boy. Daisy was out for a walk yesterday with the nurse carrying the boy – they went up as far as Grawe or so. It was cold but the air dry and somewhat bright.*

The Military Tribunal list is out. I am the only Clergyman on the island in the list of names: Uncle Thomas is on the list for the Castletown district. R.T. Corlett is also on the E. district list: not to his credit that one should have to remark on it!

Mr Kneale told me of a 'Standard' paragraph – 78 submarines had been destroyed or captured. The 'Standard' seems reliable. The effect must be of course enormous, absolutely incalculable, as the Fleet grip is now, but increasingly important.

The achievement is one of the grand things of national history. David's sling that slew Goliath is not more worthy of world-wide immortality which it so curiously possesses, than your slings that hit Von Tirpitz.'

On December 22nd Dono became 'Engineer Lieutenant'.

His ship *H.M.S. Prince Rupert* was still on the Dover Patrol, bombing the Belgian coast. However Dono was suffering. John wrote:

'Glad to know from Daisy this evening that your being on the sick list for a few days was due to vaccination.

When I was vaccinated about 25 years ago I was in bed for several days – my left arm very bad.

We have seen something in the papers about attacks on the Belgian coast, and thought you might be in it.

The nurse went off on Monday; the care of the little boy was thrown on Daisy herself plus such help as she got from Mother.

Lardy has moved back from the hit zone and is at 'the same town where he was before' – we think St Omer.'

...Lardy's Company continued working north of Albert around Aveluy and Martinsart until mid-December, when they moved back to Abbeville on railway sidings construction work. [29]

Vess and the men of the Manx Company, training at Bidston, were given leave to return to the Isle of Man for Christmas. Many of these Manx men would not see home for another year... if they returned at all. John wrote:

'Vess comes across for a short leave Dec 23rd – to return Dec 26th by midnight boat. I am glad of this – as by his last letter he was grumpy. I dare say it is very much what you used to say about the engine-room staff on a longish voyage getting sick and tired of one another. The Book of Proverbs say – 'Be not much in the house of thy neighbour – lest he weary of thee!'

The general impression is that the grip the Fleet now has of the situation is the Ace of trumps, which will take the final trick for certain.

There can hardly be a doubt but that Germany has lost 3,000,000 men; Austria probably little short of the same.

As compared with 18 months ago, with our half million, we have now 3 million: that is to say it has taken 18 months to create an army!

But the work yet to be done is immense.

There were the first bona fide photos of monitors in the last Sunday Herald. I got a copy of the paper today – one picture, not photo but perhaps fake drawing – black & white of the Humber and Severn. It was quite impossible to make much of the picture.

I see there is an indication in the press that Lord Fisher may return to the Admiralty, or a sort of demand that he ought to be recalled to the office of First Lord. Certainly he ought to be recalled as an act of justice.'

On December 28th, John wrote:

'We are as usual. The little boy is very bright. He watches the people at the table; quite interested in noting their identity one would think.

Vess got home on Thursday and crossed out again on Sunday night. He had a bad passage coming, but not bad going back. The weather was miserable when he was here, but he got a shot at some partridges. He is tired of the monotony and inaction of the Camp at Bidston; it is having a bad effect on the men. He has a good grip of his work I think.

Marge & Frank will be married on Sunday afternoon. Marge gets home on Xmas Eve. Mr & Mrs Sherriff will cross at the end of this week, and Frank Sherriff who is at the St Georges hospital, Dublin in R.A.M.C. work, will cross for Jan 2.

I hope you are feeling nearly all right again.

I heard of cases where men have been upset for several weeks from the effect of it (inoculation).'

People turned to John to enquire about anything that puzzled them:

'...I had brought to me three glass globes which came ashore at Garwick, in netting of cord. Others came ashore on the west side of the island some weeks or months ago. These are the same kind I mentioned some time ago as found at Laxey.'

John wrote to wish Dono a very Happy New Year and inform him that his wife and son were well:

'...The boy occasionally cries for half an hour or so, but I see no indication of his being unwell – mostly hunger, or some discomfort...

This week the Mersey was closed for a day – no Manx boat either way. I hear it has mines that got adrift and had to be fished up, and the channel known to be safe.

Vess writes that he has heard at Bidston that there are German 'tin-fish' in the Irish Sea, and this is the reason of the suspension of the sailings from the Mersey. At least there is some report of vessels sunk between Ireland and France.'

John later reported:

'Frank Sherriff said he had heard it was on account of 3 submarines in the Irish Sea and that one of them had been captured at the Mersey Bar. He had heard that it was on account of mines that had got adrift.

I met Robby Knox when I was in Douglas and I asked him why the Mersey was closed. He said the skipper of a small steamer had told him it was closed for light-draught vessels such as his own – say 10t – but that a submarine barrier was out as it was supposed there was a submarine in the Irish Sea.'

Lardy had written home. John wrote:

'Lardy is back from the Front at one of the base towns and has a cold and is not very well. He has written to Vess; says he is pretty well and expects leave soon.

The most interesting matter of the moment is the Government resolution to have National Service.

Our Xmas has been of course very quiet – stormy weather incessant.'

...The Monmouth Railway Companies were back on the lines of communication again at the end of 1915 – at Abbeville, Rouen and Abancourt. [13]

On the Isle of Man, the Knockaloe Camp had grown enormously in from its initial estimate of 5000 men.

French Red Cross inspections were made of the two Camps in December 1915: 22,000 internees at Knockaloe in four Camps – six compounds in each; the guards numbered 1,500. The Douglas Camp was much smaller – 2,450 internees divided into two Camps. Inspections were made of P.O.W. Camps around Europe by other Countries in order to make sure the prisoners were kept in reasonable conditions. Internment Camps generally varied greatly. The Knockaloe Camp was inferior to the Camp at Douglas and some men there were tired of confinement. In the *House of Keys* in January 1916, Mr Cormode spoke up about the uneasiness in the Camp, and some attempts by the men to escape:

'Tunnelling has been done by prisoners on a considerable scale... evidently for a good many months... It was discovered by accident.

A number of prisoners have escaped from the Camp, and found to be in possession of compass, chart, money and large quantity of provisions...

The presence of these thousands of alien enemies is a peril to the Isle of Man.' [22]

...The men broke out by cutting wires and hid in the rocks behind Peel Castle, intending to take one of the boats at night. They were discovered in the act, and taken and locked up. A public enquiry was ordered, respecting the Camp management, and suggesting that money used by the internees should be replaced by a system of paper currency. [22]

The Douglas Internment Camp M.N.H. [1]

Later, John enclosed a newspaper cutting giving an explanation of the different views in the U.K. Cabinet regarding the war. *Guardian* December 30 1915:

'The Cabinet Crisis – Two views of strategy to be adopted in fighting our formidable enemy: Long view – Germany must be worn down by sheer endurance, and finances conserved... high expenditure on weapons... hopes to win by a kind of siege against a disappointed and exhausted enemy – a coup de grace.

On other side are those who maintain that great & rapid effort is needed – no consideration of trade, and that heaviest sacrifices now will be the cheapest ultimately, whether in men or money... anxious about strain on France, and not hopeful over rapid recovery of Russia... A great deal to be said on both sides'.

By the end of 1915, the French had edged the Germans off the ridge of Notre Dame de Lorette, and the Western Front Line was further east on the ridge at Vimy, south-east of Lens. On the Southern Front in the Mediterranean, troops were evacuated from the Gallipoli peninsula.

Map of Northern France

Some places mentioned in John's later letters

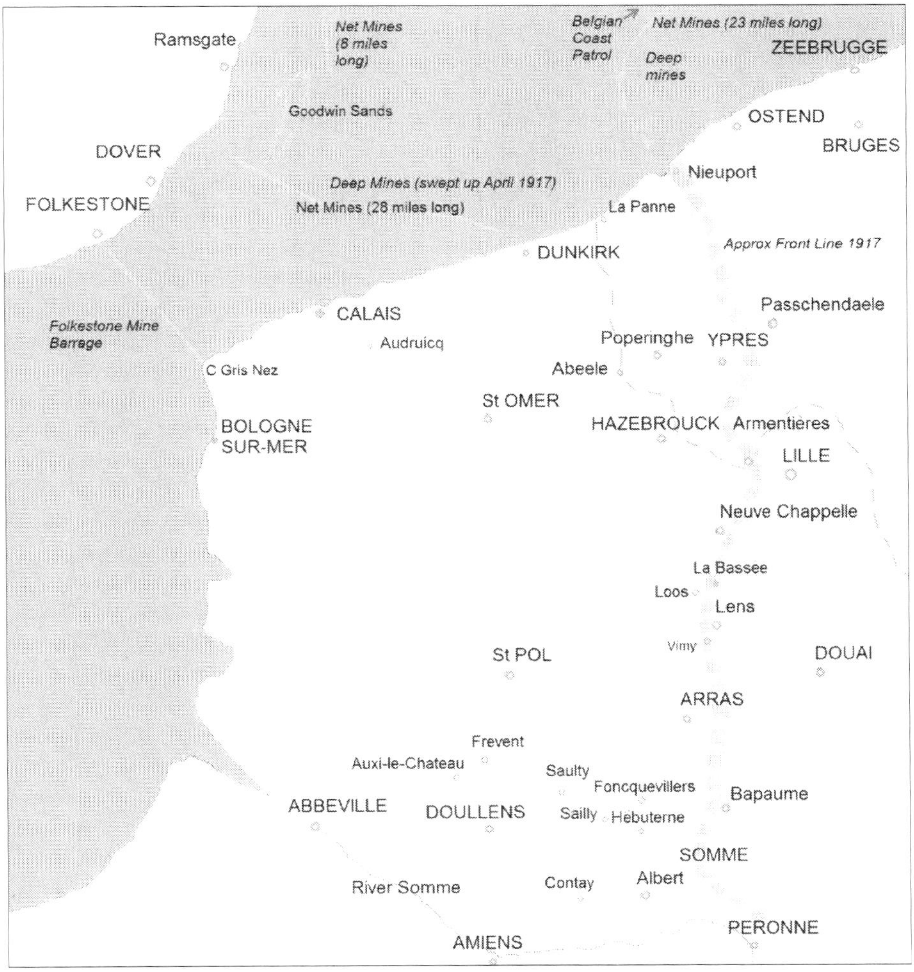

(Map drawn by Julie Quine: not to scale)

1916

1916 on the Western Front was to be dominated by the major battles of Verdun and the Somme. The British and the Allies were full of confidence for a settlement on their terms.

Dono was still on the Belgian coast patrol on board the monitor *H.M.S. Prince Rupert*. Five or six such monitors with 12" guns patrolled the Belgian coast in readiness for any land battle or firing on the gun batteries. Each night a monitor anchored fourteen miles off Ostend – a strong German submarine and destroyer base, but amazingly the monitor on duty was never attacked!' [23]

The British Fleet was inferior in some respects to that of the German Fleet, but the British Admiralty kept this secret strictly under wraps.

Admiral Bacon wrote:

> *'If she* (Germany) *had thrown every destroyer and cruiser at our fleet... she might have won the action.'*
>
> ...The German Navy were deceived into believing that the British force was of mighty strength by deceptive telegraphy between vessels and occasional gathering of ships in one area to show their 'might'. [23]

John noted that submarines were still active in the Mediterranean:

> *'The submarines have done much mischief on the Port Said, Gibraltar route. It seems likely that there has been information given of Port Said sailings west, perhaps by wireless installations on the African coast.'*

John reported some positive news to Dono from the Vicarage in the Isle of Man – Marge (John's daughter) married Frank Sherriff on Sunday 2nd January; Mr Kneale officiated:

> *'It was a very wet day, as quiet and private as possible: only the Aunts', Mr & Mrs Kelly and one or two more present.*
>
> *We went to Douglas this morning to see them off by the boat. She goes back to Over, and Frank crosses on Tuesday to Dublin, where he is in the Royal Medical Corps Service in King George Hospital.*
>
> *Frank will probably not be sent out of England or Ireland in R.A.M.C. Service – as his acceptance is for Home Service.*
>
> *A man who has been working at Port Sunlight gave me his views on the married soldier question. He says it was a terrible mistake for the*

nation. The wives of these men simply go about to picture palaces while the unmarried are everywhere scoffing at the idea of compulsion, earn their good wages and swank about smoking cigarettes. He said the streets are filled with children in the evenings because their mothers are out.'

There were rumours in January on the island that Lord Raglan was resigning. John wrote:

'A Douglas auctioneer, with whom I came in the tram from Douglas, told me a report was current in Douglas that Lord Raglan was resigning his office in the I.O.M. I could make nothing out of it, more than that it was again the man in the street!

It pretty well shows how we could get on without a regularly sitting Legislature here: the meetings during the past 18 months – for all they did, or mattered: superfluous.'

In the Mediterranean, the evacuated troops from the failed Gallipoli & Dardanelles campaign of 1915 were sent to Egypt for defence of the Suez Canal, or to Salonika in Greece to help the Serbs against Bulgarian aggression.

...The Allies continued to block Mediterranean access to the Dardanelles Straits until Turkey's collapse and exit from the war at the end of October 1918. [11]

Finally on 3rd January 1916, it looked like Vess was on the move:

'We got a wire from Vess this morning to say the 3rd Battalion Cheshire's is going off today – probably Egypt he said.

We have also a letter from Lardy – he is well – at a military base (not so well when he wrote two days ago). I fancy they had a strenuous time somewhere east of Ypres for some months past, and are having a rest. He says he is doing some 'fitting' where he is.'

John was confused as to where Vess and his Company had sailed to, and wrote on January 9th:

'Though the no. 3 Battalion sailed on Monday, we have not found that anyone knows their destination.

I was told they sailed on the Olympic and also that it was on the Britannic: I am inclined to think Olympic more likely.

Someone told me it was for Salonika, but Vess's idea was Alexandria.'

...The 1st Manx Service Company embarked at Liverpool on the *S.S. Olympic*, which had been converted into a troop ship. They were bound for the Balkans.

On Jan 6th, Vess now aged 22, was with the British Mediterranean Expeditionary Force 'somewhere in the Mediterranean', and wrote:

> *'It's really rather a wonderful experience this voyage of ours. I only wish it were a pleasure cruise. If I were only allowed to write as I liked I could fill a book with the things I have heard and seen on this boat, and with descriptions of people I've met and talked with.*
>
> *As it is, almost everything is 'verboten'.' [25]*

Photo of Manx 2nd Lieutenants: (top left to bottom right) Lace, Kissack, Quine, Gell, Captain Gateley, and Handley. Vess is pictured top right and Tommy, bottom right. M.N.H. [1]

Later, Vess wrote in his scrap-book:

> *'Arrived Mudros on Jan 9th 1916. The Company landed at Salonika from Mudros ex S.S. Victorian on Jan 13th 1916, and marched 13 miles the same night to join the 2nd Cheshire's at St John's Wood – 1.5 miles west of Aivatli on the Salonika Defence Lines.*
>
> *...Slept in snow, and next day carried on work on trenches, work which continued till the end of March.' [25]*

...The Manx Company joined the depleted 2nd Cheshire Regiment, part of the Salonika Expeditionary Force, in forming a defence line around Salonika, holding back the enemy until other Allied forces arrived later in the summer. This line was known as the 'Birdcage' due to the enormous amount of barbed wire used.

The 2nd Cheshire's were based at a village on the main road from Salonika to the Rupel Pass – the Gateway to Bulgaria. [4]

John wrote:

'We had a cheerful letter from Vess. He has asked for some things to be sent to him – a little spirit lamp, dubbin, cocoa, socks, gloves etc. He is in a dug-out with another 2nd Lt.'

On January 15th Vess wrote:

'I am just a bit disappointed to find that there is no fighting to be done here. You, however at home with your newspaper, will know more about the situation here than I do, for I don't even know where we are.

I have been slogging away all day with sledge hammer and pick, making trenches. Tommy and I have been working on our dugout – 'Grey Home' all night. I have however had some food today, bad as it was, and so am feeling better. Our mess has not yet got into working order and consequently we haven't had a decent meal since we came here.' [25]

Vess wrote later:

'We haven't been in any of the fun yet, but there is a big job here for somebody to do and it may be us. Of course there is always the chance that we may be moved, but we can't rely on it. I would rather have gone to France for some things but I'll have a much better chance out here.' [25]

In the U.K., 'Conscription', also known as 'Military Service' was due to be introduced at the end of January 1916, and applied to all single men from the age of 18 to 40.

In the Isle of Man there was some confusion in the *House of Keys* as to whether the island was included in the Compulsory Military Service Bill. Moughtin said:

'...It was compulsory service when the King could summon every man to the defence of the realm....' [22]

In the January sitting, the impact of compulsory military service on agriculture was considered, as well as the opinion that if more of the steamers had been left for use of the island by the Imperial Government, then the position of the towns of the island might not be so serious.

The resolution was put forward in the *House of Keys* for the Bill:

'...compulsory military service for single men should not be extended to include this isle without the previous consent of Tynwald being obtained'.[22]

John relates the feelings of one of its members. On January 23rd he wrote:

'I met Capt. Moughtin in Douglas yesterday, and he told me the three members of the Keys that voted (17 to 3) against the silliest resolution ever passed – were himself, Col. Moore, and Robert Clucas. Uncle Thomas was not present, being involved in the Southern Tribunal. As well might Laxey Village Commissioners resolve that Conscription should not be levied on Laxey without their consent.

We have heard from Lardy. He is on a big job that will take a considerable time – I think, railway, somewhere at the base –'not much cutting'. It is a fine place, on a plain. He is well and says it is very quiet there and that he would rather be at the Front. But of course knowing so little of the circumstances I remain without wish.'

...In January 1916, half of Lardy's Company were at Abbeville and the other at Abancourt – 'Railway work impeded by heavy snow.' [9]

Dono's wife Daisy was back in the Isle of Man in January; she spent some time with her parents in Baldrine, a short walk away from the Vicarage, where she also lodged for short periods with Dono's parents. Dono had some leave. John wrote to Dono:

'Daisy came up this morning and told us she had got a wire from you from Liverpool. We were glad to hear that, bad weather considered, you had got in well.'

...Regarding the Dover Patrol, on January 26th the group of five patrol monitors off the Belgian coast fired simultaneously in the vicinity of Westende. The firing was carried out involving aeroplane spotting, resulting in inaccurate data which led to a revision of aeroplane spotting methods. Bombardments of this sort were suspended for the rest of the winter as accurate bombing could not be carried out in rough seas. However the Dover Patrol continued its patrol work on the coast.

The guns on the Belgian coast at Ostend and Zeebrugge, particularly the Knocke and Tirpitz batteries, outranged the guns on the patrol ships, and had greater accuracy than those of the ships. According to Admiral Bacon – without smoke screens, any ships attempting such a bombardment would have been annihilated. Plans were made for a strategic surprise bombardment at a later date.

At the end of January 1916, Dono was developing a gun-sight for anti-aircraft guns; John wanted this to be officially recognised and was still unhappy that the 'net' idea hadn't received recognition:

'I told Sargeaunt point blank that you had received nothing as yet in the way of recognition for the device which foiled the submarine menace; personally I could explain it only by changes at head-quarters, unless there might be other explanations...

But history is being made so fast and memories get shorter.'

Regarding the gun-sight, John continued:

> *'I have my memorandum on a single sheet of good drawing paper (23"x15"). I give no sizes, nor useful diam. for wheels, mirror, etc. I have no book of artillery trajectory tables. Your advice is right – not to send my memorandum at present...'*

Below is a summary of Dono's ideas written by John: *in full [Appendix c]*

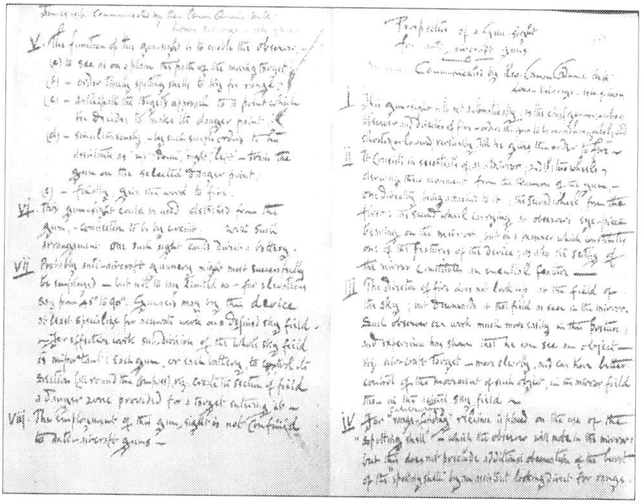
Prospectus of a Gun-sight
for anti-aircraft guns

John received a letter from Vess on January 28th and reported to Dono:

> *'Vess is assistant bombing officer and also doing some range-finding. He thinks the only way to move on is to specialize. He understands machine-guns and can work any of them, but was not given the opportunity in training of getting qualified.*
>
> *The weather has improved, but there is some idea of heavy spring rains being a feature of the climate later on. Weather there – snow, ground snow-slush, and freezing at night. He intends to build a brick fireplace in his dug-out. He seemed in good spirits, and cheerful.'*

The average life expectancy during WWI for a 2nd Lieutenant on the Western Front was just two weeks – these higher ranked men were easily identified by the enemy, as they wore a leather belt across their body. Despite the fact that Vess was not in such a high-pressure environment, he was still having a pretty grim time through monotony, and wrote to his friend on February 4th:

> *'Yesterday was the same as all days are here just now...*

When it gets light we rise, put on wet muddy clothes and boots and trudge through wire, slush and snow to our daily tasks.

At irregular intervals we devour portions of food, mostly uncooked and eaten off the earth or mud. When it becomes dark we return to our caves and dens and shiver through a night an eternity long. At times we converse with our fellow sufferers.

Our dugout is far better than the houses the Greeks live in. We have a real door that shuts and a fireplace of brick and tin, properly cemented, and a jolly good fire it is too. I am sitting beside it now, while Tommy heats his little tin of shaving water and hunts round for things to burn.

Fuel is very scarce as the only trees out here are fig-trees, which we are not allowed to cut down. The only things we can get are the roots of vine-trees (the Greeks grow the small grapes that become raisins).' [25]

The weekly Sunday 'hot tub' became a luxurious addition to the ritual in the Salonika camp. Vess wrote of the sport in the camp:

'Isn't it funny to think that out here miles from home and in the midst of the greatest war ever heard of, the British Army goes on playing football, and boxing, and holding races, just the same as ever.' [25]

Back in the U.K., at the end of January there was another Zeppelin attack in the Liverpool area and on February 1st the Manx paddle steamer *Empress Queen* ran into rocks off the Isle of Wight in poor visibility carrying 1,300 troops home on leave. They were evacuated from the steamer in a gale. Dono saw the wreck from *H.M.S. Prince Rupert* when his ship was entering Portsmouth for a refit.

John wrote to Dono a great deal about his gun sight idea:

'Glad to have your letter to hand this evening (Feb 3). I now understand the (gun-sight) idea much clearer: most interesting... I am writing to my friend John Joughin on the simplest lines – he likes to look into things and see persons that can explain things valuable in the interests of science applied to war.

I have a long letter written to Lord Raglan – lying undated as yet. Mother read it. It is plain and to the point...'

Dono was nervous of sending his new gun-sight idea directly to the Admiralty in case the outcome was similar to that of the submarine 'net'.

Lord Raglan M.N.H. [1]

John saw Mr Sargeaunt, the Government Secretary and Treasurer on February 10th and wrote:

'Today I was getting an order from Mr Sargeaunt to see a man interned at Knockaloe, in whose welfare some friends of Mr Cooper are interested. This enabled me to have a conversation with Sargeaunt.

I referred to his kind willingness and offer to send any (gun-sight) *memo... I spoke of what I considered a hardship – having sent a memo which proved to be invaluable: there was forthcoming neither recognition nor even acknowledgement...*

You were left in a position to carefully consider what was the right course to take, having evolved another device, which with the same confidence you believed – would be of great value if it materialized.

I said that conditions were not normal: national needs required secrecy and directness of communication not permitted by normal routine. I believed a personal interview or permission to submit a project personally was almost necessary. He agreed.

He told me he had sent the (submarine net) *memo of Oct 1914 to L.J., a relative.*

Sargeaunt said he would willingly write a normal letter saying that the same person (Dono), *was now an Officer in H.M.S., had a device which, with the same confidence he believed to be of great value; that opportunity to submit it was almost precluded by circumstances of Service; that the device was a g.s.* (gun-sight) *for a.a.c.g.* (anti-aircraft guns).

I had his assurance that the rights and the honour of one who could do valuable service to his country, should be carefully safeguarded... so I fell in with the proposal that he should write.

The more I think over the mechanism, the more perfectly automatic I perceive it to be... The graduating is far simpler than at first supposed – requires no artillery trajectory tables... I have all along assumed that in initial position of the gun – taking that as horizontal, the bracket's initial position also horizontal in the opposite direction; for any angle above horizon: they both rise to the same angle...'

John received regular brief letters throughout February from Lardy to say that he was well and still on the big piece of work at base. John reported:

'Lardy says it is rather livelier there now – more show of things moving. The French climate is evidently no better than ours in the Isle of Man. It has changed a little – from rainy to frosty.'

One of the costliest Battles of WWI was the Battle of Verdun, which began in February 1916, when the Germans attacked a French salient in an attempt to bleed the French army to death, and consequently the hills and ridges north of Verdun changed hands throughout March and April...

In February, Vess organised a visit to Salonika for a real bath; he was fed up of camp life. He wrote:

'I have obtained the necessary passes and permits and have arranged about getting a horse sent up from the transport lines. Isn't it funny? Out here people take it as a matter of course that you can ride and would never dream of asking whether you can. As a matter of fact I can ride about as well as I can fly, but all the same I suppose I'll just climb on board the gee-gee when it turns up and ride down to Salonika as if I'd ridden horses since the year 1.' [25]

Vess continued:

'This morning we had an inspection by the Brigadier, followed by a short crawl or route-march over the plain.

You will no doubt be glad to hear that my platoon was the best in the company on the inspection. So you see, my method of dealing with men is not so disastrous as you thought... you will perhaps be surprised to know that since coming out here, my platoon have had fewer men up at orderly room than any other in the Company. I'm rather bucked with the idea considering what everyone used to say about it.

The persistent rain, will I'm afraid, have a bad effect on our little 'Grey Home'. All dugouts get damp in wet weather. I'm jolly glad I've got a waterproof sleeping bag.' [25]

In the North Sea, the 2nd Battle of Dogger Bank took place on Feb 10th. German torpedo boat flotillas in the North Sea near Dogger Bank engaged the British mine-sweeping sloops. Knowing they were outgunned, the British boats attempted to flee, but *H.M.S. Arabis* was sunk: 56 crew killed. The three other sloops escaped. Regarding this, John wrote:

'I see there is a news paragraph that the gun torpedo boats (or destroyers) which attacked four mine-layers and seem to have sunk one of them off the Dogger Bank, came out of Zeebrugge. Probably the newspapers know nothing about it.'

John wondered if Dono might get an interview with his Admiral regarding the gun-sight – as a point of courtesy. On February 23rd John wrote:

'...You spoke to your Captain... it would be well to get any evidence of an interview sought and obtained in black & white – that what you have invented is yours... You could get leave and go up to London and patent your device at the Patent Office, then negotiate for its use. It is no longer and never was, a world in which honour counted for anything! ...So maybe seeing the Captain and Admiral is not what one should after all do – they are just as liable as you to be victims...

The value of the device is amplified by the recent haphazard hit made by a gunner in the S.E. of France, who brought down a Zeppelin – one shot and the thing dropped. But how many other hundred shells missed it?'

Later John sent a letter to Lord Raglan regarding the gun-sight *[appendix d]* to which he received a reply from Raglan... He also sent a copy of the letter to Mr J. King M.P. (Somerset). Mr Sargeaunt had not received any answer to his letter. The lack of recognition for Dono's work on the submarine net motivated John to send the following newspaper cutting to Dono:

Evening News Wed 23rd Feb 1916:

'The Tin Fish Hunt – Mr Balfour Cannot Give Away the Great U-Boat Wrecking Secret:

Mr King asked in Parliament today whether the Admiralty still retains the Services of the person or persons who devised the defensive methods which had been effectively employed against the so-called enemy submarine 'blockade', and whether with due regard to naval interests further facts would be disclosed as to the result of the means taken to overcome the enemy submarine menace.

Mr Balfour: "so far as I am aware, all the officers contributing to the scheme of anti-submarine warfare are still in the service of the Admiralty. With regard to the second part of the question, I think nothing can safely be said."'

John did not like the reference to *'all the officers'*, and wrote a letter on February 28 1916 to the M.P. House of Commons *[Appendix e]*.

John wrote to Dono, regarding the gun-sight:

'I believe that Lord Raglan and Lord Derby are well acquainted personally... This is worth something. It is no use being thwarted or set back by a failure to get in at one door, when another further on may be the right one!

There is plenty of time for things to be required yet before the war is over.'

High-angle, anti-aircraft gun-sight developed by Dono – submitted to Whale Island, Portsmouth later in April 1916

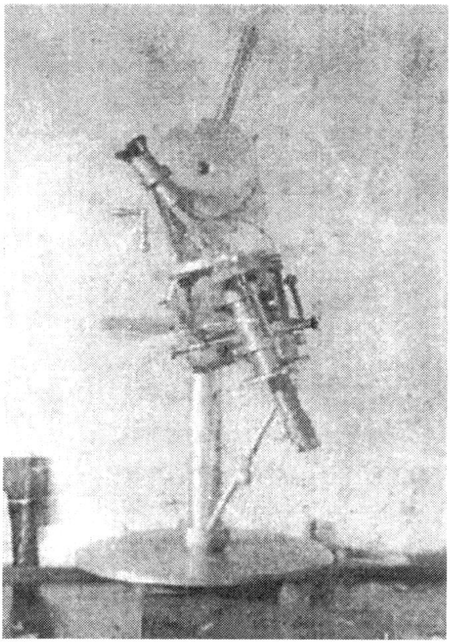

John continued:

'I was in Douglas and met Willie Knox in the street. We strolled along. He asked about you. I said you had a good thing solved – a g.s. (gun-sight) *– of which I could give him no particulars, for he started to tell me that a man named Coulthart, a Carlisle traveller who sells them*

stuff, had told him when he was over about a month ago that Armstrong's had something of a new sort which they were trying on guns in Silloth Golf Links – supposed to enable the gunner to hit!

He could not tell me of what nature the thing was, though I tried to get out of him if it had any machinery or if big or little, etc. He said he thought the gunner sat down. As they were practicing about a month ago, or rather as Coulthart was, this thing has been in hand a few months seemingly.'

John wrote to Dono regarding the larger submarines being turned out by Germany:

'The large size submarine is evidently an alarm to the newspapers. The members of the House of Commons know very little. Mr J. King M.P. House of Commons is member for N. Somerset. He is like a lot of others: they cannot get from the minister anything more than generalities.'

Daily Mail February 22nd 1916:

'The Super U – Germany's Monster Submarine. It is just 16 months since we began to receive reports of new formidable submarines in German shipyards – preparing a novel development of submarines for our discomfiture.

Last July Countess von Dagenfeld, niece of Count Zeppelin, declared in New York: 'Germany has 22 subs large enough to voyage to N.Y. and stay 2 months outside harbour before returning...'

It is known that the most successful methods of fighting the sub have been provided by destroyers & drifters, to which vessels Ad. Sir Reg. Bacon attributed the immunity of his Fleet from loss by sub attack during operations off the Belgian coast.'

The weather on the island had been harsh and bitter – snow on the hills. Vess had written at considerable length, although letters generally took a couple of weeks to arrive from Salonika. John told Dono:

'He is qualified in range-finding, visual signalling (only one in his Battalion) and in bombing. He has a big job on of range-finding just now to provide data for charts or maps. He thinks he may be required for special work and may have choice of three special jobs.

Their position in Salonika is some miles inland on a landward facing slope. He finds bad French the lingo in Salonika and gets on very well with this. I sent him a Modern Greek – self-taught, so that he could get to know something of that language too! He considers the intelligence department lacks suitable men who can grasp and report on the things important about a country – from a military point of view.

He thinks the Greeks favourable to the Allied cause, and that Bulgars & Turks would change sides should there be for us a victory of any magnitude in that sphere.

Vess says his name has been sent to Brigade Headquarters – he thinks as recommended for some work – but does not know what. He goes on with his platoon as usual.

He thinks the range-finding job is some little recognition of his previous work, or outcome of it.'

Vess wrote (in February):

'On Monday last I was appointed Signalling Officer to the Battalion, and have of course had to give up my platoon. I feel sorry in a way to leave the men and I believe some of them feel sorry that I have gone.

I still belong to the Manx Company but have nothing to do with it, as I have my own Signallers to look after and of course I am much more independent now, being responsible directly to the Company. I have to attend a Brigade Signalling class every day to learn the ins and outs of my job. Really I am progressing, aren't I?

It is just the very job for me, as I always was keen on signalling, and my wireless work comes in very useful.' [25]

John wrote:

'He still keeps on the big range finding job till he has finished, but he gives up the platoon & the bombing. The G.O.C. in the Brigade has complimented him on his mode of doing the work. Of course he has to get up his reading and sending. He can do 15 words per minute on the buzzer, and read at rate of 12 – that is after long being out of practice.'

Later, John wrote:

'Vess told me of a Salonika experience. He was range-finding, and while copying figures dictated to his Corporal, another officer came round and tampered with his range-finding instrument! Vess said sharply –"What the devil do you mean, touching that?"

Next day he was asked to report to the Colonel. He found there the man he had used the above language to:

Col: "Mr Q. you are reported to me as having sworn at a bro-officer! Is that so?"

Vess: "Yes, Sir!"

Col: "Do you know what that means?"

V: "Would you instruct me, Sir?"

Col: "It is subversive of discipline!"

V: "Yes, Sir!"

Col: "Do you know what it involves?"

V: "Would you instruct me, Sir?"

Col: "Either to apologize to him, or..."

V: "Is it your direction that I should apologize, Sir?"

Col: "That is the course!"

V: "Then Sir, I apologize to Lt. G for having sworn at him in the presence of a non Com officer!"

(Vess turns to go away as the incident is closed).

Col: "Stay a moment, Mr Quine... Now, Mr G... What the devil do you mean – by interfering with an expensive and delicate instrument for which a bro. officer is responsible?"

...and more of the same sort.'

In the Isle of Man, the Military Service Act came into operation on March 3rd 1916, but men could appeal to a Tribunal. John thought the Act a good thing, and wrote:

'...The Military Service Act affects the Isle of Man as England, by an order in Council including the island in the Act.'

When the Tribunal held its first meeting earlier in January to appoint a Chairman – the Mayor of Douglas, Danny Flinn, John wrote:

'The functions of the Committee are very much those of a jury: the Recruiting Officer submits a case to us, and we can ask the claimant questions. About 20 cases are already on a list to be heard at our next meeting.'

Later in March however, the Tribunal was scorned and John reported:

'Our Tribunal has got the execration of the people here who profess to 'have nothing to do with the war' – one might say they didn't issue the declaration of war and wish to remain neutral.

A man told me in Douglas today that our Tribunal was 'a disgrace to the island'. He made no headway, for I smiled and said: "A credit, you meant; it has saved the reputation of the island, or those left on it after the brave ones have left it! You want a back door to escape by, or a chimney to hide in: and you say to those who are not after the same things: 'you fellows are a disgrace to the island'!"'

...The Tribunal was composed of 19 members, but had a bad reputation amongst the local people. The primary duty of the Tribunal was to consider the cases of men between the ages of 18 to 41 – to decide where and how those men would best serve the national interests. There was some debate about the Tribunal in the House of Keys later in January 1917. [22]

A new Tribunal panel was elected. John wrote:

'...The new 'Tribunal' elected by the Keys has come in for much abuse. It consists of farmers and allied businesses – and the weakest men to be got! It was understood that I was marked for exclusion, and Capt. Moughtin – as the backbone of the old Tribunal that did its honest duty.

Now it will be an open back-door for any connected with agriculture.'

On March 5th 1916, John told Dono:

'Daisy and the boy were here today. They are both very well. He has grown visibly in the last week, and takes more definite notice.

Lardy reports himself much better and getting rid of his cold. This has given us much relief – as we certainly believe he had a very bad cold.

Leaves are stopped and it appears there is some considerable reason for it. He was to have had a leave about due now, but for this: probably a military movement.

We have not had a week-end letter from Vess.

We can see the glare of Knockaloe Camp (at the Vicarage) *under favourable cloud conditions, a little to the west. Yesterday I could hear heavy gun practice from Barrow.*

The French behaved very well at Verdun.

I saw that there had been operations off the Belgian coast on Tuesday (Feb. 29).'

...There was action in the North Sea between a German raider, *Grief*, which was in disguise, and an English cruiser *Alcantara* – both sunk (over 270 men died).

John continued:

'We might as well be living in the moon as here in the Isle of Man, for any chance we have of seeing or knowing anything definite of anybody... One of the great efforts that is being made in England, is that after the war (as well as during it) the same sort of people shall be enjoying the same sort of incomes, victory or none.'

There had been an incident in the Irish Sea at the beginning of March. John wrote:

> *'On Monday, people from the S.S. Tynwald report seeing a crew – German naval men – about 40 or so, landed at the stage, and versions say a submarine sunk outside, or a commerce destroyer.'*

In Salonika, Vess was in hospital on March 8th but didn't tell his parents, as he thought it was nothing to worry them about – just a fever. He was completely overwhelmed as he had flown for the first time. He wrote:

> *'I have now been an officer for exactly a year. How ancient I feel. But the crowning glory – today I have flown – yes, actually in an aeroplane and a real flight, nearly half an hour in the air.*
>
> *It came about thus – a Lieutenant Don and yours truly went for a walk to the aviation grounds about three miles from here. All the people there were French. Well we could both speak French.*
>
> *We talked to the pilots nicely and to M'sieu le Commandant with the result that they offered to take us for a short flight.*
>
> *Can you imagine my feelings – joy, excitement, just a little nervous perhaps, but keen as mustard as I donned helmet, a fur coat and all the correct paraphernalia and climbed into the neat little seat in the bows where the observer sits.*
>
> *The pilot, a sergeant, who has a name already as a daring and skillful flier, though only a boy, probably younger even than myself, climbs to his seat and tests everything. The mechanics turn the machine up wind and swing the propeller – there is a burst of sound as the beautiful motor starts up; the machine quivers and leaps forward – a short run, faster, faster, and we are away. How steeply we climb – up – up – up, then bank sharply and round we go, and below us already small, I can see the little crowd of mechanics and the hangars.*
>
> *The flight was really fine and the pilot evidently meant to give me thrills. Round and round we went getting higher and higher, then straightened out and went away cross country, perhaps ten miles – then turned back again, banking and climbing and diving all over the aerodrome, and then finishing with one grand swoop down right over the sheds with engine stopped, a slight touch, no jolts or jerks, a short run and we stop and the flight is over.*
>
> *It is the first experience I have ever had and the sensation absolutely glorious. My description is feeble...*

How can I make you realise the exhilaration, the rush of the wind on one's face, the feeling of absolute detachment from things on earth.

Description is hopeless – to realise it – one must fly.' [25]

...Vess's first flight was in a Caudron Biplane. He was given a routine reprimand back at base for the latter.

John had heard from Lardy. There seemed to be considerable movement in mid-March 1916 in his part of the country. The Company was ordered to move from Abancourt to Saulty, S.W. of Arras, where they had to put in a big gun line, and there was another move at the end of the month to Méricourt. [9] John wrote:

'Lardy seems well again and asks for some tea; we have sent him some.

...The sensation of the last ten days has been the reappearance of Mr Winston Churchill, now Col. Churchill, in Parliament. He seems not to have got a good reception, though Sir Dalziel and two or three other rather patriotic men seemed to keep him in countenance.

We are so utterly out of the world here, that we cannot really tell what is behind any of the men who figure in Parliament.

I see that some Dardanelles men are just now receiving recognitions.'

...Lardy probably moved to Vignacourt, France, in April, and continued with his work – moving materials and men for work on new railway lines.

According to the No.3 Monmouth Railway Company War Diary, in May the Company moved to the Saulty area, east of Doullens and put in gun batteries at various points including Humbercamps, Pommier and St Amand; materials for these were taken up by rail at night as there was observation by the enemy at some points. Over a mile of track could be laid in one day. [9]

In April in the North Sea Channel, a double line of deep mines – a net-barrage – was stretched about 12 miles from the Belgian coast some forty miles – from the north of Dunkerque to the edge of Dutch territorial waters north of Zeebrugge, and the task took five weeks. The 12" monitors, including *H.M.S. Prince Rupert*, took up patrol along this line. Admiral Bacon wrote:

'...It was a deterrent to German submarine mine-laying in the area.' [23]

Towards the end of April 1916, John's daughter, Marge, experienced the outbreak of the Rebellions in Ireland against the British Government on Monday 24th April – known as the Easter Uprising.

Some Irish people didn't feel the British had the right to impose Home Rule on Ireland and retaliated.

At the end of the uprising, 15 leading men were executed.

Regarding the Rebellion, John wrote:

'Marge had more experience and opportunity of seeing the active operations of Easter week in Dublin than I supposed. She actually saw the 'Shinn Fayners' – which seems to be the correct pronunciation – seize the Post Office in Sackville Street, and also was more under fire at St Stephens Green than I had thought likely.

She was not at all nervous, and was anxious only because she could not communicate to us that she was all right.'

On May 31st 1916 the Battle of Jutland was fought off the Dutch coast. It was the only full-scale WWI Naval Battle between the Grand Fleet and the German High Seas Fleet, involving hundreds of ships, and the first time that the Dreadnought Battleships built in the early 1900's came to blows. Over 8000 lives were lost.

The German Fleets had avoided unnecessary clashes to preserve their ships, and were better at military manoeuvres than naval ones, but the German High Seas Fleet was trying to eliminate some of the British Grand Fleet and thereby break the British blockade of German ports. John wrote:

'I see by Arthur Pollen's article in Land & Water regarding the Jutland battle that he holds the same view regarding last week: that it is a success of large magnitude. Though he does not insist that the German losses were in units much more numerous than ours, he says that everything points that way.

We hear that William Quine, 2nd Surgeon on H.M.S. Calliope, lost his Senior Officer through wound, and was in sole charge with a large number of cases of wounded. He had a trying time of it.'

...*H.M.S. Calliope* – one of the 5 ships in the 4th Light Cruiser Squadron, was hit a number of times during the Battle of Jutland; 10 crew killed. Fourteen British and eleven German ships were sunk at Jutland. Both sides claimed victory.

John continued:

'As you see the newspapers you are aware of the extensive Russian movement, which must seriously dislocate the Austro-German holding of the whole Eastern line, and affect the West as well as the Italian Front.'

...Early in June, four Russian armies on the Eastern Front, under new Commander Brusilov, began a general offensive in the south-west along the 300 mile Front. Consequently the Germans sent four of their divisions east from Verdun.

During April and May the Manx Company and the 2nd Cheshire's were 30 miles from Salonika. They were engaged in reconnaissance as far as Likovan. Vess was involved in this work. His flying experience was well behind him, but not forgotten.

Vess wrote of one of his experiences under fire:

'The whole of the last week has been a very busy time for us all here, as we have been away up country hill-fighting and only returned to camp yesterday afternoon. Last Monday we had 'some' air raid. The beastly things got me up at 4.30 in the morning with their buzzing and bomb-dropping.

I saw a scrap between a Frenchman and one of the Boche (German) *planes. The Boche was hovering right over our camp evidently going to let us have about half-a-ton of frightfulness all in a lump.*

He was so intent on his nasty business that he must have got a nasty jolt when all of a sudden a French plane came – whizz – over the hill behind him and opened fire with his machine gun – 'plop-plop – plop-plop-plop' comme ca. Then the Hun started his gun – 'plip-plip-plip-plip – plip-plip', and both machines swung away and we were able to draw our breaths again. Later on we saw the Frenchman come sailing back but of course we could only imagine what happened.

Then we went on our stunt. From Monday to yesterday we crawled up hills that would make Llangollen (in Wales, U.K.) *rub its eyes. No roads, no level country, no people, only goat tracks, rocks, rivers and gorges.*

Every day the sun blazed down on us till our hands and faces were raw and blistered. Every night it rained till we were soaked to the skin, and Burberry's, waterproof sheets and blankets were like sponges. However we returned safely and it was jolly good experience for us.

I saw some really marvellous country. North Wales is nothing to it, and think of the joy of getting back almost to civilisation again.

It is raining like fun tonight but I don't care – I've got back to my tent and all the rain in Greece isn't going to worry me.

I had a very hard job as an awful lot of signalling had to be done and we had to work all night as well as all day.' [25]

John told Dono:

'Vess is well. He has sent for a book on wireless in case he may have to take up that work. He has mentioned in his recent letters that he

goes to the army riding school, as he is now provided with a horse. He has three men to accompany him when engaged on trek movements. He has devised a small bivouac tent for himself about 3' high – merely a sleeping shelter. The weather is exceedingly hot – a slouch hat and shirt sleeves, the usual style.'

Vess continued:

'Nowadays I live in a tent as I think it's healthier than a dugout now the hot weather is coming on. I just seem to have enough room and have made myself very comfy with Greek mats on the floor and a good big oil stove and kettle to make cocoa on. I have made two most nutty tables and am making a camp chair.

Then of course, being Signalling Officer I have my private telephone installed and the place looks quite business-like.' [25]

Salonika: British Bivouacs 1916 [32]

Vess wrote on April 30th:

'We have had awful weather this last week but it's fine again now. We have all got our boy scout hats now so will look fearful dogs.' [25]

The 2nd Cheshire (& Manx) Battalion moved northwards of Salonika – plenty of days marching under a scorching sun, advancing over three weeks along roads which they built as they went. On May 12th Vess wrote:

'We have moved from the place that I wrote from before and have been having a pretty rough time, but are more or less settled again now. Tommy and I have built ourselves a 'bivvy' (tent) *out of water-proof sheets and Burberry's* (trench coats) *but I must admit that I have been in more comfortable billets in my time.*

Still of course I'm not grumbling and am fairly contented.

I have had a huge amount of work to do lately. I am not nearly so spick and span as I was at home. If you saw me trekking about these hillsides in a slouch hat, with sleeves rolled up to the elbow and my arms burnt by the sun till the skin has all peeled off them, garbed in breeches that are now decidedly has-beens, and my boots sadly in need of repair, I doubt if you would recognise me.

Did you read in the papers of a Zepp being shot down at Salonika? Well I saw the shooting, but only at a great distance and I didn't know until later that it was successful.' [25]

...**Zeppelin LZ85** was shot down on May 5th in the marshes at the mouth of the Vardar, Salonika. [32]

Vess wrote:

'I'm hoping to get leave to go down and see the remains of the Zepp and of course perhaps to get a bit of it as a souvenir.' [25]

...He hoped to get one of the local men to make him a memento to send home.

Vess continued:

'As I was riding round the camp this morning, my horse (not mine but a 'borrow') jibbed at a gully and deposited me neatly and effectively on the cold hard stones.

That's the worst of having to ride a thing that has no foot-brakes and a throttle that works both ways at once.' [25]

...At the end of May, Vess was thrown from his horse again during riding lessons, landed on his head and ended up in the casualty clearing station for recuperation.

Hostility continued on the Western Front with the Battle of Mount Sorrel. Fort Vaux was stormed by the German force. Later Fort Thiaumont was also captured by the Germans, but retaken by the French at the end of the month. Lord Kitchener was killed on June 5th when the cruiser *H.M.S. Hampshire* struck a mine on its way to Russia in the Orkneys.

In June, John wrote:

> *'Today there has been firing of very big guns off here on the Cumberland side, probably gun trials.*
>
> *Lardy I gather is somewhere in the Ypres sector though I do not know exactly where. He says it is occasionally 'lively' where he is now.'*

Later in June, an observer went up with the 8th Squadron R.F.C. to report on the efficiency of the new gun positions and realised that the railway lines were easy targets due to the materials used, as was proved on the 10th June when the enemy opened fire on the lines and station buildings. Two trains were moved clear. [9] Regarding this, John wrote later:

> *'Lardy said that one night they had a train of munitions in a small station, on which the German shells began dropping. They had evidently the range of it. He jumped up, and ran the train out about 4 miles to a safe spot till the shelling was over.*
>
> *A Sergeant who had been asleep and who did nothing in the matter, got a recommendation for it, but Lardy was not noticed.*
>
> *Are men to run after C.O.s and ask for justice?'*

On the Western Front, the Battle of the Somme was launched earlier than planned, on July 1st – in the vicinity of Albert, to take the pressure off the French at Verdun. John wrote:

> *'...We had a letter from Lardy. He is well. He implies that he is near Albert, viz. in the zone immediately behind the present advance. He implies that they are on railway work. Mother heard through Daisy that a young man named Leece recently gone to France is in Lardy's Co., and (by his letter to his parents) says he 'is on the same engine with Lardy'. From this I infer that Lardy is driving.'*

> ...During July the No.3 Monmouth Railway Company were working in the Contay area on the Daours line and Candas to Acheux line for reinforcements and ammunition. [9]

Dono's work continued on the Dover Patrol including bombardment of the coast. Admiral Bacon wrote:

> '...The monitors also had the job of trying to keep the German troops on the coast during the early days of the advance of the Somme.
>
> Patrol work continued until October 1916.' [23]

In the Isle of Man, July 5th is usually a day of celebration, Tynwald Day (the Island's National Day). In 1916, a high percentage of the population turned out for this event – Samuel Norris included. The people, led by him, presented a petition to Lord Raglan, Governor of the island, demanding his resignation and Government action against recent food taxes and the lack of Government funding to people bankrupted by the war. Lord Raglan was proving unpopular with the Manx people.

> ...In place of the Manx I.O.M. Volunteer Corps, the guard of honour at the Tynwald ceremony was made up of 100 British soldiers – Royal Defence Corps – imported to guard prisoners of war interned on the island; the change was not popular with the local people. [3]

John had other concerns. Later on July 26th 1916 he wrote:

> *'This evening we have a letter from Vess. The force is not moving yet. The weather is exceedingly hot, and he speaks of the strain of one's patience. He is exercised about the question of permanent stay in the Army, viz. whether to apply now or later: I do not understand what his Commission is, as he was advanced from temporary Sub Lt. to Sub Lt.'*

In July the 2nd Cheshire & Manx Co. Battalion moved northward to Lozista in the Struma Valley – an area of low swampy ground. The village of Lozista looked out across a five-mile plain and a 6000 foot range of mountains where the enemy was ensconced. [4]

Vess wrote on July 9th 1916:

> *'I suppose you will have guessed from my letters where we are. The Bulgar is quite close and we see him every day (I suppose he sees us as well), but we never have anything doing. We are more interested in keeping clear of the sickness* (malaria) *than worrying about the human enemy. This evening if it is cool enough, I'm going to ride over and see Tommy. I hear we are to get sun helmets now. I did intend sending home for some 'pukkas' eastern kit, but it would be nearly winter before the things would get here.*
>
> *Our camp is in a grove of oak trees and we are eternally worried by the 'cicidas' which are things like grasshoppers – only bigger. They live in the trees.' [25]*

But cicadas weren't a problem – mosquitoes were!

The 2nd Cheshire's were not equipped with mosquito nets or gloves, and consequently the majority of the men were struck down with malaria.

On July 16th 1916, Vess wrote:

'Nowadays I generally go about in shorts and with a shirt with the sleeves cut off.

There is no news of anything going to happen here and we hear such glorious tales of advances in France that we all long to be there.

How gladly we would quit this land of exile.' [25]

Eventually, due to malaria, only one officer, the Company Sergeant Major, five Sergeants and seven other ranks were left fit for duty. The others were so sick they had to be carried back to headquarters.

At the end of July the Battalion was sent out of the Front line for six weeks rest, moving to the hills on the other side of the Struma Valley. [4]

The Struma Valley July 1916: British soldiers being given their daily dose of quinine [32]

Vess had also succumbed to an attack of malaria.

John wrote to Dono:

'We had a letter from Vess saying he is in hospital with fever or malaria. He wrote on July 29 – the day you were at home.

He was seized with an attack the previous Sunday Jul 23, and took from Monday to Friday to get down to the 5th Canadian Hospital in Salonika. He was going to have his blood tested to see if there was malaria in the system.

He speaks of the awful monotony and tedium of the camp: the inaction is having a bad effect on the men, with the heat, malaria, and same-ness of diet!

There seems as yet to be no active operations for the force.'

Vess wrote on July 29th 1916:

'Once again, for the third time, I am in hospital and of course as usual there is nothing wrong with me.

I got sick up in the hills last Sunday (23rd), but by the time I arrived here (yesterday noon) the fever had spent itself. I just feel a bit weak and very tired.

The place we have been in is awful – a hotbed of fever with millions of flies and mosquitoes.

The journey down from the lines to here was awful. My worst effort was seven hours in a motor ambulance with a broken spring, at night.' [25]

Salonika Ambulance 1916 [32]

On the Western Front at the beginning of August, the first aerial operations were carried out by combined French & British air services, and there was a further Zeppelin raid on Hartlepool: two bombs dropped.

On the island, fund-raising was continuing. John wrote:

'There is a Red Cross fete at Silverdale, Thurs 17th August. Mother and the girls and Daisy are going.

There is to be a tea-room with five Mrs. Quine's at the tables – this includes my brother's wife from Manchester, now at Castletown, and her daughter-in-law, wife of William Quine.

Lady Raglan is to be at the fete. I am not going; I have to attend an Antiquarian meeting at Onchan – as I am President of the I.O.M. National History & Antiquarian Society this year.'

Later, John wrote:

'The Red Cross effort at Silverdale on Thurs 17th was a success: they raised £170, and will probably have £150 to £160 net for the Red

Cross. Mother and the girls were there. Lady Raglan and her daughter opened the affair.

I met Lord Raglan at Onchan on Wednesday. He insisted on my getting into his motor with him for a short distance. He looks better, but has been very ill, without question.'

As a result of the public demanding Lord Raglan's resignation on Tynwald Day in July, Lady Raglan was nervous of appearing in public. John wrote:

'Aunt Eva told me that Lady Raglan was a good deal nervous at Silverdale, where there was a crowd of over 2,000 people: she thought there might be some signs or expressions of that 'unpopularity', which no doubt they have seen in the papers. Aunt Eva and Uncle Thomas told her that there was not the least fear of any such thing, and that she would get a cordial reception. Of course the reception was cordial enough. But in any case he could guarantee it there.'

...In August 1916 Lady Raglan announced that she would not appear at any further public function due to the former outbursts against her husband.

Vess was out of hospital again and back with his regiment. On August 21st 1916 John wrote to Dono:

'Vess says the rest has done him good, and the change of diet – which had been monotonous to the limit, being every day the same, month after month. Clearly with monotony of life there ought not to be monotony of diet – for men you wish to keep fit. Of the Captain and 5 sub-Lieut.'s who went out with Manx Co, the Capt. and two of the subalterns are invalided to Malta, one with chronic rheumatism, the other with heart trouble; Vess and another were in the base hospital and are now back with Reg.: the other, a man turned 30 having escaped. The Dr told Vess his constitution was good and his stamina had resisted the malaria getting any serious hold of him.

Their Camp was in an extremely trying place.

He is now about 40 miles from the port and 2,000 feet above the sea, clear of the malaria strata, but bad enough with flies and things other than mosquitoes.'

However Vess had a secret, and wrote to his friend on August 10th 1916:

'I have practically nothing to do these days. I go out for a ride on the gee-gee every morning but the rest of the time I just read and sleep and write letters. However I'll let you into a secret! I have sent in an application and been recommended by my C.O. for the – can you

guess? – The Royal Flying Corps. I think I may get transferred with a bit of luck, and then – goodbye Salonika!' [25]

Back in the Isle of Man regarding the rest of the Quine family, John wrote:

'Marge, Margaret and Nan are all at home now. Marge is going to Dublin shortly to see Frank. He is under orders to go to a place near Salisbury Plain for training for R.A.M.C. work in France or abroad elsewhere.

We saw that German water planes had attacked a monitor flotilla on the Belgian coast. (Obviously John was fearful that Dono might have been involved in this).

Yesterday I saw the first stalks of corn of this year. The general harvest will be some considerable time yet, but I should think on the north of the island the harvest will be begun this week.

Talking of National Economy, I see no signs of the advice of the Cabinet Ministers being taken any notice of here. I should say people are almost less economical. There is every Saturday a 'tea' at the Villa Marina. Before the war the Town Council called it a 'Kursaal' (as in 'amusement park'), *but have dropped that name now; these 'teas' are supposedly for a Ladies Work Guild: the object – to spend.'*

John's brother, Thomas, was managing his business at Silverdale very well. John wrote:

'Uncle Thomas told me that his business has been better this year than in any average year he thinks, even prior to the war.

There have been a good many visitors on the island this summer and the small steamers quite crowded, especially at the week-ends.'

On August 25th 1916, John wrote:

'It is to be hoped that in the peace settlement, Belgium will get both banks of the Scheldt to the sea. Holland should be compensated perhaps with some set off elsewhere. Our guarantee of Belgium is ridiculous, if access to the Scheldt is not open to us.

I remember about 35 years ago, sailing from London to Antwerp, and noticing that 20 to 30 miles of the river is under Dutch forts.'

John was still considering the function of submarine nets and taking note of anything new in this field. He wrote:

'I saw some trawlers (sweepers) – with a device hanging in the lower rigging, pole (say 6" girth) about 12' long with buoy or fender about 6'

girth in middle, 4' long. It occurred to me that such a device could be useful to trail a net at a rapid pace. This buoy, weighted, so as to keep the forward end of the foot rope of net always at same depth, and with good length of tow-rope out, to draw the top or back and front ropes parallel, the latter at the required depth. A net might thus admit of being rushed rapidly across the course of a submarine, the lower float at some distance ahead of the end of its foot rope.'

On August 29th 1916, John wrote:

'Regarding an article appearing in yesterday's papers... it appears to me about time that the authorities took cognisance of the expert to whom they owe the creation of the net, and gave due recognition.

I do not know what sort of disposition Lord Fisher has: but it seems to me that his leaving the Admiralty at the time he did was rather unfortunate for you, as your work passed through his hands; and from him, or his secretaries, it must have been handed to the direct executive who put it into experiment and adopted it, with a success well known, and so extensive employment as to basis of this article.'

At the end of August Lardy reported from France that he was well; his Company was back with the 4th Army.

...Railway construction in Army areas became a major operation, and short branch lines were built as rapidly as possible to convey ammunition and supplies. The summer was wet and the ground heavily cut up by shell fire. [13]

John had not heard from Vess for ten days or so, and wrote to Dono:

'We think he is on the Struma Front, viz. on the English right wing. The papers say chiefly – artillery activity so far in that part.

Tom Corlett, of Laxey Glen Mills, brother of Captain Bob, told me of his two sons in the Salonika force: the elder in hospital a week with malaria, found the younger there. The elder returned to duty after light attack but had to come back to hospital again for three weeks; the younger has been sent to Malta with dysentery and may be home invalided any day. I suppose there are hundreds, even thousands of such cases, all over the country.'

Marge was uncertain about visiting her husband Frank in Dublin, as his movements were uncertain. John reported:

'His Co. seems to be intended for Mesopotamia and he wants to exchange to another Service. Frank had dysentery when he was in India, and Mesopotamia would be a bad country for him to go to. He is to go

on the Dublin-Holyhead boats as one of the RAMC in charge of wounded; he expects to be on the job for a fortnight. Marge may therefore cross to Liverpool to meet him.'

Daisy mentioned that Dono was holding over his Board of Trade application till he knew the prospects of permanent Service in the Royal Navy, and John wrote to Dono:

'Daisy says you are rather fed up with the job, which in other ships is in hands of C.E.A.'s. The point is mainly to carry through your job in a way that your Captain will express his full satisfaction with your work.

To bottle down one's feelings and keep one's own counsel in essential things is absolutely necessary, with renewed determination from day to day...

I see it reported that Deutschland has got back. I hardly know whether to believe it fact or not. Their system has been in some things; where most useful, state the fact; in other things, where most useful, the exact opposite of the fact.'

...*Deutschland* was a cargo submarine built in 1916 alongside the *Bremen*. Britain and France protested against submarines being used as merchant vessels, as they could not easily be inspected. The sub sailed from Baltimore on Aug 2nd with a cargo of $17.5 m in nickel, tin and rubber, arriving on 24th Aug. at Bremerhaven, Germany.

The Battle of Verdun and the Battle of the Somme continued on the Western Front, and there was a further German airship raid on London, the largest raid up to that point during WWI. Towards the end of September 1916, tanks were in action for the first time.

Due to the fact that Vess was in Greece, John was keeping an eye on the movements in nearby countries, and saw that the Bulgarians had started an offensive against Romania, in the district south of the Danube near the Black Sea. On September 6th he wrote:

'Russia is no doubt collecting troops for an offensive against the Bulgars, and will probably advance through the Dobrudja.

This was the direction they took about 40 years ago when the famous battle of Plevna was fought against the Turks.

The bend of the Danube away to the north is rather a peculiar feature, and it must be remembered that the Dobrudja is at the east end of Roumania (Romania). *Sofia (Capital of Bulgaria) is separated from the main part of Bulgaria by very high mountains, the true 'Balkans', which terminate at the Black Sea, south of Vorna, and separate the larger part of Bulgaria from Turkey. Following the windings of the Danube from the sea, up to the Iron Gate at the extreme west of Roumania & Bulgaria, is probably only 60 miles.*

We have not heard from Vess yet this week...

I see the Entente are taking over the Post Office and wireless at Athens. I do not know if Vess is in the running for changes of a job of that sort.

Something had been said to him about taking charge of a wireless station – but it would be probably as a military official, if he had such a job given him.'

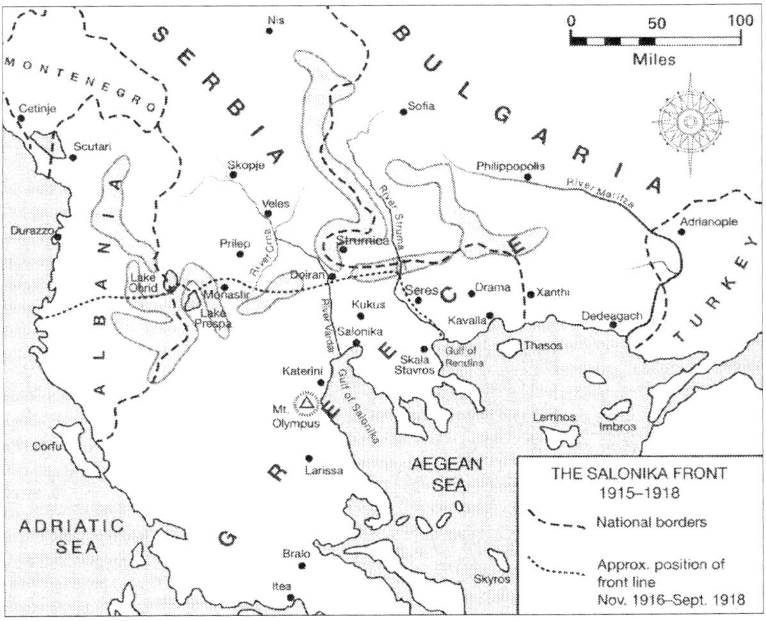

Map of Salonika nzhistory.net.nz

John wrote later:

'We have had a letter from Vess this evening. He was in hospital again (with jaundice), from Aug 22nd to 28th: Dr Godson told me it was probably a slight attack due to some congestion, not a long standing thing. He left for the Front (about 4 day's journey) on the 28th. He has applied for the Royal Flying Corps: this I think no connection with wireless. He says he is quite fit again.

Young Handley is home invalided. I expect him to come up here to tell me about his experiences in the terrible June & July when they all succumbed to sickness.'

...Lt. Tommy (Thomas) Handley was in the same Company as Vess & shared the dugout with Vess in Salonika to begin with.

Vess wrote on August 22nd 1916:

'You'll have to admit that I'm either a marvellous scrounger, or else I have no luck.

I'm in hospital again, with jaundice this time. Isn't it fierce? Here I am in hospital and the fun just beginning. However I expect I shall be out in plenty of time for the entry into Sofia, or is it Vienna?' [25]

In September, Vess wrote:

'I suppose you will have read of the Russians and Chinese landing in Salonika. I have seen a lot of both of them. The Russians especially are very fine men and splendidly equipped. The Chinese of course are French troops and look very like our Gurkhas. They are all little men and wear a sort of umbrella shaped helmet...

We hear nothing at all about the Bulgars and some of us doubt if there are such people...

I was lucky enough to see the landing of the Italians the other day. Fine men they were, very like Englishmen (I think they came from the northern parts of Italy), smaller than the Russians but splendidly clothed and equipped. All dressed in slate-coloured uniform and the officers just the same as the men.

I stood on the balcony of the hotel and watched the march past.' [25]

Vess was back with his Company. At the end of August, the 2nd Cheshire's moved back to the Struma Valley to counter-attack a dash by 'Johnny Bulgar' to capture bridges across the river.

Vess wrote excitedly on September 3rd:

'Did I tell you I had applied to be transferred to the Royal Flying Corps?

Well I have been accepted and placed on the waiting list so that in a few weeks (or months) I may be sailing away for Egypt to learn to fly.

I am to be a pilot if I have any luck.

There may be a chance of leave from Egypt. Of course there is none here just now, but you needn't be alarmed by the reports in the papers, as they are mostly 'wind' written by people who don't know the facts or the country.

Things are very quiet here but we hope to see some fun now that the Roumanians have come in.

With the exception of occasional shelling we get no excitement at all. It is quite fearsome to hear shells screaming along for the first time or two and I don't think one would ever get really used to it. It made me feel that I wasn't happy the first time a shell whistled over my head.' [25]

John had heard from Lardy in France, and reported to Dono:

'Lardy mentions a young man named Kennaugh 'who is in the other engine station about 10 yards from me!' I infer that Lardy is still on the locomotive service. In a recent letter he said he had been driving for a month, but was at the time on another sort of engine. It is probable that if he is driving, he will get a rest in the form of change of work.'

...According to the No.3 Monmouth Railway Company War Diary, a couple of trains were derailed on the lines during September causing a significant amount of work. [9] Due to wet weather, there was difficulty in keeping motorised and horse transport moving – railways reduced the length of road haul through the mud. The lines required heavy maintenance and some were abandoned due to topographical problems.

Meanwhile John was worried about documents he had in his desk! He wrote:

'The London Times has a paragraph on a recent Order in Council, practically commandeering all inventions, documents etc., and making the retention of a document of possible value to Admiralty, War Office, etc. without authority, an offence under the Defence of Realm Act. I might have a dozen such in my desk: is it the case that I am bound to ask for authority to keep them there? If I hand one or all of them up, what guarantee of acknowledgement or recognition am I to look for, if they are used? It is said that it will not prejudice the protecting of them by patent later. In one sense it is right, if also a guarantee of recognition or acknowledgement.'

On September 10th 1916 the Manx and 2nd Cheshire Battalion rallied into action. [4] On September 11th, Vess wrote:

'It seems that people at home are beginning to see that the Salonika Army have had their share of the rough, and that our time is not all spent at horse shows and gymkhanas.

The papers now occasionally have a few lines in about the Balkans.' [25]

After a three-day battle without casualties, they had crossed the river and occupied Nevoljen, a Village on the left of the Seres Road; the Company captured 15 prisoners.

...Captain May took over command of the Manx Company, as all officers with exception of Lieutenant Quine (Vess) were down with malaria again. [4]

John wrote regarding Vess in Salonika:

'Last week I noticed reports in newspapers of the British having crossed the Struma at 3 points, and today's wire says they have captured two fortified villages on that line of the Front. By a communication of an Officer (Handley) *returned from that Front, we know that he* (Vess) *and his Battalion are at Orliak Bridge in the Struma, where there is a bridge over the Struma on Seres Road. Below this, the Struma forms a long lake, with a short exit of river to the sea.*

He indicates that they were in actual fighting on Sep 10th. He wrote quite cheerfully.'

On the island, there was praise for Vess from other men in his Company. On September 17th John wrote:

'Yesterday Mrs R.T. Corlett C.P., told me that she had heard of a letter from a young soldier in the Manx Co. at Salonika, to a relative here, in which he said that 'the men worshipped Lt. Quine (Vess)*: that he would never ask men to do what he would not do himself!'*

J. Cannell some weeks ago told me he had several times heard that Vess was greatly respected by the men and was 'a thorough gentleman as an officer'.

Last evening the honours list of the Jutland engagement came out in the Liverpool Courier, and I send the paper to you by this post, though perhaps you have seen it. Surgeon William Quine is 'recommended for early promotion'. I see his Commander Le Mesusier of H.M.S. Calliope, has also a distinction, higher up in the list.

I see a recent case of graft over war contracts – a firm named Hinde, supplying brushes I think, gave over 8 months an aggregate of £1500 to a man who had only £200 a year. I wonder to what extent this goes on in honest England! The firm admitted that they made 40% profit on the goods. I know an instance recently in the Isle of Man, of a small sop offered to a man who could not have been bought for a million...

There can be no question but that the Germans are on the defensive all round the ring. The advance on the Somme is indubitable. There must be a readjusting of their line if the penetration goes on much further. I have recently asked the question, in various forms – 'Will William assassinate the Crown Prince?

Or, will the C.P. assassinate William?'

The chagrin of foiled ambition, in insane natures, is capable of such things.'

Regarding Vess, John later told Dono:

'They are seemingly aiming to cut the railway, which comes south through the Struma gorge and sweeps to the east by Seres and on towards Constantinople. He has to do some surveying or architect work, but whether for the Battalion or for his own comfort I do not quite know. Their rations just now are good as it is the autumn, and fruit and vegetables are abundant. He wants an oilskin & sou'wester, which I have ordered for him. He says that sometimes he has to wear a slouch hat and top-boots, sometimes a metal helmet and shorts with puttees (leg coverings). *He cannot use his horse much where they are.'*

Vess wrote to his friend on September 16th:

'I am camping on the side of a hill composed of soft sandstone and have excavated quite a nutty dugout which I furnish with grass mats left lying all along the roads by the refugees who fled before the Bulgars. The fields round us are full of pumpkins, marrows, beans, mealies and figs, all ripe and easy to get. We supplement our rations with these delicacies. We are getting splendid rations just at present but are also rather tired of marmalade. We get really excellent white bread from the army bakeries, almost as good as one gets at home. The weather is cooler and we are getting rather more rain and not so much thunder (the thunder is replaced by guns these days).' [25]

...On Sept 19th 1916 the Allies blockaded the Greek Macedonian coast from the mouth of the Struma to the mouth of the Mesta.

On September 23rd Vess wrote to his friend:

'Tell T (Tommy) *that the fun has just started here and that the place he left us is now held by the people I saw landing... I have a nice little dugout bivvy with room to sit up and a table to write on which is really a joy after months of living on the ground.*

I will have to stop now as there is work to be done.

I'd like to tell you what I do work at but it's 'verboten'. [25]

Also on September 23rd, Zeppelin L33 attempted to bomb London along with other Zeppelins (including L32, which was destroyed). L33 was hit and forced to land; the crew survived and tried to destroy the airship, but some of it was salvaged and new British airships were modelled on the plans.

Zeppelin bombardment was becoming a greater concern in Britain. Even the Isle of Man was not safe from possible attack! At 1am on September 26th 1916, the following W/T message was received at Government Office from a Field Marshall:

'Take Air-Raid action'.

...This was due to Zeppelins in the locality. The prearranged action was taken: lights were extinguished and the Authorities (Loyal Manx Volunteer Corps, police, fire-engines, doctors and so on) took up their allotted places in readiness. The W/T had picked up signals of other Zeppelins on their approach to the English coast, but this was the first threat of a Zeppelin raid on the Isle of Man, and the warning by W/T came before it could be conveyed by official Cable. [3] No attack was made.

The Battle of the Somme continued into October, and on the east coast of Britain there were further attempted Zeppelin raids in which airship L31 was destroyed at night by a British aeroplane at Potters Bar near London. The crew of 19 died, jumping from the burning airship. John speculated on whether Dono's gun-sight had been put into use by aircraft:

'...Today's wire says there has been another Zeppelin raid, and another Zeppelin brought down in flames. Is it possible that good results are coming from any new gun-sight in use? Or is it a new explosive in projectile? Or is it the increasing determination of our air-men?'

Regarding the island and Dono's work, John continued:

'I was surprised today to see what a crowd were crossing by the S.S. Douglas: more I think, than the day you crossed. For some weeks we are back again to the primitive conditions of the Douglas & Fenella – the Tynwald being in dock for overhaul. I understand her boilers are requiring examination.

Mr Ottewell told me yesterday of a note from Daisy, in which she said that your class of ship was to have their engine dept. under E.R.A. – except in one case. But he did not say sufficiently what it implied; only I gathered there was some rearrangement.

When you are at Portsmouth you might consider whether the notorious Captain Wardle, who in 1915 got a letter of mine to you, could have got it at the Royal Navy Barracks, or whether he intercepted it here before it got into keeping of the Postal authorities.'

...The ongoing letter saga was possibly just a good example of spy-mania, rampant in the early years of the war; it was never confirmed that Wardle was a spy.

From John's persistence it could be presumed that Daisy did not lose the letters (unless she daren't admit it of course). Wardle was probably quite innocent of any crime – just in the wrong place at the right time, but there was always a suspicion...

Jas Wilson, a relative of John's wife, was recovering from an injury. John wrote:

'On Saturday Jas Wilson crossed to spend the weekend with us, and went back today.

He had motor-cycled from Powfoot to Liverpool on business I understood, and being in Liverpool, seized the opportunity to cross.

He is not by any means fit for active service yet, still suffering effects of nerve (or shell shock). He was in the offensive on July 1st to 6th, and was at the Montauban (Somme) *sector of advance. He was upset at Trônes Wood, when a big shell burst beside him, threw him in the air and buried him in debris. He was unconscious till he came to himself in a hospital clearing station in the rear. He had lost his memory and could not tell his name, age or anything – though he recollected the flash and explosion of being thrown in the air.'*

...The wood consisted of dense undergrowth which made it difficult for the troops to follow the rules of trench warfare – the rules were very different: it was easy for the enemy to move forward unseen, and air reconnaissance was not possible; consequently, a vast number of men lost their lives.

John continued:

'Jas was 3 weeks with daily injections of morphine to enable him to sleep, was then sent to London, where the hospital being crowded, he was sent home to recover by rest.

He is recovering, but slowly. He has to see a Medical Board in Edinburgh next week.

I saw him off by this morning's boat. He told us that he understood all letters to the I.O.M. were under a rigorous censorship, since the interned alien camps were here.'

...Often there were three or four cart loads of mail bags with letters and parcels for the Knockaloe Camp. Censors had to examine everything to look for the use of invisible ink, insertion of letters into cakes and other food. Even walnuts were opened as they were found to have messages. Putting codes on picture cards or on borders of garments was another well-used method. [3]

John's wife had sent Dono some eggs. The notion of posting eggs today would be ludicrous, but at the time, eggs were scarce in the U.K. John wrote:

> *'To avoid breakages, Mother got Jas Wilson to post the eggs in Liverpool to you: but she is glad to know that they were to some extent all right.'*

On October 6th 1916, John reported:

> *'On Monday, when I was seeing Jas Wilson off, I came up Victoria St, and Broadbent was putting up a wire announcing the destruction of a fourth Zeppelin. Mr Aitken, formerly Chief Clerk at Government Office was standing beside me. I said, "That means a quarter of a million of their property gone."*
>
> *He said – "Oh dear, no – less than £100,000 – probably £75,000." I didn't dispute it, but in Tuesday's Daily Mail I saw a paragraph saying that the two, L31 & L33, could not have lost less than £250,000 apiece.'*

John did not know whether Dono was still in port or at sea again. They had heard from Lardy who was still in the region west of Albert at Contay. His company were erecting huts as living quarters for the winter and working on general maintenance of the new railway lines. [9]

Dono's ship *H.M.S. Prince Rupert* was still on the Dover Patrol in October 1916, and one morning left Dunkirk at dawn to carry out the daily patrol of the Belgian coast, approximately 10 - 14 miles from the coast, as far as Dutch territorial waters, in the vicinity of Zeebrugge. During a storm and rough seas, Dono experienced problems with the steering of the ship in the vicinity of minefields, and later with water in the engine room. Many younger seamen were saying their prayers! He rectified this by filling the 'after' tank with 40 tons of seawater. [2]

Reginald Bacon wrote:

> 'In October 1916, the danger was considerable to the monitors on the patrol line in bad weather. On one occasion Prince Rupert was caught and had to steam with both anchors down to prevent drifting into the mined nets.' [23]

Dono also experienced an amusing occurrence whilst *H.M.S. Prince Rupert* was in the Thames Estuary after one of the bombardments of the Belgian Coast: Admiral Bacon usually directed shooting from his flagship *H.M.S. Lord Clive*, but on this occasion he decided to direct the shoot from *H.M.S. Prince Rupert.*

On returning to anchor after the shooting, Admiral Bacon decided to come down the inside of the mast (probably similar to that in the photo of the other monitors). This could have had dire consequences for Dono.

The mast was unusually sooty due to a modification which Dono had made to the ship – drilling a hole in the mast to cool down the engine room. The result: a very sooty Admiral Bacon! [The Admiral Comes Down the Mast – 2]

12" Gun Monitors 'off the Thames Estuary'

Photo: 1916 by Dono from *H.M.S. Prince Rupert.*

In early October, John wrote to Dono regarding Vess in Salonika:

> *'He was for some months O.C.* (officer in command) *of the Manx Co. – as temp. Captain: at the same time carrying on his own job as S.O. of the Battalion. It was too hard to work both jobs and he is glad to be relieved of the Company by a Captain who has returned to duty from hospital.*
>
> *...We see mention of the active operations on the Salonika Front, and on the Struma Front, right or east wing, where the 2nd Cheshire's are posted at Orliak bridge... Considerable progress has been made by the Allies on the Front as a whole. Of course in the Struma sector there is all the risk of any action for those engaged. Vess has the nose-cap of a 6" Bulgar shell, which pitched about 200 yards off him. He hopes to get his additional Star or full Lt. soon, and believes his temporary Captaincy will count as credit & experience. We may take it that Vess has now had some considerable initiation into actual fighting.'*

Vess wrote on October 9th:

'You will have read in the papers about our little doings over here. I have got wagon-loads of souvenirs, but of course I'll have to throw them away when we move again. The Bulgar has had a severe doing over lately and I can't think he's feeling happy. Tommy has really missed all the excitement of life here.

I'm feeling rather good and fit now.

I had a much needed and longed for bath yesterday and it was about the best thing I've done for years. I dug a shallow pit about 3 feet by 2 feet and 1 foot deep and laid an oil sheet in it, so that the sheet covered the sides and bottom. That was my bath, and with several buckets of water, there I was – voila!

Look at the photo in 'Scenes by the Way' of Morris in his bath and picture the scheme. By the way, Morris poor chap has 'gone west'.

I'm afraid that in about a month now the weather will be no joke (it isn't much of a joke even now for that matter). I have now been out here over nine months (more like ninety to me just now).

These last few days I have been very unsettled and restless, and there has been no news of any kind either to please or disquiet me.

I had almost given up hope of getting away to the R.F.C. but I find that there are a lot of the fellows still waiting as well which makes me much more hopeful.

Did I tell you that my eldest brother (Dono) *has been mentioned in Despatches? Well he has and I'll bet he deserved it.*

I've been having such a thin time of it out here, but now that I'm in the thick of it, it's better to be thin (less target, you know). Did I mention that we are at the very 'frontest' of the front?' [25]

...'Gone west' was a term meaning 'gone east from conflict to the refuge of death where peace waits in the glory of sunset'.

Private T.H. Davis became the first battle casualty of the Manx Company; he was wounded on October 10th east of the Struma whilst scouting at the village of Prosenic, and died the following day.

The Battalion moved north to take part in sporadic fighting.

At least with the cooler temperatures there was less chance of contracting malaria. [4]

On the island there had been a 'sensation' in Ramsey in October. John reported:

'The Captain of a small patrol boat landed a guard and came on shore with a revolver and fired a shot or two in air.

The police arrived. The Captain was in Court on charge of using fire-arms I think.

It was suggested that he was not sober: but I fancy he was an irritable man who made the mistake of taking far too seriously some jokes from the quay.'

John wrote regarding British men and conscription:

'I gather that there is to be a rounding up of all single men from 30 to 35 very soon. If it is in England as here, there are still a good number about.'

Lardy had written home, and John reported:

'He seems cheerful but does not speculate much on a leave. I fancy he is too useful where he is to get a leave off.'

...As well as track maintenance and line doubling, Lardy's work would probably have included constructing bridges and ambulance train sidings, and putting in lines of communication, etc. Sappers work involved toiling around the clock, especially where lines had been cut by shellfire. Work in progress was always a potential target for enemy artillery. [14]

German prisoners were used by the No.3 Monmouth Railway Company on drainage work required due to heavy rain, as far as Acheux, beyond which the line was under constant fire. [9]

Lardy was promoted to Lance Corporal in October 1916. [26]

On the Western Front at Verdun, Fort Douaumont was recaptured by the French towards the end of October.

At sea, English losses from submarine attack & mines were comparatively slight during the summer months of 1916 – less than the latter half of 1915. However the situation assumed serious proportions in the autumn of 1916. It was thought that the Germans were preparing for a night attack in the Dover Straits – night attacks hadn't been attempted before this. Air reconnaissance spotted extra movement in the Ostend area prior to 26th Oct. [23] A German destroyer raid on the night of 26th/27th Oct. resulted in more English ship losses than German. [7] John wrote:

'...I see an English Admiral writes to the Times, complaining of want of candour in respect of the recent raid into the Straits of Dover. Any change in disposition of the patrol might lead to such a raid being attempted. My idea has been a special type of destroyer to deal with

the German destroyers that carry 5" guns; viz. equally fast, and as strong guns at least.'

Regarding the raid, John continued:

'The Norwegian question seems to me at the present, most important. I have looked on Norwegian waters as a necessary sea base for us from which to operate. (Norway issued neutrality in 1914).

If we had a base at Christian Sand or Arendal, then could we deal with the disadvantage now suffered from enemy activity in this quarter (Zeebrugge).

I have still an idea of there being such a thing as too much ship, and too many, but too small guns in naval architecture, provided that speed can be secured up to 20 knots or so in smallish vessels...

The submarine can evade large vessels better than small ones...'

Regarding the monitors on the Dover Patrol, Admiral Bacon wrote:

'Lord Clive, Prince Eugene, General Wolff, Prince Rupert, General Crawford and Sir John Moore formed the backbone of the Fleet for bombardments during 1915 and the patrol of Zeebrugge during 1916 and 1917. They were splendidly handled and absolutely invaluable. Their Captains deserve more recognition than ever fell to them for their services during the war. Of the Engineers, I can recall no single case of failure owing to lack of care or efficiency on the part of the Engineering staff...' [23]

Dono's work on *H.M.S. Prince Rupert* was about to change; he wrote in his memoirs:

'In the year 1916 the raids by the large German Airships intent on bombing our Cities, ports and industrial areas, though not very frequent, had to be treated with some concern.

It was decided to place some of our warships in strategically selected positions to intercept the Zeppelins on the way to their targets by use of anti-aircraft guns. The Admiralty withdrew the heavily armed Monitors from the Dover Patrol and distributed them along the east coast, from the Thames to the Tyne.'

H.M.S. Prince Rupert was ordered north of the River Tees for the winter of 1916, for the defence of the port against Zeppelins and surface raiders.

Meanwhile, it had been lively again out in Salonika, as the Manx Company were ordered to give cover to the Suffolk Regiment in an attack on the village of Barakli. They were to move across the enemy Front before dawn and attack the north of the village – the Suffolk Regiment attacking from the west. This was successful but the Manx Company were forced to retire in daylight across a mile of open country under heavy artillery fire.

Surprisingly there were no casualties. [4]

On November 1st 1916, John wrote:

'The Manx Co have been in action, but Vess does not say if he took the Co. into action or not. They find among the shells, different types: Bulgar, Turkish & Krupp.

One of the papers had an interesting paragraph last week, to the effect that the seizure of the Greek fleet, was to anticipate a step suspected or discovered, to slip the Greek fleet off to Constantinople and place it at the disposal of the central powers.'

On November 5th, Vess wrote:

'Barakli, Dzuma: We get shelled quite a lot where we are now and it's rather 'windy' work.

I could have gathered endless souvenirs when we came to the village we now inhabit, but I've no means of carrying them.

I am at present living in quite a good mud hut which I share with two others, a gunner and a scout-officer. We have a fire and a table and two chairs, and there is one unbroken pane of glass in the window. Quite a swell affair but a bit lively as all these Greek houses are.

Our chief worry is the legion of dogs and cats which infest the place.

The mosquitoes have now departed to wherever they go, and the flies are not nearly so bad.' [25]

On the island, John continued his letter to Dono:

'When we were at Silverdale, Aunt Eva told us that some people named Broud – in Onchan, had been told by Lord Raglan about what you had done of Service to the Country. (Re. Submarine net etc.)

I see in the papers – the credit due to certain persons mentioned by name for the idea of the 'tanks'. This sort of thing, if done at all, should be done all round!

We have had very bad weather indeed, never an October to equal it. A Douglas ketch with 4 men coming from the Mersey with coal was driven on Douglas Head and smashed up last week – all hands lost. The steamer sailings have been delayed quite a number of times.

Mother has had a lot of going about collecting subscriptions for the last two weeks; also this week for the District Nurse; after that she starts on the Christmas Box collection for the Lonan & Laxey soldiers.

We gather that you are probably at Grimsby; Daisy mentioned that you had travelled by train. I inferred you had probably been to Hull.

A report from a Swiss paper today mentions the Bremen & Deutschland as having both been lost.'

...The *Bremen* went missing on September 21st 1916 – believed hit and lost, but not confirmed. However she may not have been lost until later in 1917.

Deutschland was converted in 1917 into an armed torpedo submarine by the Germans.

The island continued to have shockingly bad weather throughout November. Lardy asked for copies of his Certificates, which John sent, and speculated:

'It may be that Lardy has in view some supervising job in railway transport. We heard that several hundred skilled engineers are being sent home for engineering jobs – maybe he is applying for such work.

We have not heard from Vess this week, but there is considerable activity on the Struma Front.

The British are attacking the line of the railway, which has its terminus at Rupels at the mouth of the pass to Bulgaria, and has also a line running west.

Mary heard from him about a week ago. He is well and keeps fit. He does a good deal of (horse) *riding now, say 15 miles a day, and has some other work at present in addition to his duties.'*

Later, Vess sent a few snapshots home, one of him riding on a mule. John wrote:

'He has not mentioned details to me about his experiences at the Army Riding School with the Salonika Force; he mentioned it in a letter to one of the girls – they evidently gave him some difficult horses, as I should expect.'

Regarding numbers of German troops, John continued:

'I have been reading H. Belloi's estimate of Germany's man-power resources in the latest Land & Water. I gather it means Germany had 10,000,000 men or over, and has lost 4,000,000 or over: so now they stand with 5,000,000 mobilized, and 1,000,000 possible reserves – far less than their wastage; the quality inferior!

We hear from Marge, that Frank Sherriff is about certain to go to Birr, an inland town hospital in Ireland – where he will probably be stationed for some months.

Graham is at Wendover (for training for the Front).'

...Frank Sherriff (Marge's husband) expected to move to England, to be sent abroad.

John had not heard from Lardy or Vess and wrote to Dono on November 18th:

'...There is still considerable activity on the Struma sector.'

Finally on November 22nd, Vess said goodbye to his camp in the Struma, but said that there was still plenty of activity, and he ***'had to dodge a few whizz-bangs'*** to get to his horse. He wrote:

'Now awaiting a passage to Egypt to go to R.F.C.' [25]

...Vess sent Letters detailing his trip from Salonika to Alexandria (from 22.11.1916 to 15.12.1916) but they never arrived in the U.K.: the boats were probably torpedoed. [25]

John speculated as to where Lardy might be:

'As it is possible that Lardy is somewhat back on the lines of communications, we can only suppose that he is near Albert. The last affair, Beaumont-Hamel, is spoken of as a very good stroke. It seems to have given our people the ridge of land north of the Ancre (river), with a chance of coming to Bapaume from the left as well as direct from the Ancre valley.'

...The Battle of the Ancre was the last of the Battles of the Somme due to increasingly bad weather in mid-November and difficulty in getting supplies through to the troops.

According to the War Diary of the No.3 Monmouth Railway Company, in November, they were stationed at Contay, working on the Contay to Daours line and Colincamp line. On the 12th a loco was derailed, blocking the main road from Albert to Amiens for a short time. The Company began construction of a new line to Vecquemont to a quarry there for ballast, work which continued into December. Again, prisoners were employed in this work. [9]

Dono was considering a career move. John wrote on November 26th:

'Much interested in your letter: all too brief. I do not know what inference to draw. I cannot suppose you could have a trip to sea in any vessel except in some attached capacity, as 'additional', or in connection with some department of work.

My idea is go steadily ahead in the path opened to you, and make your work your main concern, your one friend and defence...'

The following night, November 27th, *H.M.S. Prince Rupert* was on the east coast of England, in communication with the British air-force, and Dono witnessed a German airship raid from his ship: airship L34 was destroyed by aeroplane off Hartlepool and also L21 off Yarmouth. Regarding Zeppelin attacks, having more vessels in this coastal area proved to be a good move.

John wrote to Dono:

> *'Daisy told Mother yesterday that you have had very busy times. The papers tell us of a Zeppelin brought down on the N.E. coast. We think here partly as the newspapers bid us: for only through them do we get to know anything.'*

...At the end of November the first German daylight aeroplane raid was made on London.

Dono's drawing showing the stages of the destruction of the airship

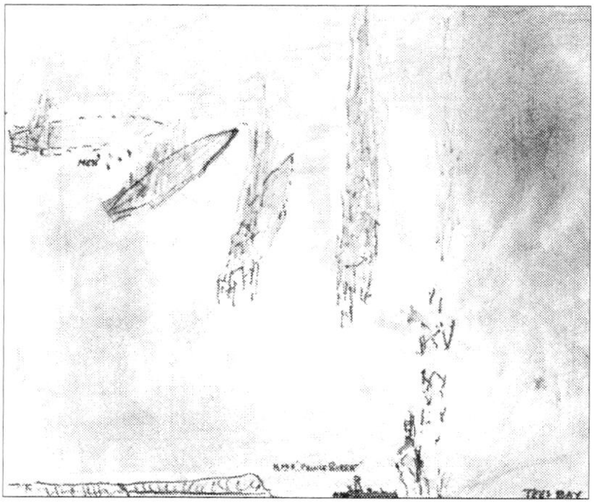

Admiral Beatty succeeded Admiral Jellicoe as Commander-in-chief of the Grand Fleet on November 29th 1916. John wrote:

> *'...We think a change at Admiralty was needed. I am not sorry to see a young Chief Admiral. My impression of Admiral Jellico was that he was cautious, rightly so perhaps: but a little more dash may be better.'*

Lardy had been home on leave and updated his parents with details of his work, although one has the impression from John's letters that 'war-related work' was only fleetingly discussed due to their briefness:

> *'...Lardy goes across tomorrow and leaves Waterloo Station at 4pm on Tuesday. Mary & Margaret will probably see him. I think Lardy is*

pretty fit. He looks a bit thin about the face but otherwise is sinewy and tough looking. I am glad to see he has no cough. His appetite is all right, so I am relieved of a certain anxiety I had with his colds and cough of last spring.

He tells me of German spies within the English lines who have passed themselves off as English Officers and ridden about, passing sentries etc., utterly unsuspected. A knowledge of English is essential; I think the Germans have been in England – fastened on the language better etc. I daresay we have some, but not many Englishmen who have studied things German so as to pass for a German.'

...Regarding Lardy's Company, in mid-December the No.3 Monmouth Railway Company took over the running of a new line from the French, from Trônes Wood to Méaulte Junction outside Albert. Parties of men were situated at Méaulte, Bel-Aire, Grovetown and Plateau, although Happy Valley and Plateau were continually shelled by long range guns. [9]

On the Western Front, the Battle of Verdun finally ceased mid-December. On other Fronts, Allied forces were withdrawn from Athens & Piraeus at the beginning of December after conflicts with the Greeks, and the Massacre of Venizelists took place on December 6th in Athens. John wrote regarding the conflict on the Southern Front:

'The Greek business may embarrass the allied authorities out there, but it ought not to embarrass them if they get a proper instruction. If it is to be all legal procedure, then I pity the soldiers & sailors who have to take action, and yet are not to take action.'

Meanwhile, the situation for German citizens was becoming desperate due to the British blockade and lack of supplies coming into the country. The typical daily food ration was 'five slices of bread, half a small cutlet, half a tumbler of milk, two thimblefuls of fat, a few potatoes, and an egg cup of sugar.' One German citizen wrote:

'If we were to starve like rats in a trap, then surely it was our sacred right to cut off the enemy's supplies as well.' [12]

The Manx & Cheshire Company in the Struma were also short of rations at the latter end of 1916, and true to Vess's predictions, it was bitterly cold with heavy snow and rain. It was not a happy Christmas for the men, far away from home in the Isle of Man.

Whilst Vess's colleagues were in the Struma, he was in Egypt taking exams and learning the rudiments of flying air machines or 'buses' as he called them – his new work apt, bearing in mind his favourite teenage pastime of making model planes. He was amongst many Australian trainees from the 6th Light Horse, a New South Wales regiment.

Vess hadn't received any letters from his parents in December for some reason. However, John had received a letter from Vess detailing some of his work, and John reported to Dono:

> *'If Vess passes his test exams in the Alexandria School, he will be sent to a Cairo School for practice with flying machines. After that, he will return to Alexandria for a more advanced course.'*

> ...The improved design of aeroplanes meant they were more reliable, and utilised in bombing with greater accuracy. They were increasingly important in reporting enemy movements (new gun Batteries, etc.) and taking photographs of the land (which changed often due to bombardment). For troops on the ground who could see very little of the enemy, this was a necessity. Balloons and air-ships were also often used for reconnaissance.

Photo taken in 1916 by Vess whilst training in Egypt

As 1916 came to a close, there was greater determination amongst the Allies to fight on until Prussian militarism was wiped away. [21 – Events of 1916]

1917

Lardy was still in France at the beginning of 1917 – his railway Company suffering from the cold weather; Vess was being trained to fly various planes in Egypt – some tough work ahead, and Dono's ship was in the Tyne area – with some food shortages on board as the effects of war grew more intense.

On January 5th 1917, John reported:

'Daisy crossed today. We heard that the Tynwald had an accident to ventilators & funnel on the passage yesterday from Liverpool, but the sea was fairly quiet.'

...Later, on January 11th 1917, the *Ben-my-Chree* (converted for sea-plane service) was sunk by Turkish gunfire – another Manx boat gone, but all her crew survived.

John wrote on January 17th to Dono regarding Vess's exams:

'Vess passed his first exam creditably with third place and 80% marks – the first candidate getting 90%. He is now near Cairo, taking work in actual flying: but of course there is, as rightly there ought to be, a succession of stringent tests before he can graduate!

He implies that he is proceeding carefully and cautiously in learning to fly – rather working to get all the instruction he can from the instructor, than eager to be too soon on his own. This is of course the better way. On the whole he is cheerful.

If you write to him, mention the regret of our letters not having reached him (in December), *and to remove from his mind any impression we made of any demur about his going into the R.F.C. (Royal Flying Corps). He seems to have an idea, perhaps from my asking whether it was a good idea to change* (to R.F.C.), *that we did not think so. We did not think or feel disapproval, believing in his own judgement to be the best guide, and knowing that he has the opportunity of knowing about the Services, whereas we know so very little.'*

Regarding Lardy, John reported on January 19th:

'We have heard from Lardy. He hopes to get a transfer to the water traction Service.

He had a cold but says he is getting better. I sent him lozenges, quinine (used to prevent and treat malaria and fever) *& iron jelloids* (iron supplement for strength).

I understand he is back at Contay at the same job.'

Lardy wrote home saying they had vile weather in France. There were some hard frosts in January, damaging equipment and water pipes. Trônes Wood Yard was damaged one evening by shell-fire from the Front.

...The No.3 Monmouth Railway Company was at Vecquemont, just to the east of Amiens, on the Somme, mining ballast for use on the Daours to Contay railway line, and prisoners of war were used to mine the ballast... On one of the lines in January a train ran into a motor lorry at a level crossing, killing one man and derailing the train. [28]

By the end of January, Vess was able to fly alone, having completed the required instruction in Egypt. John reported:

'Vess has written in an interesting way about flying. He has got through the Cairo course all right, having had no accidents except to some wires on a machine in making a landing. This course has included taking up a machine by himself.

He has now returned to Alexandria to enter on an advanced course, and seemed very well.'

...The School of Miltary Aviation in Aboukir, Alexandria, was opened in November 1916 due to the urgent need for pilots in WWI.

Vess described his work as *'full pressure, rising at 5.15am every morning'*. Regarding his work he wrote:

'After the first few flights the novelty wears off and it is just hard physical and mental strain all the while. You get into the 'bus', togged up in leather coat and cap, with gloves & goggles, and strap yourself in. Then having tested your controls, noticed how the wind is, and having looked at your instruments, you start up the engine and test it...

All this while the mechanics are holding on to the 'bus' to keep her from flying off. When quite ready, you wave your hand, the men stand clear, you open your throttle and off you go. The machine runs along the ground gathering speed, and finally leaves the ground and there you are, up in the air. After that it is just a continuous correcting of bumps, turning, gliding, spiralling...

The machine does absolutely anything you want, provided you know what you do want. Sometimes a machine will fly 'hands off' as we say, i.e. without being controlled at all, but not often. As one gets more practiced, one goes up and tries stunts – i.e. tricks.

So far of course I can't do any stunts, but I can take off and fly round, glide and land without much trouble.' [25]

Germany was turning out larger submarines in a faster time.

John was still considering ways of dealing with them and wrote:

'I cannot see why, if U boats displacing 800 to 900 tons with submerged speed of 10 knots could be dealt with on the basis of known strains, boats of 1200 displacement & 15 knots submerged cannot also be dealt with, by proportionate devices. It is very much a larger order: but it is a case of advancing from a successful device to a more extensive application of the device.'

John obviously thought that Dono's work warranted further promotion, and wrote:

'To my mind you ought to have had your half stripe and a great deal more, long ago: work for which you have given tenfold proof of capacity, to give you, as a certain high official said to you in March 1915, 'an opportunity to distinguish yourself in the war'; or rather not to distinguish yourself – so much as to render great and invaluable services. But for your part do not betray impatience. Patience and industry will in due time entitle the worthy Mason to a participation in the secrets of a Master!'

...John became a Mason in 1909 and was Worshipful Master of St Maughold Lodge on the island for a year. Dono was also a Mason.

Regarding his daughters and their husbands, John told Dono:

'Graham has gone back to Wendover. Mary is taking up some hospital work at Worthing, three days a week or so. She has some other war work in a Guild, which makes hospital necessities.

Frank has sailed, but it is not certain when, as his ship seems to have lain in port awaiting a convoy.'

...Convoy ships offered the best protection against submarines and this was the policy adopted from 1917. Convoys of around six ships escorted merchant ships with supplies of coal etc., as well as those carrying troops. The hourly movements of all convoys were plotted on a large scale chart at the Admiralty.' [7]

Regarding Graham, John continued:

'Graham is ordered to Salonika. It is vain to characterize this, as Graham is utterly unfit. But the army is now so vast an institution that no department would have time to go into matters such as the unfitness of an obscure unit among millions. We have heard that the discipline of the Army would break the heart of a lion! It is the breaking of the physical strength that I regret in his case. It is the spirit that cannot be broken, where there is an element of that in a man which I call spirit, or the will to bear and keep one's counsel. The physical breakdown is what I feel pity for and sympathy with; I cannot see that Graham can be expected to sustain what he has to go through with his physique.'

...Graham set out for Salonika in a draft from the Essex & London Regiment.

Lardy still had his cold, and John had sent him more quinine. Mary and Marge later heard from their husbands, Graham at Marseilles, and Frank Sherriff in the Canary Islands.

Daisy had crossed with baby Jack to see Dono in the Tyne area. She said that Dono was rather grumpy. John wondered why, and wrote to him:

'...It occurred to me that it might be the result of this weather, having allowed yourself to get a chill, or being too long without food.'

The crew of *H.M.S. Prince Rupert* often got ashore for some recreational shooting whilst in the Tyne, and John wrote later to Dono:

'Glad to have your letter this evening, and pleased to hear you have had some shooting. There is always a comfort in having one's own gun – even if is not so good. At any rate if you miss with it, the provocation is your own business.'

John reported to Dono:

'We heard recently that the Mona's Queen on transport Service across English Channel after being left by her convoy – 2 miles from a French port, found a submarine within her limit. A torpedo was shot, but the steamer swerved and escaped, and struck the submarine with her paddle-wheel, destroying the submarine, but damaging the paddle-wheel very badly.'

...On February 6th the Manx paddle steamer, *Mona's Queen*, was carrying more than 1000 troops from Southampton to Le Havre. Crew spotted the conning tower of a submarine, but having no weapons, Captain William Cain, a Manxman, held his course, intending to ram the U-boat. The torpedo fired from the submarine went harmlessly by, but the paddle of the steamer hit the sub, which sank immediately.

Regarding enemy submarine warfare against merchant ships, prior to February 1917 it was usual practice to give some warning before delivering an attack on vessels – by no means a universal rule – as evidenced by attacks on the Lusitania, Arabic, etc. In 1915 and 1916 – only 21% and 29% respectively of British merchant ships sunk by enemy sub were destroyed without warning... Submarines now had the freedom to destroy vessels without giving any warning, so the evacuation of vessels was not an easy option. [7]

John wrote to Dono on February 8th:

'We discover very little news in the papers, except in daily bulletin sinkings'.'

John was still pondering submarine nets in light of recent ship losses and told Dono:

'...The papers insist that it is clear that something must be done! I have still a persistent idea that submarines can be defeated by help of a net with a smaller mesh, enough to go over the nose, yet not be reached by the net cutters, and – with a sea anchor or drogue system of canvas bags, which merely hang empty until the net is pushed forward, when gradually they get drawn, and begin to act as a drag – thus letting the net be carried some distance before it is felt or suspicion aroused. Meantime it can have signalled the presence & position of the submarine; she cannot get very far, and may enable the police vessels to get into a position of advantage.

There is surely considerable possibility in the application of this. All the strength needed is not to prevent the submarine getting through, but only that the net itself shall not break by being dragged...'

John sent Dono a newspaper cutting dated February 1917, mentioning Lord Fisher and the use of submarine nets early in the war:

'...the first submarine 'blockade' was met with entire success when Lord Fisher was at the Admiralty.

That is not to say that he would be equally successful in dealing with the new and far graver menace...'

John wrote:

'As it was into Lord Fisher's hands you placed the means by which the first submarine blockade was checkmated, so with the departure of Lord Fisher from the Admiralty your immediate prospects of acknowledgement and recognition became probably very slight...

Nothing can ever alter that fact that you did this service; nothing can take it away from you. I believe that nothing good perishes, but in some way persists in existing, and in some ways beyond our powers to know, reacting for good to those that have done good.'

It looked as though Dono was about to move to different work. In view of John's earlier letter, Dono had considered ways of reducing the impact of torpedoes on ships. John wrote:

'Glad to get your letter. I am glad to hear what you say as to the possibility of a move. The higher Officer you mention cannot have forgotten your identity.

Much interested in the idea of the ship's jacket – a practical and simple idea. The only thing that occurs to me is how the action would be in a very heavy sea.

So far as the ship itself, all right I should think, acting as an outrigger; but when a ship is struck by a heavy sea – would the jacket sustain such shock? Or would that part of it above water be submitted to a smashing blow? E.g. when she lifts at a high angle, would it be subject to shock. For Channel purposes there may not be the same risk of such seas as in the North Atlantic.'

John had not heard from Vess for a couple of weeks in February, but he had a letter from Lardy, and reported:

'Lardy asks for some fish-hooks & line, as there are fish in the river near where he is. I think he is not far from a place I see on the small maps – Fonquevillers, near Hébuterne.'

Lardy had previously worked in the Fonquevillers region, but was now probably based further south than this, working on the Daours to Contay railway line. Contay had a small river, and of course Daours was also on the Somme, as was Vecquemont.

Early in February 1917, orders were received for the Company to strip and load up the steam navvy and despatch to R.C.E.1. Work was also afoot to create a new extension of the line to Pozières, and towards the end of the month a steam crane was delivered to the Company at Vecquemont. [28]

Regarding moving equipment, John recounted:

'Lardy had gone up the line on a five days journey – I expect very slow moving – to erect machinery. This job took three days. Then he was five days coming back, and had not joined his unit at the time of writing. I do not suppose it was a matter of distance, but of taking machinery up, possibly heavy stuff. He had got rid of his cold, but seems to have caught a fresh cold on this job.'

British attacks had resumed in the Ancre region on the Western Front in January 1917, but on February 25th 1917, German forces withdrew from front line positions on the Ancre, consequently impacting on Lardy's work. John wrote to Dono:

'Lardy says things are busy in his neighbourhood, and I expect that there will be moving and shifting of plant.

The retirement in the Ancre is important: it is a withdrawal and an evidence of superior pressure: very strong pressure.

I'm glad to hear you have had some more shooting, especially widgeon & goose. You only want practice to bring your shooting up to quite accurate form – I might say bring it up again, as you have not had any to speak of for a good while.

Things are very quiet here. People discuss food prices perhaps more than any other topic.'

John continued:

'Mary writes that a Lt. Werthy (I think) has been mentioned in the press, for some anti-submarine device! Curious this truly English readiness to accord prompt recognition.

Mary has heard from Graham from some port – he says he saw the Magician there. How he could confidently identify her I do not know. He seemed to write in a good spirit, but I am sure Mary is much worried; being in office work, he ought not to have been sent out on Foreign Service. There is no word yet from Frank Sherriff.'

...The Magician was a merchant ship in which Dono sailed prior to the war in 1909.

Graham arrived in Salonika on February 14th, and John reported:

'Graham writes in a cheerful tone – with a finite credit for the spirit he maintains, considering that for him, the strain must have been killing. On landing he met a Lt. Couldray, a Cousin – some little consolation perhaps that somebody there knows him & vice-versa.'

Regarding Vess learning to fly, John continued:

'We heard from Vess. He was on his fourth type of machine and seemed well. The weather had got much finer there.

Vess tells me that Mary's letters to him are censored, but not ours.'

Vess wrote:

'I am getting on quite ok with flying so far (touch wood) and am feeling quite a little tin god on wheels. It is an awfully interesting job and not a bit riskier than being on the Struma!' [25]

Vess was in Aboukir, Alexandria. He had finished 3 training courses and was going to Suez to another school. He arrived in Suez, Egypt, after an adventurous journey in February lasting 8 days. John wrote:

'I think I told you of the engine of their plane giving out between Alexandria & Suez, and the pilot being obliged to come down 12 miles from nowhere in the desert. I think they had to rescue the plane and get it conveyed to Suez. The whole thing would be somewhere on the general line of the Canal. At the moment I do not know if there is a railway from Port Said to Suez, but I rather think you said there was. He seems quite well.'

John later wrote:

'Vess has been in hospital at Suez for dysentery, but only for 4 or 5 days – seemingly a slight attack; at the time of writing the second letter he was back at work. He complains of having lost some time, no doubt by the delayed journey from Alexandria to Suez as well as by his being ill.'

The Russian revolution began in February 1917 when the Tsar stepped down, resulting in a Provisional Government. John wrote:

'The news of the revolution in Russia is interesting. Revolutions are infectious: but the hope is slight of Germany being infected by it extensively enough to produce a similar effect there.

'Lie Power', an expression used in Daily Mail for one of Germany's resources employed in the war, has been believed in by the common German, as much as by the aristocracy, and sufferings and injustices will not produce a revolution.

There must be a conviction that there is such a thing as right and of course wrong, as distinct from rights and wrongs, in order to produce a revolution!

They talk about England being regenerated by the war – that soldiers will make their political voice heard, etc. I am not too ready to believe that. I think the soldiers will have become independent, but that the industrial matters and poverty may drive them to politics. There will be more wealth accumulated in the hands of a limited number, and a greater multitude of relatively poor people.

As we have in this Country what they have not got in America or France, viz. an aristocratic class, with an Englishman's obsequious deference to a Lord, there will be in addition to the pinch of poverty, a greater and not a less chasm between classes.'

On the island, March brought a violent change of weather with snow and considerable drifts. John wrote:

'The mountains of course lie white. There was no English mail last evening and none this evening. The Tynwald went from Peel on Monday and the Douglas only arrived during last night.

Today the Douglas did not get out of harbour and the Tynwald is expected to go round to Peel.'

Dono left his ship *H.M.S. Prince Rupert,* as he was appointed Temporary Engineer Lieutenant on March 17th 1917 to *H.M.S. Termagant* stationed with *H.M.S. Lucia* and the 10th Submarine Flotilla. The Flotilla was based between Risa Island and the Island of Hoy until the autumn of 1917, although they were only there for a day or so at a time, unlike some Grand Fleet vessels.

John wrote to Dono:

'We were glad to hear of your move. It is a stirring, arduous, but responsible branch of Service. I hope you will get your half-stripe, and although vague about it, I assume (unless you say otherwise) that it will be as Senior Engineer Officer, as on old ships.

'Termagant' is often understood as applying to a woman, a fish-wife trawler: but it is really a man, and in that sense only used in Shakespeare and the early English writers.

The word is supposed to have come from the East in the time of the Crusades, and was a Mahommedan hero of the most violent storming temper. It was the fashion of men in high rage to swear by 'Termagant' the furious. Shakespeare speaks of the Scottish Douglas as a 'Termagant', etc. The application to a raging fish-wife is of later date, but it is not correct. As to pronunciation it is -gant, not –gent. I hope you may get a good Captain.'

...*H.M.S. Termagant*, one of the four destroyers of the Talisman class, began building in 1915 for the Turkish Navy, but was taken over for use in WWI by the British Admiralty and completed in 1916. The destroyer had taken part in the Battle of Jutland in 1916.

Dono wrote in his memoirs:

'My next ship, the new destroyer, H.M.S. Termagant, was an experimental ship as far as W/T was concerned. We had Fessenden underwater, Poulsen arcs, and Thermionic Valve Diodes – Marconi sets were the usual. Knowledge of the theory of W/T was not widespread, and it was only when Marconi explained at an enquiry about group frequency in Morse signals, that the light was turned on in the subject...'

Dono was in Hull for the refitting of *H.M.S. Termagant*, and John enquired on March 18th:

'I should be interested to know several things about the new vessel – tonnage, speed, no. of personnel. But as it may be against rule, I prefer not to know rather than that you should set aside any rule...

I'm glad your interview was quite satisfactory, as it seems to have been. I have considered that for more than a year past your services have not been utilized, and your experience was being wasted in a job which once set going, might be handed over to a good 1st class engine room artificer.'

With regard to Dono's work with his new Captain and ship, John wrote:

'Of course now your turbine ship experience will come in, and it will make a world of difference to you, having that experience.

The confidence that comes from understanding the machinery must be totally different from what is called mere empirical acquaintance with it.

I hope you'll find your new Captain a good stamp. I hear he has a D.S.O., and that being so, I should excuse him for being extremely proud of it. I do not know his name, but that is because I had no means of fixing it in memory when I read the honours list. I hope also that you have reliable artificers – I mean men of the right sort.

At first I expect, after a slow heavy ship, you will find a very fast one very jumpy.'

...Cuthbert Patrick Blake was the captain of *H.M.S. Termagant*.

On the Western Front in mid-March, there was a German retreat from the Somme to the 'Hindenburg Line'. Roye was occupied by French forces, and Bapaume occupied by British forces. John reported:

'Yesterday we heard that the British are in Bapaume. The possession of the place can only be regarded as an incident now, as many much stronger points must exist on that line of German defence. Lardy seemed to think Achiet-le-Grand a more important point to get possession of – as it is more a focus of a railway junction.'

John continued regarding the movements of Graham and Frank:

'Graham has got a job in the Q.M. stores (in Salonika)*, more the sort of thing he should have had from the start. He writes cheerfully, and finds the warmer weather agreeable after the cold of the winter Camp in England. The hot season will be on in about a month; I hope he has less exposure and a better sort of billet.*

We got a picture postcard from Frank Sherriff from Cape Town.'

Regarding Vess, John reported:

'Vess is Gazetted as 'full Lieutenant' ...A friend sent the Liverpool Echo, with extracts from the Gazette Tuesday March 16...

He is back from Suez at Alexandria (Aboukir) *again. He has to go up by himself to 10,000 feet before qualifying. It hardly does for me to think of it: I do not understand it! I would not wish this repeated for the world: for I know it is done, as all sorts of other wonderful things are done – the running of engines for example, by those who have got themselves to acquire the power of doing it!'*

Vess wrote later in March:

'I have now left Suez and returned to Aboukir. I have done 15 hours solo flying and am at present doing a machine gun course. I expect to get orders in a few days now, either to return to 'Blighty' (slang for 'Britain', or home) *to finish off, or to stop out here to get my wings.' [25]*

There had been a German destroyer raid on Ramsgate & Broadstairs – on the Dover Barrage, and there was further movement in Lardy's area in March. Péronne & Noyon were now occupied by Allied forces.

John wrote on March 20th:

'We hear from last night's papers that the Germans are still withdrawing on the Somme, and over a wider front; this will mean that

Lardy will probably move forward. As he has been erecting machinery I should think it likely he may be moving forward in that capacity.

The British have now Achiet-le-grand, which is an important railway point. That is a case of men with knowledge of machinery not being utilized. For Lardy to have been two years out there and in every juncture the one man in the Company most available for any mechanical problems, to be left a Lance Corporal is ridiculous.

The developments of the Somme battle are now interesting, but we have not a sufficient large-scale map.'

On March 22nd 1917, John heard that Lardy had re-joined his unit and the Company were busy in preparation for movement. The No.3 Monmouth Railway Company received orders to move as soon as possible to Ancre Junction at Méaulte, just outside Albert. [28]

A 15 ton steam crane arrived on 29th March in the Méaulte camp dump in France (possibly the same crane which was delivered to Vecquemont in February). Lardy later recounted his experience of moving the machinery to his father, who told Dono:

'Lardy had an interesting experience, taking charge of a digger, or big machine for excavating, a sort of crane, working a dry-land dredger. With two privates, fitters or assistants, he had a three day rail journey with six wagons containing the machinery, which he had first taken to pieces for transport. On arriving, a Sergeant and twelve men came forward: they were going to erect the machine. He fought that out by saying that all he would permit them to do was to sign a paper he had with him, acknowledging that the machine had been erected and was properly working; when he had the machine working, he would call on the Sergeant to sign.'

By 1917, the Isle of Man was suffering from some food shortages, as was the Internment Camp at Knockaloe due to its sheer size; changes had been incorporated to make the Camp more self-sufficient and provide some activity for the men, such as growing crops and so on. The men were also employed on other projects outside the Camp under supervision. John wrote:

'So far as I can see, the work done by Hun interned prisoners in clearing ground for cultivation is work scarcely worth doing. The ground, so far as I can judge, would not repay cultivation, and I should not be surprised if all or most of it went back to the wilderness in a very few

years. Lack of judgement, want of judgement, is a characteristic of many people entrusted with the direction of affairs.'

...At the end of March 1917 the Manx Government provided guidelines as to what individuals on the island should eat in a day. The guidelines: '9oz Bread, 1.75oz sugar, 6oz meat' per person, were brought in as a result of discussion in the *House of Keys* in November 1916 regarding the high price of food and the serious implications for working and middle class families on the island.

It was mentioned that the 30,000 aliens in the internment Camps could consume more potatoes than were grown on the island.

People were told to buy substitutes, leaving potatoes for poorer people, and to use turnips in April instead. Fishing parties were urged to catch fish for people in towns in lieu of meat, and bread was subsidised as in the UK. [22]

John wrote:

'A man who knows much of our alien internment camp work, accused the other Keys on Tuesday, by his account of new regulations as to rations...'

In April 1917 the daily diet for prisoners of war held on the I.O.M. was:

'...8oz bread, 3/4oz flour, 5oz salt-cured herrings, 6oz fresh or frozen meat on 5 days a week, 3oz tinned meat on 5 days a week, 12oz salt-cured Codfish or herring on 2 days a week, 1oz margarine, 3/8oz tea, or 3/4oz coffee, 1oz sugar, 1/20th of 1lb tin milk (condensed), 1/2oz salt, 1.72oz black pepper, 3oz oatmeal, 1oz syrup/jam, 2oz split peas/beans/rice, 10oz fresh vegetables.'

...This was added to for employed men; the amounts were reduced in 1918 when food shortages became more acute. [3]

The U.S.A declared war on Germany on April 6th. Regarding advances on the Western Front and America's entry into the war, John reported:

'The papers tell us a little of advances to gain contact with the positions; the Huns may be taking up for a further stand on the Western Front; it seems from some of the Correspondents articles that the Hun troops are not first rate.

Now we have the papers fitted with American decision. I do not know how to take this business.'

...Germany felt that the entry of the United States would be of little help to the Allied cause due to lack of sea-vessels. However, Vice-Admiral Sims ordered protection of some trade routes by the U.S. Navy, and fast production of some vessels by the U.S. for use in European waters. [7]

A great deal of news arrived at the Vicarage in April from family. Local matters probably faded into insignificance! John's daughter, Mary, was anxious about Graham in hospital in Salonika, supposedly with measles.

Marge had heard from Frank Sherriff at Bombay; despite some reluctance to go there, he was thought to be bound for Mesopotamia.

...There was ongoing friction in this part of the World. Politically a success in Palestine was believed to be a less costly way of defeating the Germans than the losses on the Western Front, hence British men were being sent there as reinforcements.

Regarding the food shortages of 1917, John had taught all of his children to shoot animals and birds, the girls included. Even John's wife had a shot at a rabbit or two, particularly when they attacked her garden produce; it wasn't unknown for her to fish in the local rivers either. These skills came in very useful when food became scarcer.

At the beginning of April 1917, Dono's ship, *H.M.S. Termagant* moved to Scapa Flow and was being refitted. Dono wrote to his wife on April 8th about food shortages there:

'My Own Darling Di, There is little to write about regarding our refit...

We are having a very trim time indeed as regards food, and our dinner tonight is a cormorant or black diver which I shot (flying) with a rifle.

At the time of writing we are anchored in deep water (very clear) close to an island, and yesterday, the tide being low, some matelots went ashore in a sandy cove and found a cockle bed in the sand; we are having a few for tea.

I cannot help feeling very anxious about you and Jack as the food question gets more serious...

I am longing very much to get back to you both. I have heard a buzz that we are to stay up here till October, but one hears so many buzzes now that it's almost impossible to believe them.

As a matter of fact I fully thought I would be with you this afternoon but it has not materialised. I have been hoping to hear from you every day... Remaining your own boy, Dono.' [2]

The day after Dono wrote yet another letter:

'My Own Darling Di, I have not had a letter from you today and am feeling rather miserable in consequence...

Here we are so much out of the world and out of touch with civilisation that it has a depressing effect...

There are no fish to be caught here so we go to the cliff which is about 300 yards from the ship, and shoot shags.

Yesterday – Easter Sunday we dined off cormorant pie, which was not so bad, the meat rather good, not fishy; in fact tasted something between a hare and a rabbit. The birds were very tame.

Today an old seal has been sculling round the ship, and if he stays for a day or two longer, we will probably sample him...' [2]

Due to the meat shortage, Dono took a pot shot at an eider duck. This was seen by the crew of *H.M.S. Lucia* and Admiral Jellico immediately issued an order that no eider duck were to be shot!

Dono's ship *H.M.S. Termagant* was back at work after their refit; John wrote on April 10th:

'We are hoping that things have turned out fairly satisfactorily in your first cruise in this ship. It is a great change from a slow ship with not very powerful reciprocating engines, to a very fast ship, turbines and oil fuel. However I believe that given the time to classify your cares, you will hold the whole business completely in hand.

I saw William Knox. He was quite delighted over your going with a fast turbine boat. Certainly your specializing on turbine work has given you an unspeakable pull in this job!

Last evening we heard from Lardy. He is still at the same place, preparing to move forward – the weather is very bad, including snow. He reports himself well.'

John had also received a letter from Dono detailing his trying cormorant for the first time. John wrote on April 13th:

'We cannot form a very confident idea of where you write from. At any rate we were glad to know you enjoyed the new dish – cormorant pie, as it is one of the three important considerations – get sleep, keep warm, and keep up your appetite – enjoyment of food. I have not yet heard of any collection of gulls eggs here (as recommended in Daily Mail), but your cormorant pie has made us rather keen to taste such new dishes generally.

Your walk inland up a glen, to a hill ridge and along the ridge is interesting, and I followed it carefully.

You mention red grouse which are peculiar to the British Isles: so I suppose you are within the limits of that region. But whether the absence of fish is consistent with any of our conjectures I cannot be sure, as I thought that some sort or other could be caught around all these coasts.

We heard incidentally from a young man's letter, who is in the Royal Monmouth's, that Lardy has moved up to the Front again – no doubt in the extension of the Railway lines and accessing establishments.'

...Lardy's Company were involved in the construction of the railway lines and branches of Dernancourt, Longueval, Pozières and Trônes Wood lines near Albert. [28]

The Battles of Arras and Vimy Ridge ensued from April 9th to 14th. John continued:

'We hear today of a success on the Western Front – 6000 prisoners, 119 officers and Vimy Ridge in our hands, with other advances.'

Some submarines were believed to be in the Irish Sea around major ports. John wrote:

'We get to know nothing of the reason why the port across (Liverpool) *was closed, but I think that submarines must have got into the Irish Sea. I heard three were captured or accounted for.*

The other story is that a neutral flag vessel was captured with evidence of mine sowing on board.

...It appears that some of those mines which sink to the bottom and rise to near the surface after a given period, have been laid in the Mersey Channel. We hear of a liner on Friday or Saturday that was wrecked by a mine near Formby Light.'

...These mines when laid, sank to the sea-bed and rose again if disturbed – sometimes weeks later, so proved difficult to locate. On April 9th 1917 the American liner *New York* – struck a German mine just outside Liverpool on a voyage to Liverpool in stormy weather, tearing a large hole in her hull below the water line. The Steam Packet Co. Manx boat – *S.S. Tynwald*, which was about a mile away, went to the rescue of passengers.

Viscount Jellicoe wrote:

'In the spring of 1917 the situation on the seas was so serious that we could not carry out experiments involving grave risk of considerably increased losses of vessels. A force of six destroyers was used in the Channel solely for hunting submarines... it was not long before the destroyers had to be taken for convoy work.' [7]

John had noticed an increase in activity at sea since the problems of mines at Liverpool. He wrote:

'Two small vessels passed this morning, and one returned and repassed later at a high speed; I should think 25 knots, if that be possible for so small a boat. I was told they were 'submarine catchers' or hunters. I should say this vessel was not more than 50' or 60' long – or 70',

no funnel but a cloud of steam from the side, and a long wake of foam from the screw. I could not make out distinctly any gun; but think it possible there was one for'ard.

I have since heard there is another 'submarine catcher' on the west side. They carry a small gun, and have a search light and possibly wireless. I was told they drop an explosive astern which has powerful action. They must get clear of it by 500 yards or so, to escape its effect. I was told they can do 19 knots. As evidence of the want of reflection on the part of an ordinary seaman, an I.O.M. S.P. Co. hand told me 35 or 40 knots, but this I think physically impossible.

A large steamer (light) passed up yesterday, a very rare sight here: I should say carrying 6000 to 8000 tons.

A three-masted schooner passed up on Tuesday, and down on Wednesday under light sail, with a flag, seemingly Norwegian on the aft topmast. These are all the breaks in the sea monotony for weeks. I have the old binoculars mended and they are fairly useable.

The news from France is good this week: but the weather there is as bad as here, and the conditions must be extremely bad for men in the open.'

Later in April, John had a letter from Lardy. In his region, the Contay line was to be closed down and picked up, as was the Longueval to Bécourt line at the end of the month, but there was generally a great deal of work in delivering supplies to rail heads. [28] John wrote to Dono:

'Their weather is still bad; their work the same, moving up and erecting plant. I am sending him quinine at his request. I find that 'Easton's Syrup' tablets may be had – a very good energizer or tonic. I sent him some before, and am doing so again.'

John had not heard from Vess for a while, who noted later:

'My letters from 22.3.17 to 9.4.17 were not received and presumably lost in mail boats torpedoed about that time. I left Alexandria on S.S. Saxon on 9th April 1917 bound for London.'

Regarding Vess, John reported:

'On Fri April 20th we got a letter from Vess from Southampton. He left Egypt on Easter Monday. They were 7 days travelling to Marseilles – ashore 2 hours at Messina (Sicily) – and ashore for three hours near Bastea on the coast of Corsica. The troop train to Marseilles and to Havre was 53 hours; Havre to Southampton: 16 hours. He went on to

London to Regent Palace Hotel, Piccadilly Circus. He reported to the O.C. Air Board on Apr 21, and will try to get a short leave: this uncertain. He seems quite well. He lost kit (£25) through transport Service bungling but will try and get it, or recover cost. It had some curios and photos.'

John continued his letter to Dono:

'I met Lord Raglan at a Masonic meeting in Ramsey on Thursday. He was enquiring for you, but I had no further opportunity of conversation...

There has been a round up for classification of young men, with a view apparently to calling up for Service as required.

Mother has a small egg collection for naval and military hospitals. It seems a drop in the bucket, but better than nothing.'

Due to the massive destruction of merchant shipping by submarine, English airships (Submarine Scout class) had been speedily developed (airship stations were established on British East, South and West Coasts and at Scapa), and were used for spotting submarines – they were more useful than aeroplanes: more reliable, could carry heavy equipment including bombs, and stay in the air for a day or so if necessary. [27]

On April 23rd 1917, John reported:

'I saw a new English Zeppelin today steering towards Maughold Head from E. or S.E., and afterwards going back. It was not (tapered) airship style, but 'lozenge' shaped.'

There was a 2nd German destroyer raid on the Straits of Dover on April 20th; action by British destroyers *H.M.S. Swift* and *H.M.S. Broke*. John commented:

'I see the Dover flotilla have had a scrap – two or three German destroyers sunk. I cannot understand why the German boats fired on the coast, unless they wished to report a 'shelling of the English coast' in the papers.

The sinkings this fortnight are shocking. I suppose Broke & Swift were of your class: they seem to have done well.'

On April 29th 1917 John wrote to Dono:

'We got Daisy's card, saying you had got into port, and that a short leave was possible. Glad if it comes off. We shall be delighted if you get across.

It would be far wiser if Daisy and boy stayed here, so long as your present cruises are as now.

We have not heard from Lardy this week. I sent him quinine etc.

I am hoping that the weather is mending there. I assume that he is moving things forward, as there must be such movement on his sector. We hear today of heavy fighting about the Arras sector.'

...The movements on the Western Front meant constant making and dismantling of railway and branch lines to enable supplies to be transported to the troops. Battles continued in the Arras sector during April and early May.

John told Dono:

'Mary has heard from Graham in a convalescent hospital outside Salonika. One could wish that he might be invalided home. Marge has not heard from Frank in Mesopotamia.'

...On April 24th 1917, Samarra was taken by British forces on the Mesopotamia Front.

John continued:

'Things are dull here. The weather is dry, but of late a cold north breeze and no sunshine.

The boats run quite normally now and generally make good trips.

Vess is stationed at Dover to continue training I think. Mary went up to London and met him, and he also saw Margaret. Mary says he looks well...'

John had heard from Vess and reported:

'On Tuesday I went to St Maughold's Lodge (Masonic), *and Mother went to Silverdale till Wednesday evening. On our return we got three letters from Vess. He crossed to France on Wednesday. It seems he passed all his tests; in response to some notice put up, he gave his name in to fly in east Africa, but was put in the draft for France. On Tuesday he was reporting to the Air Board in London, and packing up. The machine is 140 hp – 90 mph.*

Mary has since written to say that he was very well, confident and fit.'

...April 1917 was the worst month for the hazardous business of air reconnaissance – the average life expectancy of a British pilot on the Western Front was 93 flying hours. It was known as 'Bloody April'. Vess would need to utilise all his training skills to keep him safe!

Vess wrote May 23rd from France:

'I have now arrived at my squadron and am settling down alright. My address will be S.L.Q. 3rd Cheshire's att. R.F.C. No.21 Squadron R.F.C. B.E.F. France. I cannot of course tell you where I am, nor about my work (haven't done any so far). I have a decent tent which I share with another chap and have quite a lot of comfort – e.g. a camp bed and any amount of kit. The weather here is very hot and sticky just at present with lots of mist. The old guns banging away make it very like Salonika (but I hope without the malaria and mosquitoes).

So far I have only done about 1 hours flying since coming out to France.' [25]

At the end of May, Vess wrote the following letter to Dono:

'Dear Dono,

Just a line to let you know I am doing O.K. Don't you think I got pushed over here very quickly? I had just time to rush down and see Mary at Worthing. I have already settled down to work and have been over the lines once or twice and got 'Archied' like stink. The weather here is none too good just now. I am not anywhere near where Lardy is, but further north. How are things going in your world? Ok I hope? If I'm lucky there might be some leave going about the end of Aug. Drop me a line when you have time. I hope Daisy and the youngster are both well. Cheerio! Your affectionate brother Sylvester L. Quine. P.S. I met Cousin Willie at Dover and found him quite a decent sort of chap.'

...'Archied': Anti-aircraft fire or gunnery. It is said that the name came from a British pilot who reacted to enemy anti-aircraft fire by shouting the line from a music hall song, 'Archibald certainly not'.

Vess was flying in the vicinity of the Ypres canal in May in the action on the Western Front. He experienced a bad spin on May 27th whilst on a shoot, and was 'Archied' in reconnaissance work on the 28th, and crash landed. Generally according to his log book, throughout 1917 he was involved either in shooting or photo work in the Ypres Salient area. He had another attack from malaria early in June, but he recovered quickly due to quinine sent by his sister Mary, and continued with his work.

John wrote:

'Vess is considerably north of where Lardy is; I think about Arras perhaps, or even further north. Vess found the actual work a bit awkward at first, but his O.C.'s are helpful and considerate. He has done a couple of small flying jobs already and is getting into the way of it.

He told his orderly at Dover on May 14th to send on his washing here... but the parcel has not arrived yet.'

Regarding other family members, John reported:

'I have a long letter from Graham. His Battalion is doing navvy work, probably roads. He mentions a river and lake – it looks like the Struma. I hope he is not in that malarial sector with the hot season on. He writes cheerfully: it is amazing to find him able to do anything at all after what he has come through.

Daisy and the boy were up today, both very well. The boy is around everywhere and is the reverse of timid. Indeed, one has to be constantly watching him

The country here looks very well at present, though warmth & sunshine are wanting. I have recently been noticing the visibility over the sea – and a good light is the exception, some sort of obscuration the rule.

Considering the handicap in favour of submarines, I still think that a net device readjusted to the new boats is the most effective instrument against them. The handicap in favour of surface vessels is considerable, in spite of the most energetic patrol. Even if the departure of every Hun submarine from its base was known to the British patrol, the chances in favour of the submarine are immense.

Some submerged method of intercepting them on a known track is the only panacea for the evil – plus guns on every merchant vessel etc.'

...During the first four months of unrestricted submarine warfare in 1917, the percentage of British merchant ships destroyed without warning rose to 64%. [7]

On June 8th 1917, John wrote:

'It appears that May 1917 was the warmest since 1868 – 5 degrees above the temperature of an average May. We cannot say we had that impression of the month: but vegetation came on very well after the cold spring.

Today we hear of an important affair just south of Ypres – the Messines ridge captured – 5000 prisoners taken – and the salient straightened out, so far as no longer to include the ridge which is only about 200 ft. above sea level, and perhaps 100 above plain.

I should think if counter attacks are broken, this is an important move.

I hear some report that Jap troops are being, or are to be employed.'

...The Battle of Messines lasted from June 7th to 14th 1917.

Lardy had had some neuralgia and John sent him quinine, Easton's syrup tablets and menthol. John reported to Dono:

'We had a letter from Lardy dated Sat 9th Jun. He is still at the same place. He occasionally has to go out a few miles to do some necessary work.

He has heard from Vess, and has a good idea as to where Vess is.

I think Vess is about 50 miles N.N.E. from Lardy; at any rate Vess is on the actual Front of last week's operations, and had been over the actual salient, now flattened in.

On Jun 5th he was 'Archied' badly, his machine holed a lot, and his observer wounded. On Jun 6th he wrote, 'Have been in the thick of things the last few days'. He dropped into a group of seven Hun planes, but kept away and assistance arrived.

On Sunday Jun 10th he says they were having a 'comparatus easy' after the previous strenuous days.'

On June 6th Vess wrote:

'We have been having a most strenuous time and I have had no sleep for nearly two days now. I hope the rain holds till tonight. I have had a rather rough time lately.

A few days ago when several miles over the lines with an observer, we suddenly found seven Huns aiming right for us, and one of them tried to attack. However we managed to get away alright and several of our scouts coming along made things quite safe.

All the same, half an hour after we found a Hun right over us again, but this time he didn't attack. We were getting 'Archied' very badly all the time.

Yesterday my observer was wounded, and several holes shot in the planes. However there wasn't much harm done really and I went up again.' [25]

Vess wrote on June 10th 1917:

'The weather today is not fit for our job. All the same I have been for a flip round.

The news in the papers is very good and cheering isn't it?' [25]

Later, John reported regarding Vess:

'His work at Messines (7th to 14th June) where his squadron directed fire, resulting in 72 Hun batteries being silenced, was relatively easy work, as there was a minimum of Hun planes on the scene, and little interference.'

...British land forces intended to push westwards and cut off the German forces from the ports of Zeebrugge and Ostend.

...This was a prelude to the Battle of Passchendaele.

The air work on the Western Front was just the beginning of the important work Vess had to carry out later during July 1917.

Daisy stayed at the Vicarage for a few weeks in June. Dono, on *H.M.S. Termagant*, was ill. John wrote on June 14th:

'Daisy has a letter from you this evening; you say you are still keeping on your feet, but if you are so ill as that seems to imply, is it not better to lie up or go into hospital? Daisy herself has been ill somewhat this week. I went to Laxey, ordered Quayle's trap, and got the Dr to come up. She was a great deal better on Thursday morning, and the nurse who had come up again, said she was all right.

As Mother had too much to do she sent for Mildred (Daisy's sister) *to come and take the boy out and about so that Daisy would not be forgetting about him.'*

In the summer of 1917, Dono's ship was still stationed at Scapa Flow. As well as being on the northern patrol, *H.M.S. Termagant* had orders to clear all surface vessels from an area north of the Shetland Islands. The reason for this was to give a clear field of view for British submarines to attack any German 'U' boats passing through on their way out into the Atlantic to raid British shipping.

A skipper of one fishing vessel was stopped by a small crew on a boat from *H.M.S. Termagant* and the skipper was very generous with their haul of fish, which, with a crew of 150 men on the ship, was very welcome. The leftovers led to 'A Good Catch of Lobsters'. [2]

H.M.S. Termagant was also given other missions during the summer months. Dono wrote in his memoirs:

'One special mission the Termagant carried out during the summer of 1917 was to take a signal party with Wireless Telegraphy apparatus to Fair Isle, a small island situated midway between the Orkneys and the Shetlands; the apparatus was installed on top of the highest hill, 480 feet above sea level.' [2]

...Due to the fact that German submarines constantly used their wireless installations when operating at sea, the wireless stations were able to fix the positions of the submarines by cross bearings.

Wireless telegraphy was essential in escorting cruisers, so that the course of a convoy could be diverted to avoid the path of a submarine. [7]

Vess was having a difficult time through hot summer weather. He wrote the following Letter to Dono from France on June 16th:

'We are having very good weather from the pre-war point of view, but for us now it is not so good. It is very hot and sticky, with brilliant sunshine, but of course this causes a lot of mist and cloud, making things absolutely beastly, and the air as bumpy as a stormy day at sea. These heat-bumps get your 'bus' and chuck it all over the place. Sometimes you drop a hundred feet or so. Other times the whole machine is lifted up just like a boat rising on a wave. Inside the clouds is absolutely beastly too, holes and side-winds, and above all absolute loss of the sense of balance.

I wonder why people talk about 'trips to cloudland' etc. Not for me thanks! I have now done about 40 hours flying and any novelty there may be has worn off and it's just as monotonous as any other job. Of course I have the advantage of a comfortable tent and good grub and plenty of kit so really I've nothing to worry about.

Pater wrote and told me he was doing some fishing with the rod you gave him. I think it's a good idea for him to have something to occupy his mind and take him away from all the little beastliness of people like the L-B. By the way did you notice that the Bishop has signed the petition protesting against taking reprisals for bomb-raids. That ought to make him popular (I don't think!)

Well old man, I'll stop now. Take care of yourself. I'll let you know if I hear anything of your G.S. (gun-sight). *Your affectionate brother, S. L. Quine.'*

On June 20th 1917, John wrote to Dono again regarding his health:

'I have been hoping all week that you may have got rid of the chill you had, and that you feel fairly well again.

On Monday we heard from Lardy. He is at the same place, and fairly well. The weather is hot, but also subject to changes that make it disagreeable.

This evening we heard from Vess, dated Sun 17th. He is fairly well, but the weather is hot and also rather trying: not suitable for air work.

He has had a good deal of flying – 40 hours in all he says: but I do not know whether this is much or little – having no idea what length of time it is usual to be up.

He has got over the newness of first acquaintance with the actual work. He mentions that a Battalion of his own regiment has done very well in recent activities.

Mary says she is not surprised that Vess was sent to an important sector, as the O.C. had said to him something to the effect that he would rank as a 1st Class pilot, and generally classed his work as excellent – I think for plain flying – not for the acrobatic flying.

I see by papers that there is a partial evacuation of the Struma sector (Salonika Front) due to the malarial conditions.

Sydney Corlett, who was out there, is home waiting for an opening into a Cadet School; he still suffers recurrences of malaria and some days has to lie down nearly helpless for hours together.

We have heard from Marge and Margaret. There was an air-raid recently of which a report or account was in the papers: Margaret says that she heard a number of the bombs explode, and that of course, they had a nervous half-hour.'

...Generally there had been a number of aeroplane and airship raids over the south of Britain during April, May and June, the most recent being on June 12th 1917 – when 100 bombs were dropped: many missing their targets.

For the first time, children in cities were evacuated in large numbers to the countryside away from the threat of bombing. A further 7 air-raids took place during the following three months. [6]

Regarding the island, John continued:

'Both country and town are very quiet, the town seeming more so, as in fine weather (as it was yesterday) the total absence of visitors made Douglas look very deserted.

The boy (Jack) *is developing finely. He has a few words of his own making, which he seems to think are rather better than the usual words used – e.g. he calls rhubarb – 'babbum' – quite ignoring the suggestion that it is not an improvement on such words as 'rhubarb'.'*

John wrote to Dono on June 22nd:

'Daisy had two letters from you this evening – which gave us great satisfaction to know you were rather better. Daisy is now all right, and read out parts of interest to us.

The drawing for the boy was very good, and the gun you sent him arrived last evening. Daisy also showed us a sketch you enclosed – of his interest in the screws to turn up stove-wicks, very true to fact.

I assume that the Huns are able to bring vast masses of troops to Western Front now, and that our people are of course aware of these extra reinforcements.'

In relation to Vess's work – in mid-1917, German High Command formed the air squadron JG1, as they felt that they would always be outnumbered in air operations on the Western Front; JG1 was larger than the previous Jasta11, to try to obtain air superiority over the Allies. In January 1917, Richthofen was appointed leader of this new squadron. He painted his aircraft red and was notorious for his combat victories. Vess found himself in combat with these aircraft later.

Vess wrote on June 22nd:

'We have had a bit of thunder and rain this week and so I haven't done much flying lately. The other day (18th June) I had a scrap with four Hun machines, but was lucky enough to come through alright and nearly got one of the Huns.'

Regarding the incident involving Vess on the Western Front, John wrote on June 28th:

'Vess has had his first serious air-battle. Four Hun planes attacked his. They scrapped at close quarters – he could see the heads of the Hun pilots say at 30 yards range: but after a time they had got enough and went off. He says it has given him increased confidence to know that four Hun planes have been beaten off by one of ours. As he was pilot, it goes without saying that he kept his head and nerve throughout.'

Vess described his work (later in September) to John, who wrote:

'In photo work the airman is too high up to make out the detail, perhaps any detail of what he is taking...

The camera makes its record, which when developed, printed and submitted to magnifying power, gives the details and admits of exact identification in its place on the map.

When engaged on the photo work, he has had 8 to 10 one-seater planes keeping off the Huns, but even then it gets sometimes too 'hot' to carry on work.

The Huns use 6" Archies, with a scatter of 50 yards in every direction, and get the height of a plane very accurately.

This is a constant condition under which he flies. A plane flying into a spin is so strained that it has to be rebuilt. The life of a plane (average) in hard service is a fortnight.

This idea is that there should be unlimited augmentation of the service, and never a shortage of men.'

...Reconnaissance work was becoming increasingly important for the troops on the ground, to know the positions of the enemy and positions of guns as well as the constantly changing terrain.

John wrote at the end of June regarding ships in disguise:

'I met Lace (of S.S. Tynwald) this evening, who told me one of the Hun boats he saw going to sea some days ago – was painted to deceive the eye. He called the engineers on deck to look at her. She was light grey all over, except on the hull – on which was black or dark paint, showing a smaller vessel turned the reverse way. He declared the deception very good!

I had not heard of this dodge before. I assume there was similar painting on other side of ship.

A fine ocean tramp, painted light grey, passed west yesterday, say 12 miles off. At first I thought it was a cruiser, but then easily made out it was a tramp vessel up to 10,000 t carrying power – seemingly going down channel.

A good deal of fish is reported being caught by Ramsey fisherman – all sold to exporter or exporters, who ship it to English market.

Very little seems to be caught off here, though a few mackerel are now being caught.

We have had a postcard from Frank Sherriff. I see the London Times has the report of a Commission on the Mesopotamia campaign of the earlier period, and it contains censures. I am too little acquainted with some of the data to form a judgement.'

On July 6th 1917, Lardy was at the same place, although he said he went some distances off for occasional work – though he did not say what kind of work. His Company was still working on railway lines in the Albert area of France during June and this continued into July on the Dernancourt to Bel Air, and Dernancourt to Pozières lines, and dismantling the Longueval line and yards. [28] Both Vess and Lardy said the weather was bad.

John related some further praise for Vess's previous work in Salonika:

'Caley, a soldier in the Manx Co. at Salonika, home on leave recently, was telling people in Laxey about Vess, as the best Officer they had: very considerate to the men and never asking a man to go into a dangerous job, but going himself first. He said they were all sorry when he left Salonika, and that he was the only Officer they would have been sorry to see transferred. Mrs Parkes told me that one of your Manchester cousins is a nurse in a military hospital in Malta at Thalis; Aunt Mary Ann told me the nurse had written home that she had come across Manx Co. soldiers from Salonika invalided there, who had told her the same sort of thing, and mentioned things Vess had done which had impressed the men, which had made him regarded with great respect and affection by the men.'

Regarding his present work in the air, Vess wrote on July 3rd:

'I suppose that little things like being chased by Huns are really just routine and quite the ordinary everyday life out here, for everyone else seems to have the same experiences, and the old hands consider them quite normal and not worth speaking of.

I am very annoyed to find that I haven't been gazetted yet, though I've been out here nearly two months now.

I have heard that several fellows whom I knew in Egypt and who came out with me are now either missing or prisoners.' [25]

Vess wrote later on July 8th:

'I have put 'Sunday' at the top of the page just to remind myself that it is the day of rest, for otherwise it is just the same as any other day here. It has rained all day so flying is off thank goodness.

The sky is so stiff with 'hate' these days that there is not much fun in flying. I went over this morning to another squadron to see a chum of mine only to find that... but never mind about that...' [25]

...The Battle of Passchendaele, also known as the Third Battle of Ypres or 'the battle of mud' began on July 11th. Vess's work in this area continued until November 1917.

John related the success of the 1917 Silverdale fete on the island to Dono:

'At Silverdale there were a great lot of people as usual. Uncle Thomas said his business was up to the usual. He has a Government Sanction, subject to some rationing rules to be observed.'

John complained:

'The newspapers, that do much good by their existence, are the vainest of voices. They talk incessantly of 'after the war', and 'war rendered impossible', and 'permanent peace', and 'disarmament': but in fact do they think there are going to be no navy and navies, no army & armies?

My opinion is that the professions of sailor and soldier have as big a future as past.'

Lardy reported that he was in hospital, and John told Dono on July 26th:

'...His letter of Jul 20th says he is in hospital, with an accident which occurred three or four days before. It turned out not to be as bad as was at first thought. From the fact that he was writing himself, and his handwriting quite firm and good, we draw the inference that it had not unnerved him in any degree.

He mentions that he might be in hospital a fortnight or so with a slight wound in the leg – but does not say of what nature the accident was. Later he sent a card to say he was getting on well and not to worry, and later a card stating 'wound – slight in leg': so we are disposed to be thankful that it was not worse.'

...The injury occurred at Méaulte North Yard, near Albert, on July 18th, where Corporal Nuttall was in charge of a working party.

Corporal Nuttall wrote:

'Sixteen men under Lance Corporal Quine were carrying a 36' rail on their right shoulders. Lance Corporal Quine was on the opposite side of the rail at the rear end, and was using his left shoulder. The word to throw the rail clear was given by the sappers at the leading end of the rail.

When the rail was thrown clear Lance Corporal Quine was knocked down by the extra weight coming upon his shoulders. The rail struck the ground clear of him, but the end sprang up and tore his right trouser leg from thigh to ankle. He was not cut, but his shin was bruised. He appeared to be badly hurt so I sent for a doctor.' [26]

...Vess later mentioned that Lardy had sustained injuries to his leg and arm, and was suffering in consequence.

At the end of July, Dono wrote to say he had not been receiving any letters from home, and was obviously concerned to hear how his wife Daisy was after her illness. John wrote:

'Your letter to hand of Jul 25th...

I am rather at a loss to know why my letters have not reached you.

As to Daisy, there is absolutely no necessity for you to be anxious. She has not been well off and on, but the weather has been very warm and rather trying, in the sense of tiring.

Daisy and the boy are well. He is getting very strong and energetic.

Vess wrote on Sun 22nd. He says they are very hard worked, and that he feels fairly done up at the end of the day sometimes, and that it produces irritability. But he notes this as noticeable in other airmen, who seem to suffer in the same way in the present strain of the strenuous work.'

Vess wrote on July 18th:

'I was up this morning but could hardly find my way about in the clouds. 'Archie' saw me and gave me quite a lot of hate. However, as he 'archied' some of his own machines that were after me, and so enabled me to get away, I almost forgave him...

I have done quite a lot of flying this last week or so.' [25]

Vess wrote on July 25th:

'I had another scrap with the Huns the other day (July 23rd) and got some bullets through the planes but got off alright and managed to drive the Huns off another chap's tail.

One member of the Black Hand has 'gone west', poor chap, and another has been injured (but not in flying).' [25]

Vess later recounted his experience of another of his actions on the Western Front in 1917 to his father. John wrote:

'Vess described a most serious experience he had, in being attacked by 'Baron Richthofen', (Manfred von Richthofen) *who claims to have destroyed 60 of our planes.*

The method is scientific and cautious, as the man is too valuable, or his prestige at least to the Huns, for him to take risks. Therefore he flies with a convoy of 15 planes, arranged say 10 planes at 9000', 5 planes at 8000', himself at 7000': and he watches out for solitary English planes on reconnaissance.

Having spotted one he manoeuvres for a head off advantage, then attacks.

As no English plane can fight 16, there is only one course – to rocket off to the shelter of our anti-aircraft guns. But a plane of 90 mph speed has not much chance with his 130 mph plane – followed by a flotilla.

Vess calculated his distance from our lines and his height, and loosened out his engine, which does 1500 revs, but in this case (for a short while) did 2500 revs or more – 160 mph. He seems then to have used gravitation in a spin – which seems to be hurling himself down into space with this circular movement of a bullet from a rifle. To recover, it is all important not to do it too suddenly.

One might say nothing is dangerous which brings one into safety!'

...Richthofen was severely wounded in the head on July 6th, but resumed flying on July 25th for a short time.

John wrote to Dono regarding family on August 12th:

'Marge crossed home yesterday – crowded travelling – no getting on the first boat – but no harm as the second was the S.S. Tynwald – rough passage of 5.5 hours.

She is very well. We hope to see Margaret at the end of next week.

Marge showed me a letter from Vess, with a brilliantly clear description of a 3.30 – 7.30 morning fly, scouting I suppose over his sector.

She says Frank has kept remarkably well in Mesopotamia, and Graham also keeps well in Egypt. The heat is severe as they have moved from the shore farther inland.

Lardy sends postcards from 1st Gen Hospital at Étretat (Roche), about a dozen miles or so east of Havre on the coast.

From the postcards, the scenery is fine – as he says, not unlike the Chasms neighbourhood in the I.O.M. He is cheerful; says he is getting on well, and will soon be out. He expects to go back to his Co., but has sent an application to transfer to water transport, the same service he applied for before. Daisy says she has seen somewhere that in that service they are all B1 or B2 men: so perhaps even if he recovers completely, his chances of transfer are slight.

We heard from Vess on Thursday. The weather has been extremely bad, but he seems to keep well. The work is strenuous with the weather conditions – indeed under all conditions.'

Vess wrote August 12th:

'Tomorrow I am down for a beastly job but hope for the best.

I'm longing for my leave to arrive but there are still 22 long days to be got through.' [25]

The following day he wrote:

'I have just returned from the job I spoke of. I wish I could describe it to you. However, I was several miles over the lines and got 'Archied' like anything. I got back with a large chunk of 'Archie' through the 'bus'. Several nasty Huns came after me, but found they'd made a mistake as our scouts were about. There was quite a pretty scrap going on when I left, but I know how it ended.' [25]

August was a fund-raising month in the island. Earlier in the month, John's wife had a flag-day for the disabled Manx Sailors & Soldiers Fund – she sold 600 flags at 1d each – which brought in £5. This was followed by a Gramophone Recital at Lonan Church later in the month. John wrote:

'We had a grand Gramophone Recital at 6pm after evening Service today – which raised £4/11/1 for the war memorial; the church was filled in spite of showers, which probably kept a lot away.'

Regarding fund-raising, John continued:

'Mother has organized a fete or carnival at Garwick Lake on August 23rd (for disabled Manx Sailors & Soldiers Fund) – a Committee of ladies – admission, tea, some concert programme, Girl Guides, side shows etc. – the object that when the grants are made hereafter, the men of the parish may be in line for the same treatment as elsewhere.

This has taken up a lot of time on my part, seeing singers etc.

The people on such Committees are helpless: everything has to be done for them. They're like the woman who said to her husband, "get me bacon, dripping, a frying pan, a fire, coals of course, plates, knives, forks, cups, saucers, kettle, teapot, sugar, milk, a table, chairs, in fact a house and complete outfit, and I'll get you breakfast!"

I had to get the permission for the ground, and men to cut a wilderness of grass, as well as tents, forms, chairs, singers, dancers, a good gramophone, a piano, etc. I have got most of the things and now have to get someone to open the show!

Uncle Thomas & Aunt Eva also have a Red Cross Carnival at Silverdale – Lady Raglan & daughter to be there, etc. I think Mother and Marge, possibly Daisy and the boy will go.'

Later, John wrote:

'The Carnival organized by Uncle Thomas & Aunt Eva last Thursday, to which Mother, Daisy and the boy, Marge & Nan went over, was a

success; I understand about £300 were taken.'

Regarding boat crossings to the island, John reported:

'Margaret crossed home yesterday – the first boat was too crowded to get on it, but she got the S.S. Tynwald, as Marge did last Saturday; the passage was equally bad – nearly half a gale.'

...John remarked later that there had seemed a good few visitors on the island during the summer of 1917, considering the few boats on the service.

John continued:

'Daisy seems to me ever so much better now, and has recovered normal energy. The boy is most energetic and very amusing. His vocabulary of words understood is considerable, but his practical vocabulary only comes out in occasional surprises.

Lardy (after being discharged) *sends a card to say he is in hospital again, but that he expects to be out again soon in the convalescent depot. He probably presumed too much on being all right, before he was so. I have urged him to be cautious and allow time to bring him right again before exerting himself. I had a note from Lord Raglan a few days ago, enquiring how you were all getting on.*

He mentioned his son who is an instructor to a base camp in France.

I made a note of the sea-trout, to try them in the evening. I may get a shot at grouse later on.'

John reported bad weather on the island on August 25th 1917:

'...We have had frequent heavy rains, wind to fresh gale, and temperatures from sultry to cold and glass 28.8".

Mother's Fete for Disabled Sailors & Soldiers Fund had to be postponed from 23rd to 30th August.

Yesterday I had to go round Douglas to see the various musicians etc., who had promised to come out, in order to secure their services for the postponed date. This is a sorry sort of errand; I can do it but I do not like it! I must have walked a few hundred miles in the last few months – as I found when weighed a few days ago that I was 20lbs lighter than I was. I find I can walk fairly untiringly, and perhaps it is better than having a motor car!

Vess says the weather is still against their work. I do not know exactly where the squadron is; he has said nothing of any change of sector: so it is probably opposite Messines. The present centre of activity is farther north according to newspaper reports.'

...In August there were battles at Hill 70, Lens on the 15th, Langemark, Ypres on the 16th, and the 2nd offensive Battle of Verdun on the 20th.

Vess wrote to his friend on August 26th:

'I only hope my leave will go as slowly as the days are going just now.

I am being very careful these days and I had the 'wind-up' awfully yesterday, when 4 'albatross' planes sailed right over me just about 500 feet above me. Fortunately my observer got busy with his gun in time and they didn't have the nerve to dive on me.' [25]

Regarding the island, John wrote:

'I see two M.L. (U.S. Motor Launch?) *boats are still in Douglas, and occasionally one of them crosses this bay. The men in charge are R.N.R. – I think with rank of Lt.*

Mr Lansborough told me this evening that he had seen a lot of American troops landed in Liverpool.'

...By June 1917, around 14,000 U.S. soldiers had arrived in France, but American troops played little part in the war activities of 1917.

By May 1918 however, over 1 million U.S. troops were stationed in France.

John continued:

'For some reasons it would have been a better thing for the native people of this island if they had not been so isolated: for most of them don't know there is a war; they have not the imagination to realize anything beyond what they see!'

On 30th August, John's wife held her Fete in aid of the Disabled Manx Sailors & Soldiers Fund at Garwick Lake, Baldrine. John reported:

'Quite 1000 people were present, and the gross receipts exceeded £100. I daresay mother will be able to give the fund £80 in all, as there are considerable expenses.

Today we were clearing up, returning seats, chairs, flags, etc., borrowed for the occasion. I was down at Garwick at 8am and had to work till 1pm, getting things sent off.

If yesterday had been a very fine and bright day, we should have had, I believe, from 1500 to 2000 people: but it is a matter for satisfaction that it turned out so well as it did! The people bought and sent flying over the place £14 worth of confetti, on which the Committee made some profit!'

Later, John wrote:

'The Garwick Fete fund realized about £110 – which will give about £90 net for the fund. We sent £7 before – so we hope to get near the £100. The Nunnery Fete for the same object netted £88: so this I think will at the very least equal it. It is exceedingly good for a country parish.

Mr Kneale told me he thought no country parish on the island could touch it.

In fact it was organized well: Mother and I practically doing all that, with some good helpers to carry it out.'

John continued:

'Lardy writes from the Convalescent Depot, from which he expects soon to be sent to the Base, where he thinks he will be for some time before re-joining his Co. I warned Lardy not to attempt walking or any exertion too soon.'

On board *H.M.S. Termagant*, Dono had encountered problems with his deck Lieutenant. John wrote:

'Daisy tells me that after you have insisted on not being precluded from having your breakfast, he starts some complaint against you...'

Painting of *H.M.S. Termagant* by Dono

Regarding his work, Dono related the following story in his memoirs:

'The German submarines (U-boats) raiding merchant shipping with no mercy in 1917, were known to pass to the north of the Shetland Islands on their outward journeys and return by the Fair Island channels. Termagant was at Scapa Flow on submarine patrol.

On one occasion in the autumn of 1917, the destroyers were given the signal to proceed on patrol at 0400 hours under the command of the senior Officer, Commander Benson on H.M.S. Medea, an 'M' Class destroyer (a slower, older ship).

The command was given to steam only on one boiler, making it impossible to go all out in an emergency if the other two boilers were not operating.'

...Due to the submarine attacks on oil tankers bringing oil fuel to the Fleet, fuel reserves became perilously low during 1917 and it became necessary to limit the speed of oil-burning warships except in an emergency. [7]

The command given may have been due to the fact that some of the ships in the above convoy were of this type, so all the ships were to move at a slower speed.

By the end of 1917, the situation had greatly improved as destroyers were escorting the oil tankers through the most dangerous zones.

Dono's sketch of the attack on the U-boat

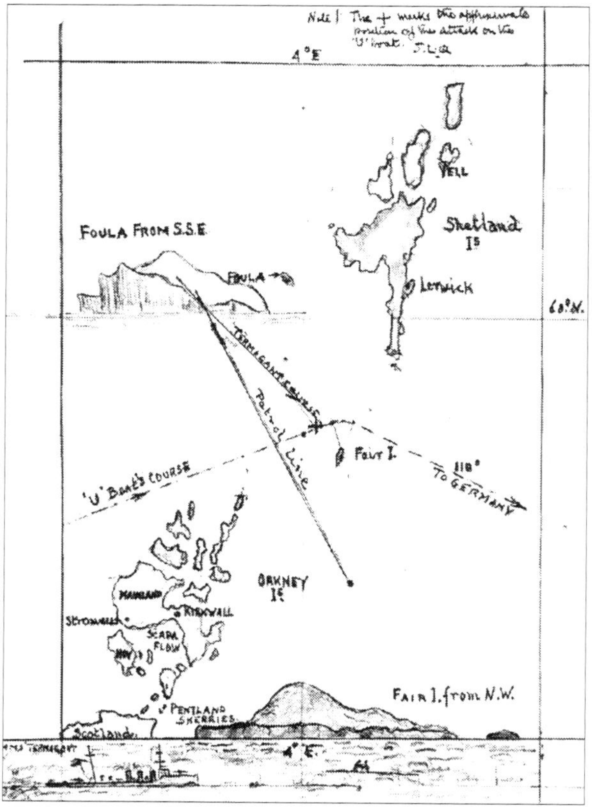

Dono was proud of his engines and ship and decided to disobey the order to steam on one boiler. On the twenty mile beat, about ten miles to the west of Fair Island, steaming behind the 'M' class leader, with speed limited by his one boiler, Dono was aware of the sudden acceleration of his ship's propellers and by the fact that they were making a rapid turn.

He wrote in his memoirs:

'A signal had been received from the Chief at Scapa Flow, Sir David Beatty: 'Commander in Chief to Grand Fleet, Senior Officer of patrol. Fair Island reports:

'Enemy submarine on surface proceeding on N easterly course, distant, 6 miles, four of our destroyers in sight but do not appear to have seen him! Why the hell don't you do something about it?'

Termagant was first on the scene due to the fact that she was steaming on three boilers rather than one.

The destroyer sent down depth charges after the 'slow to submerge' submarine, caught unawares by Termagant.

It was uncertain if the charge had hit the submarine as there was no flotsam.' [2]

Dono later had to explain, using some technical jargon, as to why he was steaming on three boilers, as Captain Medea was rather upset and not fooled by Dono's explanation, having seen wisps of smoke from *H.M.S. Termagant's* three funnels!

After the war, Dono wondered if the submarine they saw was U-88 – commanded by Walther Schwieger – Captain of the U-20 which sank the *Lusitania* in 1915, and was responsible for the sinking of 48 other ships.

...As Schwieger was killed in the autumn of 1917 this was possible. However information suggests that he was killed on September 5th 1917, when his submarine U-88 hit a British mine while being chased by *H.M.S. Stonecrop*, north of Terschelling.

John wrote to Dono on September 7th:

'We were much interested to hear from Daisy that you had revisited the scenes of two years ago and more. We gathered that perhaps you had since then returned the same round back, though I wondered if perhaps you had gone the complete round.

Daisy thinks you were at Oban, but how you came there, or where you were when you called on your old friends of more than two years ago, she is not able to say.

On Monday we had here a Lt. Young of Melbourne, son of a first cousin of mine, daughter of my father's brother, Thomas Quine, who lived and died in Australia. This Lt. is 26. He served in an infantry Regiment in France and got the Military Cross. He told Uncle Thomas that he got it for holding the Major's overcoat while his Major went over the top: but as the Major was a long time in returning he sent the coat back by an orderly to the base and lo – there it found its owner: result – a decoration!

He is not particularly humorous and hardly invented the story, but he was bright, spruce, and intelligent; by training an engineer.'

Vess crossed home on September 10th for a few days much needed rest. John wrote:

'Mother and I met Vess at the boat. We were very glad indeed to see him so well: and though I think he needs a rest and change from the active strain, sustained so long, he seems to have stood it very well indeed.

He went with me to Douglas this morning. He saw Mr Dickinson, went to the hospital, saw Uncle Thomas, Mrs Parkes etc., and seems bright and fit this evening.

Tomorrow he goes, I understand, to Silverdale.

What he says of the Service and of things in France is all very interesting; but we are wishful to let him be quite free to rest and recuperate imperceptivity by avoidance of 'shop'. 'Leave' days slip by very quickly, and the value of them is in the reserve of recuperated force unconsciously gathered by a certain renewal of familiar scenes and easy goings about.

Vess saw Lord Raglan in the street today and was struck by his looking so aged or feeble.

I see there has been trouble at Immingham, three persons (civilians I think) arrested for defrauding the Government or Admiralty – in respect of work supposed to have been done on ships.

When an airship passed some day last week, I calculated its speed as up to 40 mph perhaps; Vess tells me this is about their speed.'

...Later, in 1918 an airship landed at King William's College (pictured). It had a top speed of 57.5 mph, and cruising speed of 42.6 mph.

The airship shown was delivered in March 1918 from manufacturer, and totalled over 800 hours flying time.

Photo: Canon Stenning M.N.H. [1]

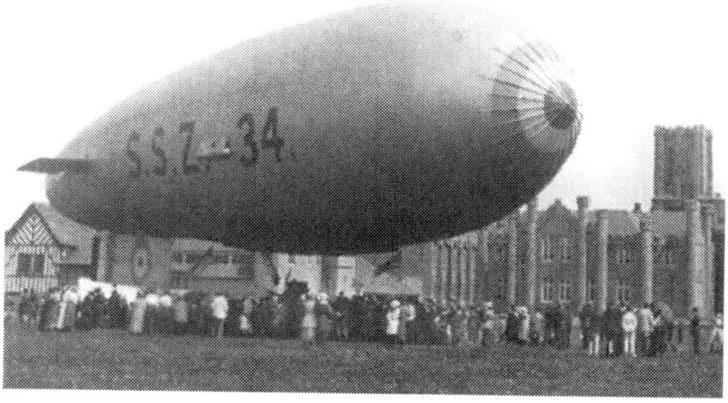

Whilst Vess was home, John decided that they should do something interesting. John wrote on September 15th:

> *'Yesterday Vess and I had a pleasant excursion to the north of the island – 10.30 tram to Ramsey – half hour with Fred Brew – a trap (high, one-horse, four-wheeler) with driver, first to Regaby where we spent half an hour seeing Kneale's place, had a glass of milk & biscuit; then on through Andreas village to Croc-e-dooney (Jas Martin's) where we had a meal and spent about an hour and a half* (and discussed the events of the previous two years).
>
> *Vess had mentioned previously that he had never been much in the north, so I arranged this drive: and we got a very fair day – which I think he found quite enjoyable.*
>
> *One thing has occurred to me, that his leave has been rather dull, there being none of the girls at home.'*

Vess returned to his work. John wrote on September 18th:

> *'Mother and I went to see him off per S.S. Douglas, not getting away till 10 am. The day turned out fine, but he wired to say the passage was long. He was going to the Reg. Depot at Birkenhead to see a Captain, and Sub Lt. there on light duty who was in the Manx Service Co. in Salonika with him. He was going on to London today to report 6am at Victoria for the train for the Channel boat.*
>
> *He described to me slightly what photo work is, what directing of shoots is, and general reconnaissance work. These are what he has been engaged on. Vess's account of his work was profoundly interesting. There is no question that it is a most dangerous and trying*

Service. It is extremely difficult to exactly express my impressions of Vess, first as to how he was, and second with regard to the Service.

He seemed to the eye remarkably fit and well, considering what he had come through, but there was a sort of tiredness which I explain as nervous strain. It did not mean that he wished to rest: he went out every day, to Douglas, Silverdale, Castletown, to the north with me, etc. He slept very well and his appetite improved: and when he went away he looked very well indeed. Naturally he was if one may say so, older: but his spirit seemed firmly set and indomitable.

The service is so arduous that any shortage of men entails on those there so much extra work, and the result is break-downs – physical & nervous. This nerve strain is hard to diagnose: for it is tested by the medical men by an examination of the eyes chiefly. At any rate I was very thankful to note he had come through so well, after nearly four months of it. I only hope his physique and constitution will enable him to carry on.

As to the Service, he says flying itself is nothing, no more than driving a motor car: but the continuous interference from accidents, gun-fire, Hun plane attack, etc., make it a certain high-strung atmosphere of tension, strain, excitement, of which I know nothing.

Vess took some small photos, which Nan took to get developed.

I think that his practice in photography was easily recognizable in the skill with which the essential object was caught and fixed.'

Vess crossed back to France and reported to his squadron on 20th September. John wrote to Dono on September 23rd:

'As you know there is a resumption of the offensive on the Ypres sector since Thursday. His squadron operates on the right wing of that offensive, in the direction of Gheluvelt or to the right of it.'

...The Battle of the Menin Road Ridge, Ypres, ensued from 20th to 25th September 1917.

Vess was back to his usual work and wrote on September 29th:

'We have been having quite a busy time since I got back, but the weather hasn't been up to the mark.

You will no doubt have read in the papers all about our activities out here.

I had another forced landing the other evening but managed to get down alright without breaking anything. It was just getting dusk when we landed and we were splendidly entertained by some gunners (officers) who gave us dinner and opened a bottle of 'fizz' in our honour.

Of course the people back at the squadron thought we had 'gone west' as we didn't return when it got dark, and were getting quite worried, until our message arrived to say we were ok. Then of course they sent a car to bring us home.

I've just been watching a Hun getting 'Archied'.

It looks awfully pretty to see the little white bursts all round the sky, but I know what it's like for the man up there.' [25]

Regarding Lardy and the others, John wrote to Dono:

'I have written at least four times to Lardy at R.E. Base Depot, BE7, France; he says he has had no letters from us since Aug 23. He got one from Margaret – to the same address as on my letters. Later he says he has got two – one containing copies of his papers. He says he thinks he will be returning to his Co. soon.

We have heard from Marge that Frank Sherriff has been sent from Amara to Bombay with enteric fever. (Later in mid-October, Frank was convalescent from his fever.)

Last evening we had a letter from Graham, somewhere about Gaza, as he jestingly alludes to Samson carrying off the gates of Gaza. He suffers from dust: the wind brings it dashing across the camp in small whirlwind. I should say it was deadly monotonous for him: great heat, desert sand, and dust. He thinks that he is neither being made fit to be a soldier, but unfitted for civilian life: of course Graham was never fit to be a soldier.

Things are very quiet here. Daisy says she thinks you have had a run down the east coast.

A few mines off Douglas have been sighted or picked up by herring boats fishing now from there, and sunk by the M.L. boats on this service'

...By September 1917, an efficient mine had been developed by the British, tested in the Heligoland Bight in September and October. This was found to be successful against enemy submarines, and mines of this type were laid in November 1917 in the Straits of Dover. The Americans had also devised a mine in 1917 which they used on part of the North Sea Barrage from Orkney to the Faroe Islands and up to Iceland, to restrict all vessels to a certain area.

Regarding Vess, John wrote:

'We had a letter from Vess dated Oct 2: he was contriving to keep fairly fit, and they were very busy. He had just had a sharp air-fight: he was attacked by 3 Hun planes, one of which he sent down, 'unfortunately' he says 'on the German side of the line; the other two hooked it'. He says in this case it was 'easy'. I take it he found himself complete master of the Hun in the art of manoeuvring his plane. They do more flying than in the summer months.'

The disturbed weather on the island continued. John reported on October 7th:

'It is very cold and squally. Yesterday the same little three-master went south past here, putting up a top-sail off Garwick bay.

I expect she had been wind-bound at Ramsey since Thursday.

Both Daisy and the boy have had colds, and he spent one day very quiet in the dining room; he is three-parts all right again. Daisy is better.

Last evening's paper gives an account of the most recent stint up to Friday's results. It is clear that the army has gripped a big length of the (Ypres) ridge – say 3 miles. The ridge seems related to Ypres much as the Bride hills stand in respect of distance and height to Ramsey.

I was surprised to note in the Times, that, from Broodseinde on the ridge, one can see Bruges, viz. a distance of quite 15 miles or probably more – which implies an absolutely level country, to be seen over from a height of less than 200 feet above sea-level.

There are evidently no other ridges towards Belgium. Bruges is about 7 or 8 miles from the sea: and the point reached is about 30 miles from the sea.'

...Bruges was the control centre for the German Army. Battles in the Ypres sector continued in September and October: Sept. 26th to 3rd Oct.: Battle of Polygon Wood, Oct. 4th: Battle of Broodseinde.

During August and September there had been a number of air-raids by German aeroplanes on England, but on September 4th, German aeroplanes raided London in force for the first time, and the raids became more frequent towards the end of the month. Further airship raids also followed in October.

John continued:

'Margaret's letter received last evening is all about the air-raids. She is much less nervous than she was.'

Hilda Toulouse (pictured) – the friend to whom Vess wrote, and later married

Regarding the latter air-raids, Vess wrote to his friend, Hilda, on October 6th:

'I hope you enjoyed the moonlight walk you speak of. No doubt it was one of those very nights that old Fritz (the Allied nickname for a German soldier) *was over dropping hate on us by the ton...*

We have now gone into huts, for the weather is becoming fearfully cold and there's a lot of rain and fog.

We have been rather busy lately as you may have noticed, and are giving the Hun quite a lot to think about.' [25]

On October 9th 1917, *H.M.S. Champagne* was torpedoed by German submarine off the west coast of the Isle of Man with a crew of 34 officers and 271 ratings. Peel lifeboat was launched and together with fishing boats they rescued 217 of the crew. Additional survivors were found later.

Vess was flying in the Ypres area early in October. On October 10th, John told Dono:

'The weather on the Ypres sector has been bad: some days no flying possible: but I understand the artillery directors of shooting were at work, so I expect Vess was having a turn of that.'

...October 9th 1917: Battle of Poelcapelle, Ypres.

Vess mentions using his front gun in an air mission in a letter dated October 17th:

'I was up on another 'nasty job' today but it turned out quite well as it happened. I had another 'bus' from our flight escorting me and he stuck on splendidly. Old 'Archie' got very excited and fair hurled hate up at us but didn't do any damage.

Then three Huns dropped down out of space and came for us. I saw them a good way off so opened up with my front gun and made some decent shooting.

Then I let the observer get a shot in, but his gun jammed. The Huns however didn't feel like a fight after that...' [25]

...Prior to 1915, the main work of planes was reconnaissance and observation, but pilots often carried hand guns and some planes had rear guns fitted for the observer to use (but you had to be in front of the enemy to shoot at them; shooting forward from the pilot's position was not possible as the propeller was liable to be hit, with serious consequences).

...By 1917 the machine gun was fairly reliably coupled with synchronisation (known as an interrupter) – giving the pilot the ability to shoot forward through the propeller. From this point, the work of the pilot and his passenger became a very different one, revolutionising World War I in the air. [24]

Lardy had been sent from the Railway E. Base Depot back to the Western Front again. John reported:

'This evening we had a letter from him, part of 2nd leaf torn off, I assume by censor. He gives address as his old Co. – (No.3 Ry. Co.).

...In October the No.3 Monmouth Railway Company was working on the lines at Dernancourt, Bel Air, Pozières and Rocquigny (north of Reims), France.

Work was also carried out in painting the Ancre Junction bridges, and covering water pipes to protect against frost. [28]

Dono had sent a parcel of trout home to his parents at the Vicarage, and John wrote to him on October 21st:

'Thanks for the parcel; we enjoyed the trout very much. Daisy had no share of them, as she had gone to Silverdale with the boy to stay from Tuesday to Saturday. He had some very distinct impressions of things there. His chief impressions were of the big water wheel, and of the feet of the ducks swimming. I asked him if he saw the big wheel; he threw up his hands with a gesture and said, "The wheel stopped." Daisy said he had seen it stop. I asked him if he had got a sail in a boat on the pond, and he said, "Too wet!" Daisy said that they had looked at the boats, but they were partly filled with water, and too wet to attempt to get into.

Things are very quiet here, and the weather very wet indeed.'

Dono's ship, *H.M.S. Termagant* was re-commissioned in the autumn of 1917 and given a new crew and Commander. Dono remained on the ship and in control until the new crew arrived. He became 'Engineer Lieutenant Commander' of *H.M.S. Termagant* under the new command of M. Bernard, and on the 8th November, the ship left the Tyne for Dover. Dono wrote in his memoirs:

'Termagant had been allotted to the 'Dover Patrol'. Captain Donaldson on H.M.S. Lucia wanted men who had been trained to work with the 10th submarine Flotilla.

As I had previously served as an Engineer Officer in Prince Rupert for nearly two years in the 'Dover Patrol', I looked forward to serving there once again in what would be the fastest and best gunned destroyer to be stationed there at that time.

Termagant joined a strong force of destroyers including H.M.S. Swift with a new 6" long range gun – Admiral Bacon's idea – to outrange the guns of the Germans.' [2]

...The Dover Patrol Policy: the Straits should be impassable for enemy ships – to protect cross-Channel communications of the British Army in France, for protection of trade in the Channel, and to prevent Germans from landing military in the south of England or in that area of France. During mid-1917 twenty transport and hospital ships crossed the Straits daily. [7] Constant vigilance, mine-sweeping, and abolition of night sailings, meant that over five and a half million troops crossed to Boulogne by the end of 1917 without loss. [23]

...Secret plans were afoot for a bombardment on Zeebrugge and Ostend once again. Earlier in the year, the British Admiralty thought Allied troops on the Western Front would have pushed the German army further east, cutting off the Belgian ports under German control; in readiness to support these troops, large guns had been secretly installed within range of some of the largest German gun batteries.

Meanwhile Vess had carried out the following important mission, reported later by John:

'On Oct 30 – in a gale of 50 mph – rising in gusts to 60 or 70 – two planes of his squadron left the ground in this gale: one of them getting into trouble a few hundred feet up, falling, and both pilot & observer killed.

Vess got up, and worked right over Passchendaele and over the Hun line about Moorslede. He discovered that a great many Hun batteries were in action, not already located: so he started on these and called up our batteries and gave them the ranges. He sent in 34 demands in all, and totalled over 700 signals sent in. He was flying for 3.5 hours in this gale, fighting the wind and directing the shoots.

When he found it necessary to return, petrol supply a consideration – it was quite dangerous to come down in such a wind. He hesitated several times, but at last trusted to his staying power and made a good landing.

Meanwhile the Canadians had been in difficulties on Passchendaele Ridge at Crest farm, in consequence of new Hun artillery concentrations, making it impossible to hold the position. This artillery however gradually slackened (being silenced by the English batteries), and the

Canadians hung on to their position on the ridge. The Canadian Brigadier General wrote a letter from his Brigade, thanking the R.F.C. Squadron for its work that day – work really done by one plane! Later in the day – the wind moderated and other planes went up: but Vess had put in his day's work; quite enough for one day.'

On November 6th, Passchendaele was captured by British (Canadian) forces.

John wrote on November 18th:

'Vess writes this week. He has completed six months flying and continues to keep fit and well. He describes vividly 'a fly' where the mist prevented anything being done; he could find no break in the cloud envelope underneath, so decided to return; and after 25 minutes flying against a strong S.W. wind, calculated he must be well back of our lines, so plunged down 3000, 2000, 1000, 500, even to 200 feet. His compass began to spin, so all guide to direction was gone. He got some sort of visibility at 200 feet and found himself just over our extreme front line, then switched backed over the terrain! What made the compass spin?'

John continued:

'The progress of the Palestine force would be interesting to watch, if it were not for the concern about Graham.'

...In October and November there were battles on the Palestine Front.

On Nov 25th, John wrote to Dono on *H.M.S Termagant* on the Dover Patrol:

'I gather that you have gone south as you conjectured likely. There is the satisfaction at least that you can teach your crew; and there is something in this of possibilities for yourself – to make them a thoroughly efficient lot: there may be need of men that can do this.'

Dono wrote in his memoirs:

'Shortly after arriving in Dover, H.M.S Termagant was proceeding with 7 other ships in line at 30 knots on a north-easterly course in the vicinity of Zeebrugge, expecting to encounter German Flotillas.

An order had been given to the ships to maintain W.T. silence until further orders.

For some reason the Telegrapher broke the silence, and was ordered to draw out of her 7th position in line and take a position abreast of the leader – over 1 mile ahead. This was a difficult manoeuvre, but H.M.S. Termagant managed it.' [2]

On the island, the Needlework Guild was conducted by various ladies who either issued wool & flannel to women and girls who were paid to manufacture these into socks and shirts for sale to the Government War Camps, or wool and flannel were provided to anyone willing to manufacture them into socks and shirts for troops at the Front, without payment.

John wrote:

'Mother's needlework Guild has sent about 20 parcels, and will conjecture to send more per week as the work is completed.'

Regarding the Cambrai advance on the Western Front, John reported:

'There was some talk here of ringing Church bells for the Cambrai advance: but I took a more serious view.

The advance is good, if it results in the capture of Cambrai, and the cutting of the railway lines converging there. Church bells are superfluous; the tangible success is the important thing.'

...The Battle of Cambrai lasted from November 20th to December 3rd 1917.

John complained to Dono regarding news:

'Some of the Correspondents write well, but give nothing of the actual situation. One long-winded thing I read gave me no information in any way new, except that there are thistles in France.

Cannot these writers get to a point of view that war is war, which when realized makes it a hard and earnest thing, and not a thing of eternal 'smiling' and 'cheeriness' – which are vulgarity itself.

War is a particular and peculiar sort of work, not any kind of escapade or picnics. It is not a thing the result of which should be infinite babble of talk; but rather a tendency to silence.

I shall be glad to know how you get on with your new crew and conditions.'

At the beginning of December, Lardy was home on leave after some time in convalescence from his injury and further work. John wrote:

'Lardy arrived home the day before yesterday – very well and cheerful – just the boyish temperament unaltered. His work is close up to the last or rather present stunt, getting the lines forward for transports. He seems to stand all right with his O.C. etc. He goes out with him on a small motor forward up the line, Lardy driving at 45 mph.

At the D.G.T. Base Depot he had unpleasant experiences, as it appears that on coming out of convalescent camp, men are not sent to their old units; but he stuck out and insisted on it, quoting an Army Order or King's Regulations to that effect.

He wrote to his Captain asking to be definitely called for to re-join the Co: the Captain seems to have been only too glad to do so.

As to the application for transfer to water transport Service, he said he was told it was hopeless, as he could not be spared from the Co.

Lardy told us that when in hospital, a soldier there named Shimmin who had been in the Manx Service Co. in Salonika, asked him if he was a brother of Lieutenant Quine. Lardy said, "Yes."

He said that not only the platoon, but the Co. and the whole Battalion were very sorry when Vess left; that he could have got promotion to anything; he was most considerate and respected, and best signalling Officer in any Battalion there.

Lardy says his own captain has told him he is next on the list for promotion: it is slow; his Co. is in work with few casualties and is at full strength...

I expect he is rather disappointed over the fact that he has only been made Lance Corporal after all his long and arduous work, in which I am certain he has not spared himself, nor ever shirked the most dangerous duty.

Lardy was 'the man with the iron nerves' in his Co., but that is not the man who is promoted.'

...Records show that during WWI, 173 men from Railway Companies lost their lives.

...Of course, as well as constructing railways, the Company was responsible for moving tanks by rail, making ramps for unloading tanks, and making gun-bases. There had been another accident in November 1917 – a collision between a motor lorry and light train, the driver of the lorry, killed. Tanks were moved by train to Heudencourt. [28]

Vess wrote regarding his work involving flying under hard conditions:

'...wind 70 mph on the ground, and going up when it seems impossible that any plane can leave the ground.'

John wrote to Dono:

'Vess has been recommended for 'consistently good work' – he himself adds – 'whatever that may mean!'

He is hoping for a leave as he finds the strain telling on him.

The others seem well. Graham has been transferred to the Salvage department. One can only conjecture it is in the rear of the Palestine expedition.

As to the results of the war, apart from U.S.A., there is no conviction, no idea held (in common), no fixed principles animating Englishmen, by which alone a nation can achieve such an achievement as victory in a war!

Your main concern is your work... Carry on.'

Lardy was due to cross back to France. John wrote on December 5th:

'We went to see Lord Raglan on Monday at Castle Mona, where he is residing at the hotel. He is aged a lot and seemed to me, while wholly genial, quite gone off in vigour of mind.

He said Lardy ought to be getting a Commission now, but Lardy said he had no wish to go into the infantry.

Lardy is well, and several persons have remarked that he looks much better than when at home last.

He was telling me of a number of things in the way of big casualty bunches, which I am sure never appeared in the press – in some cases unavoidable, in other cases the result of stupidity of persons with that want of mentality which makes them incapable in the sense of responsibility.

Vess is in London, and last evening we had a note from him. He was reporting to the Air Board on Monday, having strong recommendation for a flight and Home Service, after over six months flying on the war Front. He hopes that he may perhaps get home for a few days and also see Mary.'

On December 6th, John reported:

'This morning a wire arrived addressed to Vess, O.H.M.S. London – wire from France states that he is awarded the Military Cross (M.C.).

I suppose these awards are made by Headquarters in France. I do not know the value of the distinction, but of course it is given on the basis of the report 'consistently good work', which he says was the nature of O.C.'s report.

We are much relieved by his getting a change to England, if only temporarily, as in one of his most recent letters he said that he much needed a rest and felt the work telling on him.'

Later, John wrote:

'He told me of this M.C. – got in part no doubt for good work, but yet for a definite service specially named. His work on October 30th was the knife-handed feat for which the M.C. was awarded.'

John continued:

'The release of masses of troops from the Russian Front will enable the Huns to concentrate heavily on the west: and I expect extremely severe fighting will take place there.

The recent counter movement on the Cambrai Salient has a character that indicates desperation.

Weather here has been extremely bad – very wet & stormy. I think it has rained every day that Lardy has been here.'

Lardy returned to Liverpool on Friday December 7th. John apologised to Dono for not writing, due to Lardy home, then Vess, plus having got a chill, and neuralgia or toothache. He wrote:

'Vess met Lardy in Liverpool, and they went up to see Marge. Margaret met Lardy in London and saw him off by the military train. We are hoping to hear any post now – believing him to be very near where he was the winter of 1915-16: that is at the head depot of the Co., and not so near the Front as he was just before coming home on leave.

Vess thought Lardy had suffered a lot through his accident and ought not to be set to work as if he was efficient again.

Vess crossed home on Monday and has been to Douglas to see the necessary people e.g. Mr Dickinson, Aunt Mary Ann, Mrs Parkes, etc. Today he went to the College and is spending Sunday at Silverdale.

He looks very well indeed. It is in fact wonderful how well he is – considering the strain, physical & nervous in the Air Service, which breaks down so many.'

...Whilst he was at home, Vess expressed a desire to become a Mason, and so John wrote to Rev Mark Harrison, W.M. and Mr Brew – asking them to get him put through as emergency.

The Dover barrage was supposed to direct the German vessels north, making their journey longer to points of attack. In December 1917, Admiralty noted that German submarines had been passing through the Dover Straits, the barrage no obstacle to them, and were concentrating attacks in the Channel and Liverpool area, a campaign against the convoy system.

Dover Patrol Mines and Nets [23]

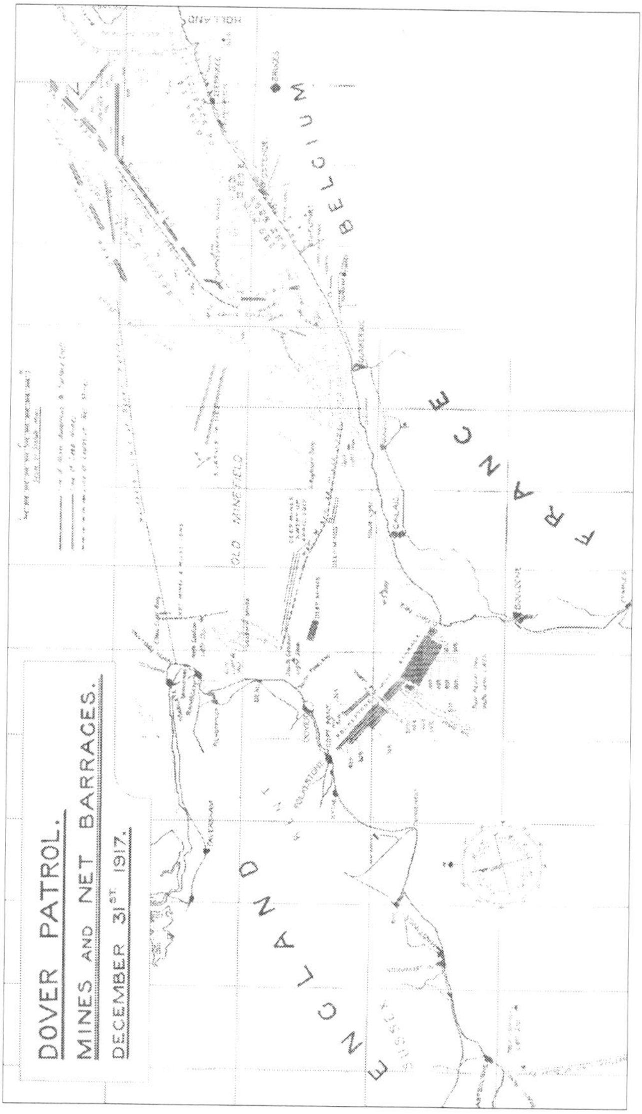

On December 14th Admiralty ordered Admiral Bacon to concentrate destroyer patrol craft (including *H.M.S. Termagant*) on the deep minefield from the French coast to the Varne, instead of the Dover barrage line.

Bacon argued that German vessels would then be free to use whatever entrance and exit routes they desired from Zeebrugge. [5]

In Dono's memoirs, he mentioned that during Admiral Bacon's command in the winter nights of 1917, German destroyers were often in the Straits to raid British submarine defences; some serious tactical errors had been made in night shooting, resulting in British ships firing on each other.

It is interesting to note that there had been a conflict in December in which *H.M.S. Termagant* had been involved, with some shooting between ships, although details are difficult to find. John wrote:

> *'I was much interested watching scraps of news regarding the affair on Dec. 22nd/23rd. I see now from what Daisy has told us, plus your letter to Mother – that you were in the affair. I expect it is the old case of being out-weighted or outranged by a heavier class of gun – in effect as helpless as a man with a shot gun against a man with a service rifle, who has 2000 yards of extra range.'*

...The above scrap was possibly masked by the news that on 22nd December 1918 three brand new British destroyers were sunk off the Dutch coast going to meet a convoy – they ran into a minefield there: over 250 lives lost.

John was still wondering if the submarine problem could be solved by nets:

> *'I cannot get rid of the idea that there is still scope for the net, even cotton, or whatever material there is. Had they held up all cotton intended for Germany two and three years ago, there might have been enough!'*

...At the end of 1917 it was estimated that the enemy had a total of about 130 submarines of all types in home waters and about 20 in the Mediterranean. [7]

On December 27th, Vess crossed back to Liverpool via *S.S. Tynwald* – it was a fine passage. He expected to go to Winchester on January 7th after seeing Mary and Margaret in London and possibly Dono. John reported:

> *'He goes to Winchester for instruction work, not a flying School, but to lecture on the cooperation of artillery & infantry, and which I am sure he thoroughly understands. A medical exam to find out any nervous strain, if it exists, will be part of the programme.*
>
> *He seems physically & nervously all right, but a little high strung at times: I wished there had been some exhilaration or amusement at home to distract and make things gently exciting.*
>
> *Today was very fine, as was yesterday when Vess crossed. He was lucky – for the next three days the port of Liverpool was closed, and no*

boats, no mail etc. Three air-ships were off Laxey working in concert, and it transpires this evening that there was no boat from Liverpool or from Douglas to Liverpool today, and the trawlers forbidden to go out etc.'

...During World War I, Liverpool Port was a strategic western port in keeping Britain supplied with food and essential supplies. On December 28th a mine was hit by a pilot vessel at the Mersey Bar; 30 lives lost. So the closure may have been due to mines or submarines in the area.

Regarding Vess going back to France, and his idea of army strategy, John continued:

'We heard from Lardy after his arrival in France at his Co.

Vess tells me that General Plumer, gone with the army to Italy, has the highest reputation among those in command of armies. He was an Engineer Officer, his methods characterized by mathematical precision and calculation. The others are Cavalry Generals.

Army experience shows that Engineer Officers have made in a large number of cases, a great success when in command of operations in respect of strategy!

Officers are wanted for the tactics, or managing the contacts of forces and particular experience that detail needs. But at Cambrai, cavalry was not used extensively: a matter of a few hundred! The papers talked of cavalry being used – the effect is that people think it was used where it ought to have been used – when in fact it was not.

I see Admiral Jellico has retired with a Peerage.

Things are quiet and dull. We get circulars now, calling on us to warn people to economize. I do not know that there is any waste, but any extreme efforts at asceticism, where not much saving can be effected, is probable anywhere in these parts.'

1918

At the beginning of January 1918, Dono was still working on *H.M.S. Termagant*, grouped with the Dover Destroyer Flotilla.

Admiral Bacon was swiftly replaced by Roger Keyes on the Dover Patrol. He expressed his sadness in leaving the patrol, and the fact that his successors took the credit for work he had started – plans for the mine barrage in the English Channel, and an attack on Zeebrugge and Ostend, to take place at the end of February 1918. Dono wrote in his memoirs:

> *'Sir R. Keyes came to Dover and replaced Sir R. Bacon (sacked at a moment without notice) who had successfully guarded the vital Belgium coast and English Channel for three years.'*

John obviously thought that this was due in part to the incorrect magnitude of the guns on the ships and wrote to Dono:

> *'...I was very much struck with brief touches (in your note which Daisy showed us) regarding your saying goodbye to V.A. Bacon. In a general way I draw inferences, that whether the stunt was his or the Huns, he had not managed well; also, authorities roused by certain other affairs farther north, were more prompt to come down, possibly even too hastily. But what earthly use or sense in keeping light guns afloat to cope with heavier guns?'*

Later on January 13th 1918 John wrote:

> *'I see that Vice Admiral Bacon has a post in the Ministry of Munitions. I remember well what you said some two years ago regarding out-ranging!'*

In January, German destroyers had been in action again and bombarded Yarmouth in Norfolk, but outside the Dardanelles, two notable battlecruisers (belonging to the Ottomans since 1914) were not so lucky in the Battle of Imbros: *Breslau* (renamed *Midilli*) was sunk, and *Goeben* (renamed *Yavuz Sultan Selim*), was beached after striking a mine. *H.M.S. Raglan* was also sunk.

John was concerned about Lardy and wrote:

> *'We have not heard from Lardy, but Margaret has...*
>
> *Lardy complains that he suffers much inconvenience from his arm and leg.*

Vess thought that Lardy must be suffering inconvenience when he was at home and saw him.

I went to see an elderly General Jones yesterday – who seems disposed to say a word for Lardy. He gave me a form of application for a Cadetship, for R.E. or water transport work.'

...John filled in the form and sent it to Lardy.

...Regarding Lardy's injuries, it is thought that at some point, Lardy's loco was bombed whilst carrying ammunition and he was pinned under the engine, sustaining some injury to his arm. His leg injury was from the earlier dropped rail incident.[30]

John heard that Dono had been recommended for an advance in rank on January 22nd (in Royal Navy Reserve – R.N.R.).

On the island, Vess was congratulated by many people regarding his Military Cross award. John wrote:

'The I.O.M. Times had a very friendly paragraph noting Vess's Military Cross; a crowd of people evidently glad to see it.

Lord Raglan's third son has got the M.C decoration.

Today I met a Baldrine youth, home on leave – R.N. or R.N.R. – his ship is in Leith after a collision with a destroyer. I asked him about his ship. He said it was a 'decoy ship', an oil steamer, really an oil steamer (5000 tons) but carrying 4 guns and 2 T tubes; and had actually destroyed several submarines. She was 'nearly cut in two' in a collision with a destroyer, 12 miles from Aberdeen; the destroyer smashed the ship up to the bridge, but both vessels got in, 'towed' in. A collision where a destroyer cuts one of our oil steamers or two twelve miles off land seems unnecessary.

Parliament is now very severe with regard to the Higher Command in France – some strong speeches recently.'

...Decoy ships were used by the British Navy. During 1917 when the unrestricted submarine warfare was in progress, many decoy vessels were fitted with torpedo tubes. German submarine commanders became more wary and developed a dislike of coming close to merchant ships. Disguises or identities of ships were often changed to confuse the German commanders. [7]

In January, President Woodrow Wilson of the U.S.A. gave a speech listing 14 points towards war aims and peace – the blueprint for the final peace negotiations at the end of WWI. John wrote on February 3rd:

'It is difficult to judge as to Pres. Wilson – whether he is all the time sending documents or making speeches intended for Germany & Austria. Perhaps the newspapers in order to fill up where real news is

wanting, think Pres. Wilson can figure as a sort of cartoon caricature of Uncle Sam 'talking'.

There is nothing locally to mention except that Dr Godson is in the hospital with pneumonia, and at present in a serious condition. I am sorry that so good a man should be struck down, even temporarily. Ramsey has lost its best doctor recently with pneumonia: and with the demand on the time of Dr's in attending the Aliens in the Camps, the community is very much without medical men.'

Etching of Knockaloe by an internee 1918, looking towards Peel, giving an idea of the scale of the Camp [21]

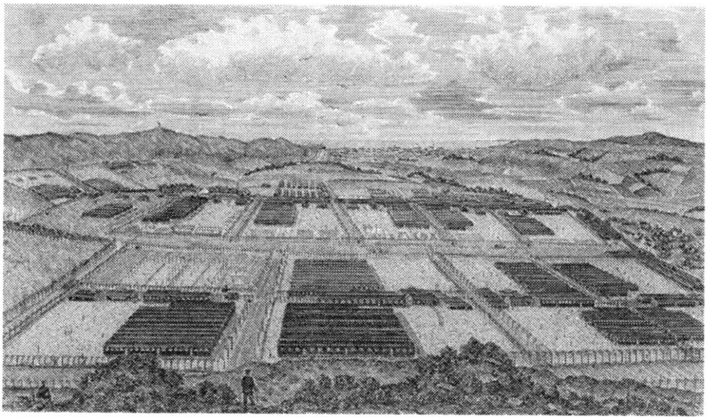

Dr Godson was a Laxey doctor, well known to John and the family, and he kept an eye on the health of Vess after his attack of pneumonia in 1914. He was also one of four part-time local medical practitioners at Knockaloe, along with around five other full-time medical officers.

There were 5 hospitals in the Knockaloe Camp and one at the Douglas Camp.

Unfortunately Dr Godson died on 9th January. John wrote:

'I am sorry to have to mention that Dr Godson of Laxey died at Noble's Hospital of pneumonia. He was overworked at Knockaloe Camp, and had had a bad illness from which he had not recovered to anything like his old form. He attended a Dr Sugden of Ramsey who died of pneumonia, and seems to have contracted pneumonia by infection.

He was an exceptionally worthy man, able, and a gentleman throughout!'

Food rationing was introduced in Britain in January 1918. On the island, the impact of war on food supplies was becoming more noticeable.

No rationing was implemented on the island.

In February John wrote:

> *'Really with the inferior bread we get and the shortage of other things, one has enough to do to keep, or in my case, recover normal physical strength.*
>
> *Just now we have no serious shortage of food, assuming war conditions, to imply privation, but it looks as if things are being tightened very much.*
>
> *...The island is perhaps not badly off, but the nakedness of the shops is plainly visible, and prices are going up still – decent bacon is now 2/8. The bread is far from good.*
>
> *We have enough ground apart from the Glebe field for all the vegetables we need. If I had been at all a gardener, certainly the Glebe field could have been made a garden long ago.'*

Dono's mother also wrote the following letter to Dono:

> *'My dear Dono, You will wonder to get a note from me. I want your advice about some of our ash trees in the garden. There are five which I think we could do without and the Government are giving 4/6 a foot for all ash wood, so I think we might fell them. I hear that they plant another tree in place of the ones cut down...*
>
> *I am going in for more bees this year and I only hope I may be successful.*
>
> *We are looking forward to your holiday. Hope Vess will be home as well but I am afraid we cannot hope to have Laddie (Lardy) as his leave will not be due. I am sorry you are all having a not very good time as regards food as I heard from Mary, Marge & Margaret.*
>
> *Here we cannot say we are badly off. Sugar we get a half pound each week each. Bacon & butter we can get. Bacon is 2/8 per lb, butter 2/6, margarine 1/4. Government controlled stuff is in nearly all cases very inferior. However we must be thankful we have plenty of eggs, and the worst of it is that we are not allowed to send any off the island. I must close now with love. Hoping to see you before long. I am your aff. Mother.'*
>
> ...As the war progressed, a permit was required from Government Office to send eggs, potatoes, live-stock, meat, oats and other essential good off the island, due to

the quantity of food required to feed not only the islander's but the prisoners in the Camps as well. Despite this, Manx oats were sent from the island for a great deal of the duration of the war, with just a short restriction, Manx oats becoming renowned. [3]

John wrote to say they had heard from Daisy and told Dono:

'In the pressure of your work we do not expect you to write much.

Yesterday a destroyer passed south – a long time since anything of the kind seen here; today two minesweeping trawlers I think.

It is a fortnight since I sent the form of application to Lardy: we not have heard from him since my last letter.

Vess seems as usual. We heard from Mary, Marge & Margaret. The last raid did not come so near to Margaret's part of the town.

I see Admiral Jellico has been speaking at Hull, and confessing in complimentary ways to Lord Fisher – who in 1911, said Germany would use submarines against merchant shipping, while all the other people of position and consequence stated it was impossible, unthinkable! Also Lord Fisher knew or confidently asserted that Germany meant war, and that it was inevitable!

What strikes me as an odd comment is that only when your memorandum reached Lord Fisher in Oct 1914, was anything done really to deal with the menace, and even that was not pressed to its full development – perhaps by Lord Fisher going out of office.'

John sent Dono the following newspaper cutting regarding Admiral Jellicoe's Hull speech on U-Boat Losses:

'For the odd battle on the surface of the sea between surface ships, this country was prepared. For the battle under the sea neither this country nor any other, including Germany, was prepared. Even the Germans did not find out until after the war began the possibilities of undersea warfare...

When the Germans discovered the possibilities of such warfare they had the advantage of their great scientific appliances, in which they were unrivalled.

When the war started we were not in a good position in regard to destroyers. The Germans were able to build their submarines faster than we were able to build destroyers.

Lord Fisher started a great programme, and the gratitude of this country was due to him. The shortage of destroyers was partly due to the fact that before the war this nation thought in Dreadnoughts.

The destroyer... was the great antidote to the submarine. We had it on the best authority – from the German people – that what they did fear... was the British destroyer. With regard to the destruction of the armed forces of the enemy, so far as surface ships were concerned, the Navy had not been given many opportunities...

> The first Lord of the Admiralty, speaking last November, stated that between 40 and 50 % of the German submarines... had been sunk...
>
> The mercantile marine up to the end of last year had transported oversea... a total of 13 million troops, and total loss of life due to enemy action was 2,700 officers and men. In addition, 25 million tons of supplies had also been carried oversea.
>
> ...Our destroyers were continually open to attack by surface craft and submarine and to the danger of mines, and we must wonder if occasionally, the destroyers of the enemy got past our patrols and inflicted damage, as they did recently...
>
> One heard so much of what the enemy submarine did and so little of what our own submarines did. There was never a day when there was a German ship at sea in the North Sea... therefore our submarines had no targets on which to work...'

Regarding the speech, John wrote:

> *'The speech makes me wonder why the authorities permit such speeches, which raise and simply disappoint expectations.'*

There had been no major attack by German flotillas in the Straits since April 1917, but German submarine Commanders had reported that the Straits were increasingly difficult to pass and wanted a raid on the barrage. [5] On February 14th, German destroyers made a devastating raid on the Channel vessels; the day after, Dover was shelled by German submarine. John sent Dono the following cutting from the *Times* regarding the attack:

> 'The German destroyer raid into the English Channel on the night of February 14-15 had for its primary aim the destruction of the auxiliary patrol forces on outpost duty. This was evident from the deliberate and systematic manner in which, in the inky darkness, the attack was carried out. A large force was chosen for the enterprise, comprising 10 at least of Germany's largest and fastest destroyers...'

John wrote:

> *'The papers mention a raid of 'large' Hun destroyers into the straits of Dover, sinking seven or eight trawlers, and retiring before our ships could interfere. By 'large', I assume armed with 'larger' guns: if so, have we vessels as fast and as well armed as these 'large' destroyers on this spot? I attach no importance to an incident of that kind if our vessels there are capable of dealing with it on equal terms – speed, range, etc.*
>
> *Things are very quiet and depressing here. The weather has been quite trying...'*

In his memoirs, Dono gave the following account of his experience:

> *'Captain Lieutenant Von Heinke led a force of German Destroyers into the English Channel. Coming down the North Sea, he passed close to Dover and proceeded south-westward down the Folkestone Gate*

along the submarine barrage steel net, which stretched across the Channel. Turning southeast at this point, he led his Destroyers along the line of the net, with its supporting fleet of Drifters and other vessels, and destroyed them all by gunfire. The net barrage vessels, which were defenceless, tied to the net and dependent on the Dover Patrol Destroyers, were massacred.

Returning the way they came, the Germans arrived safely home without having been brought to action by our own Destroyer patrols guarding the straits of Dover.

That same night, Termagant leading her division of Destroyers, was on the eastern barrage patrol, off the French coast in the vicinity of Cape Gris Nez and Calais.

Flashes of gunfire had been seen down channel during the night, but it had not lasted long; nothing had been seen of the German ships; it hadn't aroused any curiosity in the Officers on Termagant's Bridge.

Early in the morning I was on my way along the deck to the Engine Room hatch... On our port beam I saw a steam drifter about half a mile away and kept my eye on her. As I went down the hatch, I saw her fire a 'Very light'.' [2]

...A 'Very light' was a coloured flare fired from a pistol, named after inventor – Edward W. Very.

Dono reported what he had seen, but Captain Bernard did not act upon it. Dono continued:

'...We were soon ordered to proceed to the line of the net barrage to the scene of the slaughter. A few of the vessels with their upper structure and decks blown away remained afloat, the open shell of their hulls a shambles.

I personally looked down into them and shuddered at what gunfire at short range could do, to both men and ships. There was nothing we could do but run alongside floating hulks and see if there were any survivors, but we found none alive and the dead were a pitiful sight.

Due to the above blunder, the Captain was assigned to a different ship and a new Captain was appointed to Termagant.' [2]

...Troops were not transported across to France during hours of darkness due to the prospect of such an attack.

Dono was clearly unwell – the recent work had been very stressful. John wrote:

'It is difficult to know what to do in your case – becoming ill: except that you absolutely must call on the Dr to declare you unfit for duty. Surely the Regulations contemplate such cases as your chill, which must be dealt with at once, and provide for your going, if necessary into a naval hospital...'

John continued:

'We have heard from Vess, who is well, but we have still not heard from Lardy since I last wrote.'

Vess was training pilots at Netheravon for the Artillery Squadron from December 1917 until May 1918. To date he had flown 19 different types of plane.

Vess (standing) in February 1918 at Netheravon with an RE8 of the Artillery Squadron [25]

Regarding Armistice on the Russian Front, John wrote:

'The news from Russia is the most complete discrediting of the wild notions people had three or four years ago, of Russia's 'steam-rolling' – showing how utterly out the newspapers were – the only sources of information.'

...Earlier, in October 1917, the Russian Bolshevik Revolution took place, capitalising on the February Revolution, resulting in a Provisional Government.

In the October Uprising, the Provisional Government was overthrown by a Bolshevik rising organised by Trotsky, giving the power to the local Soviets who strongly supported the Bolshevik party. On February 18th 1918: Armistice terminated on the Russian Front. Later, on March 3rd, Soviet Russia signed a Treaty with Germany, ending its participation in the war. Harsh terms imposed by the Germans forced the Russians to yield a quarter of their pre-war territory & over half of Russia's industries.

[www.historyplace.com/worldhistory/firstworldwar]

Back on the island, small boats in Manx waters felt increasingly susceptible to submarine attack.

...On February 23rd 1918 the I.O.M. Peel fishing boat *Girl Emily* was fishing for cod about 10 miles off shore. A German submarine came alongside and the Captain asked the skipper if he was fishing, to which he answered, "Yes." The sub moved off about 100 yards and opened fire on the fishing boat. Skipper Hughes was severely wounded in the face by splinters from his boat. The sub then came alongside and demanded the fisherman's catch of fish. [4]

With regard to war on the various Fronts, John wrote:

'They say a grand offensive of Huns has begun against the French line: but the papers only imply some attacks which may be in order to disguise other intentions.'

...Occasionally it was leaked that troops would be landed in force in certain areas to make it look as though there was going to be an attack, whilst the men were landed in a different area, having drawn the enemy to the former place. Many different subterfuge tactics were used by ground forces, and naval authorities.

John continued:

'J.P. Callow was at home this past week. He is in Lamport & Holts Office, Liverpool. He told me that he had seen in the papers – a thing I missed – that the army of 140,000 Turks under German Officers going to counter the British advance in Palestine, had 'deserted en-masse' – simply sloped off to their native homes...

I think Callow possibly came across (to the island) *in connection with his licence for the hotel for the summer season. He implied that the Defence of Realm Act was making people exceedingly cautious, watchful and suspicious, lest every stranger might be a detective or spy; and it was unsafe to express sentiments in hostile criticism of existing authorities. I attached no importance to his ideas on war prospects – e.g. an early peace with Turkey & Bulgaria etc.*

We are hoping to hear soon of your having a leave, and a rest from the tension and strain of the present arduous service.'

By mid-March, Dono was still feeling unwell and John wrote to him:

'We know from Daisy that you have had, and are having, a hard time – more especially of late, when you must be feeling the effects of over-protracted strain, and too long continuation of worry of things.

I hope you will get some rest when you get into port for refit.'

...Vessels were laid up for long refits due to collision or damage, in addition to the usual four-monthly refits.

In his biography, Jellicoe wrote:

'Anyone familiar with the delicate nature of destroyers – and the conditions of life at sea, will appreciate the strain the conditions imposed on those on board, as well as the machinery; the personnel and the machinery of these vessels at sea were approaching the limit of endurance by the end of 1917.' [7]

John complained to Dono:

'...The newspapers have very little news. The public mind is without that succession of stimulants in the way of news on which it has been keeping going for as long as the newspapers could keep it up. Dullness and vagueness is now the general feature of the man in the street.'

In March there was further destroyer action in the North Sea between Allied & German flotillas, and on the Western Front, battles continued around St Quentin, and both Bapaume, & Péronne were taken by German forces.

Vess was ill – with a cold, and swollen glands. He wrote the following letter from A.C.S. Royal Flying Corps, Nether Avon, Wilts on March 24th:

'Dear Daisy, just a line in answer to your note. There's not a hope of my being in Liverpool before Easter and as far as I can see very little even then. We expect to move to some new aerodrome about the 29th but we haven't been told either when or where we're going. I'll write or wire if I do get any leave. I'm suffering from neuralgia and a cold just now. The news from France today is very grave. I hope Lardy is safe, for the very worst fighting has been on his Front.

The weather here is topping. I've been to Bournemouth twice for lunch, yesterday and today. It's only 35 minutes run from here by air, i.e. about 50 miles. On Thursday I had a crash but didn't get hurt. My wing hit a tree and the bus was absolutely wrecked in no time... Yours affectionately, Sylvester.'

Battles on the Western Front continued with the Battle of Rosières in the Somme, and the 1st Battle of Arras.

Incidentally, earlier in 1918, a conversation was overheard regarding the Isle of Man Internees in a large factory in the north of England:

'Six enemy submarines would be in the north Irish Sea between March 29th and April 2nd – and no vessel would be immune to attack, all except one from the Isle of

> Man with a large number of German prisoners on board – internees who would have broken out of the Knockaloe Camp.' [4]
>
> ...About the same time, censors at the Camp discovered a chart of the Irish Sea in the false bottom of a box sent to a prisoner. [4]

There were several submarines in Manx waters at the end of March, and the White Star liner *Celtic* was torpedoed 12 miles from the Calf of Man: 17 engine-room staff killed. Precautions taken at the Knockaloe Camp meant that the escape plan was scuppered...

> ...In the same attacks, the fishing boat of Manx-fisherman Dickie Lee was captured by a German submarine. Dickie Lee was taken on board the submarine and kept there overnight; he was interrogated about Manx affairs, and told that the submarine would sink other vessels; they put him in the lifeboat of one of these vessels.
>
> Back on Manx shores, Dickie told the Manx authorities about his capture and that he had seen a chart of the Irish Sea in the submarine, marked with 'interesting information'! The 'course' followed by the Manx Steam packet ships was marked as 'protected'; the Manx boats were immune from submarine attack because the ships possibly carried German prisoners or visitors to the camps. [21: Chapter 5]

John was probably aware of the local attack on the Celtic, but the situation in France was so grave that he had more than enough to occupy his thoughts.

On the Western Front, in the great German attack offensive of March (recapturing ground lost in 1916 in the Somme) and the Allied retreat, the Railway Companies were responsible for the demolition of railway installations, including bridges and track – a colossal task. [13]

Lardy was in this melee, and John had received no communication from him for a while.

Lardy's work had continued on much the same course until March 20th, when he suddenly found that he was in the thick of the developments in the Ancre region. On the 21st March, bombardments commenced with mustard gas shelling, and the Front line was broken.

According to the No.3 Monmouth War Diary, an order was received on the 24th March for the Company to demolish the railway line to Pozières and move valuable material, and the Railway Company moved to Buire.

That night, heavy bombing was carried out by enemy aeroplanes, and the following day, a party was sent to demolish the railway, and charges were set on the Ancre bridges, as the enemy were advancing from Bazentin, Longueval and Albert. At 2.30 on 26th March the enemy were reported to be around 400 yards away:

'Gas shell, high explosives, shrapnel and machine gun fire from aeroplanes was intense.' [28]

John wrote later (in 1919) regarding Lardy's experience in March 1918:

'Lardy tells us of his experiences in the great avalanche of March. The German advance was a surprise: many officers of ours supposed to have been afterwards shot for utter incapacity and ignorance of what was coming.

Mist and moonlight both greatly assisted the Germans – who were able to pass through barbed wire systems unopposed, probably after smashing them with shell.

The first word Lardy had, was to hurry back to dumps, get gun cotton and return up the line to the extreme Front, and blow up the railway line completely and all bridges at the same time, returning and sending all railway stock back.

When the Germans approached the Ancre (south of Albert) his company were thrown into the fighting line for three days – where he faced (day and night) advancing waves of German infantry – waves as heavy as any described by correspondents – driven on from behind, as no troops could have faced the destructive fire except by forcing on, irrespective of loss!!

He lay in the corner of a garden with a low hedge of 2' thorn trees, looking out on an open field of fire along a railway line to the Ancre Bridge and to the open across it. It was a case of continuous rifle fire, and the destruction immense. He thinks the Ancre River below them was bridged solid with Germans killed.

There were three lines of rifle fire, he in front: then gradually driven back across a high road lined by houses forming a village, and ultimately to a railway embankment on top of which he lay with rails as his only breastwork!! Eventually our heavy artillery behind got onto the German Front line and that stopped their advance.

The heavy shells from our guns were burst right in front of him, a matter of merely tens of scores of yards, flinging their burst forward.

As for the German artillery during those three days, it was shooting over his head – being directed to the roads behind, along which the reserves were advancing.'

...After this the No.3 Monmouth Railway Company moved by train to Vecquemont and on to Vignacourt, north of Amiens, where they were to be employed in making new defences until April 5th. [28]

John related Lardy's further experience:

'After being relieved, the Company was sent back to construct a line of defence – trench and barbed wire, some miles behind Albert. Their task individually each day in trenching was a section 16' x 6' x 5'6": but half of it only 3' deep: the earth thrown forward 1'6" high, tailing away.' (...part of John's letter shown)

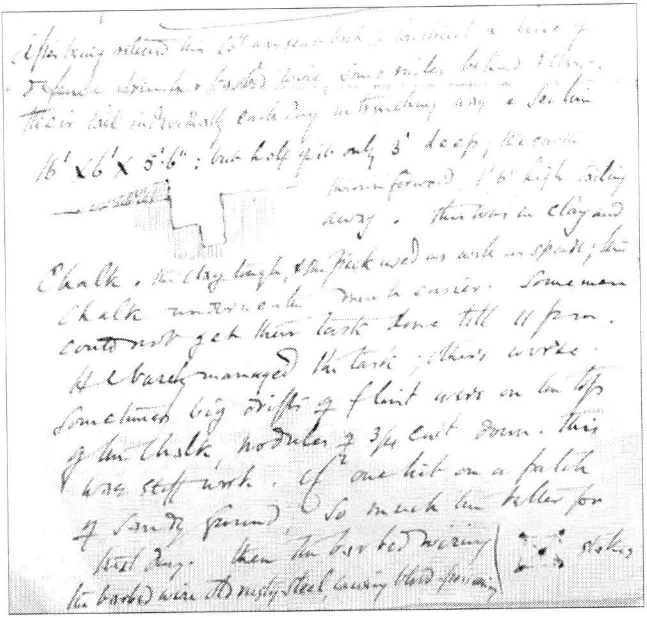

After being relieved the Coy was sent back to construct a line of defence trench & barbed wire some miles behind Albert.
Their task individually each day in trenching was a section
16' x 6' x 5'6": but half of it only 3' deep; the earth
thrown forward 1'6" high tailing
away. This was in clay and
chalk. the clay tough, & the pick used as well as spade; the
chalk underneath much easier. Some men
could not get their task done till 11 pm.
He barely managed the task; others worse.
Sometimes big drifts of flint were on the top
of the chalk, nodules of 3/4 cwt down. This
was stiff work. If one hit on a patch
of sandy ground, so much the better for
that day. then the barbed wiring | stakes
the barbed wire old rusty steel, causing blood poisoning

John continued:

'This was in clay and chalk, the clay tough, and the pick used as well as spade – the chalk underneath much easier. Some men could not get their task done until 11pm. He barely managed the task: others, worse.

Sometimes big drifts of flint were on the top of the chalk, nodules of 3/4 cwt down. This was stiff work. If one hit on a patch of sandy ground, so much the better for that day.

Then the barbed wiring; the barbed wire stakes were old rusty steel causing blood poisoning.'

...Battles continued in April on the Western Front in Estaires, Messines, Hazebrouck and Bailleul.

Regarding Lardy's Company, John wrote:

'Later they came some 30 miles north and made 28 miles of railway – which was hardly completed till it was condemned as not required, and taken up again.'

...On April 5th 1918, Lardy's Company marched 20 miles to Fortel, then to Wavans, north of Doullens, where they commenced railway construction once again in the directions of Frévent and Auxi-le-Chateau, making an ambulance siding near the latter yard. [28]

To John and his wife's relief, Lardy finally sent a letter home on 10th April saying he was well, and some distance from where he was before, but no hint of course as to where or what had happened to him. He asked for quinine, as he was getting frequent wettings and had been feverish.

Meanwhile, Dono's ship, *H.M.S. Termagant* was under repair and refit at the Shipbuilders in Hull. On April 10th 1918, John wrote to Dono:

'We got your wire before tea-time, saying you got in at 3.15.

We hear today of another German advance of 3 miles. Have the newspapers been putting a face on things merely to keep the public in a comfortable state of mind?'

Whilst Dono was waiting for completion of the refit of his ship, he unknowingly dined with the new Captain appointed to *H.M.S. Termagant*.

Due to the necessary precautions taken when meeting anyone new, Dono was cautious not to mention his name or that of his ship, and it was a while before they each discovered they were to be on the same ship.

Dono wrote:

'I first met Sir Andrew B. Cunningham in the West Riding Club in Anlaby Road, Hull, where I dined. This was also the same night as the Zeppelin raid, when five or six Zeppelins came over Hull (12 April)*.' [2]*

...The latter was the last airship raid over England. There had been around 50 raids and well over 500 people killed by bombing from them. German aeroplanes had now overtaken the airship regarding speed, control and reliability.

John wondered about Dono's new Captain and wrote:

'...Assuming you are going with a new Captain, do not expect to know him throughout too soon... what you want ultimately is strength and capacity and character, not the particular external guise of it. There are men who are only husk and no kernel... But remember what we were saying when fishing one day, that it is not wise for another to suggest to yourself that the engineering profession is not a scientific profession with a great deal in it...

If he is a man who knows his job and works at it, he will be sure to find out that you know yours...'

Marge came home to the Vicarage mid-April due to her school being closed on account of an epidemic of whooping cough. John wrote:

'She looks fairly well and is in good spirits. It is quite wonderful this equability of disposition. Frank Sherriff has been sent from Bombay to S. Africa in the transit of a lot of mental patients.

The sun-stroke cases he had are described as very bad indeed.

He got to Cape Town in March, and remarks that between Bombay and Cape Town, they never sighted a single ship. They may have taken a course off the beaten tracks. He says he feels very well now.'

...Frank, after convalescence from sun-stroke, spent time in Hospital near Bombay with dysentery.

John continued:

'Mary heard from Graham from the convalescent camp near Jerusalem, and later from Cairo Red Cross, where he is back again: he fainted, his heart bad. Some light duty in Egypt must be all he's fit for.

We have no letter from Lardy this week, but have heard from Vess, whose squadron are under orders to hold themselves ready to move.

On the Irish question, my view is that our Government show a weakness, fatal in the present situations: for if they cannot master a dog, how do they hope to master a tiger; if they cannot control Irish Sinn Fein, how do they hope to master Germany?'

John wrote later on April 17th:

'We have a card from Vess from Hoylake – he hurt his right arm with a blow from the propeller of a plane which came down with engine trouble. As he was on the field he went up to see what was wrong, when the engine started again. No bone was broken, but the muscles bruised, and he got a few days leave at Hoylake. J. Clarke met him in Liverpool, and told me he looked very well except for his arm...'

Regarding other news and affairs, John wrote:

'I see the Man Power Bill exempts clergymen. This is not as it ought to be: there are a dozen young men I should think here, who ought to go to military service... they could be very well done without where they are...The news from France is not reassuring just now. Of course so little is told us, and we know so little of the relative numerical

strengths, and nothing about the disposition of our forces; still less, if possible, about the strategic intentions of Gen. Foch (the French General)*, that one has to possess oneself and wait.'*

John told Dono about the Laxey mines strike:

'Laxey has a strike. Six months ago the miners or workers formed a Union, affiliated to the English Trade Union. I said at the time they would have to act on their orders: now those orders have come. The mine directors say they will make no advance in wages; in consequence of the enormous expense entailed by the flooding of the mine some years ago, no dividends have been be paid up to date.

If the directors do not budge there will be much distress in the place, and 2 things must happen – the exempted men will have to go into the army and others will have to seek work in England – possibly a few may get work on farms...'

Laxey Mine Water-wheel

Later, John reported regarding the strike:

'The big wheel was stopped but has started work again. This stoppage was simply a flooding of the mine.

The Laxey strike ended with work to go on as before. I know nothing of advance in wages.'

Daisy had seen Dono whilst he was in Hull for the refit of his ship: he was still feeling ill. Daisy told John that Dono's Captain was more capable than his previous Captains, but possibly not an easy man to get on with. John advised Dono regarding work and health:

'...proceed carefully and do not say too much...

Perhaps it would help you a little if you took somewhat systematically a little gregory or sulphur, or cream-of-tartar. If you think so, I can send you some.'

The refit of Dono's ship took seventeen days. On April 21st, John wrote:

'We are supposing that by this time you are away from Hull, and perhaps back to the same station.'

Cunningham wrote regarding his new Captaincy of *H.M.S. Termagant*:

'After our refit, we arrived in Dover – too late to take any really interesting part in the pending operation.

The Dover Patrol was very different from the Grand Fleet; the proximity and enterprise of the German destroyers kept it lively.

The raid on Zeebrugge took place shortly after our arrival.'

...The blocking raid by British light forces on Zeebrugge & Ostend in April 1918 was led by Admiral Keyes – the plan – to neutralize both ports.

Cunningham continued:

'The Termagant was to escort the 15" monitors along with two other destroyers to their bombarding position close to Dutch territorial waters not far from the entrance to the Scheldt... in thick fog!

After anchoring I was told to steam half a mile to a Dutch navigational buoy...

The monitors fired deliberately through most of the night of the 22nd April... now and again one heard the burst of a shell fired back by the enemy's big guns. Nothing came close to us.' [11]

...Although publicised as a British victory, it did not stop the Germans from using the ports for more than a few days. [10] *H.M.S. Termagant* was mentioned in the subsequent honours list for her part in this raid. [5]

John saw the reports of the raid, and wrote on April 24th:

'This evening we have an account in the Times of the affair against Ostend and Zeebrugge, as it was organized by the Dover Admiral. About the Ostend attempt very little is said.

We suppose that your ship may have been engaged in it, and at the moment we are wishful to know if you are all right.'

Later, John wrote:

'We were very glad to get your wire on Thursday 25th, saying you had returned all right – as we had calculated you would be engaged in it.

It would be extremely interesting to us to know – though perhaps you cannot yet tell us – what part your ship took from beginning to end. Daisy's letter this evening merely says you brought the Iris back...'

Regarding towing the Iris away, Dono wrote in his memoirs:

'It did not come into the province of an Engineer Officer to concern himself with signals, navigation, gunnery and the like, but in destroyers at that time, the Engineer Officer was in charge of the whole equipment of the ship.

This responsibility resulted in a difference of opinion between Cunningham and myself when ordered to take the Mersey ferry in tow to a safe distance from the coast after the attack on Zeebrugge (she had 75 dead men on deck, a shell hole in her funnel). He put out a 6-inch wire as a towrope and then rang 15 knots to the Engine Room – the wire snapped like a shoelace.

Cunningham blamed me for not having better wires. Only when those on Daffodil gave us their anchor cable to use as a towrope, were we able to do the job properly. In the meantime I had recognised in her war paint (as one I had travelled on many times), as the ship she was, at least 500 tons deadweight. So I ignored the 15 knots ordered by Cunningham, accelerated Termagant slowly, and she took the tow nicely. Incidentally, I was temporarily blinded by the brilliant flash of one of the enemy's shells, which pitched some distance away, but close enough. Once in the open sea the tow was released and she proceeded under her own steam. Termagant escorted the ship to Dover.' [2]

...The *Iris II*, a Liverpool ferry, with Royal Marines on board, was initially towed to Zeebrugge by *H.M.S. Vindictive*. The ferry was heavily shelled in the raid, killing 46 Marines. Both ferries, *Iris* and *Daffodil*, arrived back in the Mersey later, on 17th May 1918.

John wrote to Dono:

'We were glad to have your letter, and very glad to have so definite an expression of your favourable idea of your new Captain. I am quite sure that to you it must make a great deal of difference to be serving under a better man, than to be more or less worried by seeing a man not completely his own master or not knowing his own mind... I am

glad that you think your new Captain earnest, capable and patriotic – giving you substantial ground on which to relate yourself to him?

I hope that you are no worse in any way and that you were able to carry out your duties to your own satisfaction.'

After the Zeebrugge raid, *H.M.S. Termagant* was stationed at Dunkirk, which Cunningham preferred to Dover. Cunningham declared:

'There was more chance of action, and one was relieved of the rather monotonous duty of escorting troop transports from Folkestone and Dover to Calais and Boulogne... My opening experience of the Dover Patrol was eighteen consecutive nights (and days) at sea with the men at action stations practically the whole time'. [11]

John had heard from Vess: he did not expect to be sent to France immediately. John pondered:

'...but we do not know why, yet have no definite cause to think that he is still under nerve strain. He thinks they will move to a new spot, which he himself observed and called attention to as site for a drome.'

There was news of the death of Richthofen, the German pilot encountered by Vess in 1917; he was brought down near Amiens on 21st April 1918. John reported:

'I see that he was brought down within the English lines on the Somme, his plane a mass of wreckage and gunshot wounds, showing that he had been hit in the melee before the crash.'

During April, the Belgians battled to hold on to what little of their country they had left on Kemmel Ridge in the region of the Lys. The Germans were hopeful of breaking through to the North Sea around the 25th, and in the ensuing battle, thousands of French soldiers were slaughtered.

Towards the end of April 1918, John had a letter from Lardy saying that the weather in his sector was not at all good. Lardy had heard nothing of a Commission or the papers he had sent in, and did not expect to hear anything further. John reported:

'Lardy is some considerable distance from the Albert sector where they were stationed, but gives no clue as to what direction in which he has moved.

The news this evening is not good... The news from the Western Front is very serious just now, but the probability is that reserves are being husbanded; I can see no other explanation of the constantly repeated statements that our men are fighting at a great disadvantage in the positions of defence.

One cannot say that anything has taken place here. I was in Douglas and saw Lady Raglan crossing the street to speak to me: so I crossed to meet her, and she asked me to wait a few minutes to speak to the Governor.

He told me that the Monmouth Battalion had had some casualties – I gathered in the first part of the offensive soon after March 21st.'

...The No.3 Monmouth Railway Company was working on the Auxi-le-Chateau, Wavans, Fortel railway lines and sidings later in April. [28]

Early in May, John wrote to Dono, suggesting he ought to have a rest after the recent high-strung affair at Zeebrugge:

'Daisy read a paragraph from your letter received Thursday evening. We infer that your patrol work is going on as before, within hearing and sight of the actual Western Front, probably some 25 miles or so away.

We have also heard from Vess; he does not expect a flight for 3 months yet, he thinks. Also he implies that in the Air Force, the new organization is not regarded favourably by the men in the service. He knows Trenchard and thinks highly of him.

It would be a pity if social influence is again to get the upper hand and the spirit of the new army, which is to recognize personal merit not position, had to take a back seat.'

...On April 1st 1918, the Royal Flying Corps (R.F.C) and the Royal Navy Air Service (R.N.A.S.) were amalgamated to form the Royal Air Force (R.A.F.).

Regarding American airmen on the Western Front, John wrote:

'According to a paragraph in this evening's papers the American airmen have been achieving much success, exceptionally great success – if one is to believe the papers; but they have a lot of soft talk, intended (they would probably say) to promote the growth of cordial relations with the U.S.A. mind towards ourselves.'

...American airman, Rickenbacker, attained a reputation as a fearsome ace, with 26 'kills' by the end of the war.

Following the April Zeebrugge raid, Cunningham asked for *H.M.S. Termagant* to be given a front seat in the next blocking raid; this was promised. [11] Due to unfavourable weather conditions, the next blocking raid on Ostend could not be carried out until May 9th 1918. Despite the promises made to the Captain of *H.M.S. Termagant*, Dono's ship played no part in the raid, as the date clashed with the ship's boiler cleaning period. Unfortunately the raid was no greater success than the previous attempt.

H.M.S. Termagant spent most of her time at Dunkirk after this, periodically disturbed by the attentions of a German long-range 15" gun whilst moored in the harbour. Dunkirk had a pretty hot time from German aircraft. [11] Dono also wrote in his memoirs that *H.M.S. Termagant* was responsible for laying the mine-field off Ostend.

Dono was still unwell. On May 10th, John queried:

> *'Your wire to Daisy arrived this morning. She mentioned that you were not well when you last wrote, though I did not hear it mentioned before – only that you were feeling the strain: that indeed not a slight matter however. I hope that you are feeling better again. It may be that an aperient might be worthwhile.'*

Later, John wrote:

> *'We were glad to have a note from you, though Daisy tells us anything of direct concern to us in her letters. I have gathered what you say of the strain entailed by the routine as well as the special work. The question is, what to say – that is, with a wish to help you under the weight of it.*
>
> *You must use your plain conviction as to consulting a medical officer on the point of the necessity of sick-leave – for to be unable to carry on is to absolutely require hospital rest. The fear of not getting as good a ship, were you to have a sick leave, is not sufficient reason on the one hand, against the certainty of a break down on the other hand.*
>
> *You have done your duty in the highest degree. Endeavour to carry on as long as you can: but use your judgement in deciding if you have found the point reached where your physique and reserve of physical resources demands a hospital rest.*
>
> *Willy Quine is mentioned in Pearson's magazine this month in an article on 'Medical Heroes of the War' – a brief mention of what he did in the Jutland affair.'*

On May 17th 1918, John wrote regarding the family to Dono:

> *'First to mention that we have heard from Lardy, who is well, but evidently working very hard. He got the quinine I sent him – though I*

overlooked putting the 'contents' on the packet. He is very busy, but gives no hint where he is. He seems to have an impression that the situation is very serious, though he does not distinctly say as much.

When Marge was at home I was moved to admiration at her equability and strength with regard to the absence and illnesses of Frank, and I find Mary's letters full of an indomitable spirit, never a trace of a murmuring tone. They both of them have deep and intense feeling, yet a strength to repress it and hold themselves in control.

Daisy may not have the same natural resources, but she maintains a fairly good spirit. Mother is certainly very particular, and I should think succeeds very well indeed in keeping the right atmosphere.

Indeed from my point of view it is for you I am concerned, on account of what must be a terribly trying and wearing strain.

Where it is a case of something entailed on all alike, it is one thing to set oneself and suffer oneself to bear it: but where a certain number evade their part – as I see constantly in the case of young men of military age, by the view taken by Tribunals in favour of their exemption, a sense of injustice has rightly a place.

The cold-blooded evasion and shirking, and that without any sense whatever of the baseness and cowardice of it; the greed and swinish glutting in making money; the total want, I do not say of patriotism – but even any consciousness that they have any right at all to serve the country, not to speak of every bit as much right as those who are serving, drives me at times into a sort of hate of the system, which allows any man of military age who possesses property to get scot free.'

During May there had been a number of aeroplane raids by both British and German forces; planes were still very dependent on reasonable weather to fly. On board *H.M.S. Termagant* towards the end of May, when out with the monitors on the Dover Patrol of the net barrage, Captain Cunningham spotted heavy firing inshore and German destroyers shooting at some British sea-planes. He wrote:

'We made off towards the enemy at full-speed... The Germans were reinforced by five other destroyers.

We opened fire. It was fairly rough, but... I have never seen such wretched shooting of the Termagant and the others.' [11]

Dono wrote:

'16 torpedoes were fired at the line of 9 enemy destroyers – no hits.' [2]

Cunningham wrote:

'To be 5,000 yards off the enemy and unable to hit them was exasperating and a poor reflection on our gunnery... The Dover destroyers were so desperately hard worked that they had no time for firing practices or exercises...' [11]

Vess was posted to Salisbury, and expected to go to France on June 6th. Regarding the rest of the family, John reported to Dono:

'The boy and Daisy are well. He came in to see me this morning in my room. I was nearly ready to go out. I said "Now I must get on!" He said, "You must get a move on?" He is constantly repeating expressions he has picked up when no one was aware of his noting what was said. (Dono's son, Jack, was now two and a half.)

Marge has heard from Frank – in India again – set up by sea voyages to the Cape and back. He would have liked permanent service on sea transport, but getting papers through is such a formidable delay that he gave the idea up. Graham has been sent to active duty again (Palestine).

I heard that Tom Kelly (son of a Laxey man known to John) *in the Harrison-Rennie service has been ill with malaria, at Durban or Lourenco Marques. He had been down with enteric* (typhoid) *fever at Durban, but was on the way to be well again.*

The news of the Huns offensive is rather bewildering – 26 miles in 4 days – seeming like an unopposed infantry march.

We know nothing but the meagre news which the newspapers serve out to us.

I hope you are able to get some sleep and able to keep carrying on.'

The Battle of the Aisne was followed by the Battle of the Matz (in which, despite the French being aware of the impending attack, they still had significant losses).

Lardy wrote home from *'a part of France he was in before with two fine rivers, several large woods'*.

...The War Diary for the No.3 Monmouth Railway Company states that they were working in much the same area as before – Auxi-le-Chateau, on the river Authie, with frequent gas mask parades. However, the enemy had the range of the Frévent yard on the river Canche, bombarding it with 14" shells. [28]

John reported on June 9th 1918 regarding Lardy:

'He has tried fishing, but not successfully. He seems well.'

Around the middle of June however, many men in Lardy's Company were reported to be coming down with a fever, which was probably what Lardy also suffered from, as John wrote later in the month:

'We have heard from Lardy, who is some distance back from the Front. He asks for more quinine – which I am sending him by first post.'

...Later in June, the pay for the No.3 Monmouth Railway Company (5250 francs) was stolen from the O.C.'s office on the 'living train', and a sapper injured when a loco rolled down an embankment. [28]

Cunningham had only been Captain of *H.M.S. Termagant* for a couple of months. Shortly after his appointment, there was mutiny on board! Dono related in his memoirs:

'The previous Captain had been more lax in his control of the Deck Officers and the ratings associated with them.

One day the 'hands', upset at losing their previous Captain and not liking the discipline of the new one, had barricaded themselves in the mess decks and refused to turn out for work.'

...This resulted in Dono taking the watertight door off its hinges. Some of the men involved were consequently sent to jail for 90 days. [2]

John wrote to Dono regarding his Captain:

'I note what you say regarding your Captain, also regarding your 1st Lt. and I am very glad that you had officers of that excellent stamp with you. It is a satisfaction to know, to have known, men of this sort.

I also note your remark about 15" gun sniping.

The papers have some severe remarks - John Bull, Daily Mail etc., on a Danish machine gun of much improved type, not being produced for our army after having been secured and orders given first.

There is also a serious leakage in accounts of a great munitions department: I hope some move will be made to bring home to the offenders their deeds.

But John Bull, widely read I believe, particularly by soldiers at the Front, has a spirit not likely to influence the best sort of people – I do not mean socially, nor religiously, nor anything of that kind: but people of character.

There is little news or incident here.

Vess is not going to France yet. He is engaged on a job to enquire into causes of smashes etc.; his legal training will help, as will his mental keenness.'

Vess crossed home Mid-June for about a fortnight. John wrote:

'Vess had trained his flight and got it ready for France, when doubt arose as to his physical fitness for flying in France, and he had to have a Medical Board – who decided he was not fit.

He has had recurrences of malaria – the effects of Salonika; he has also neurasthenia, and some heart weakness, which would make it risky for any flying over 5,000 feet.

They gave him three weeks leave, then spoke of two months ordinary flying in England, and then to go to a warm climate – Egypt or Texas – to do instructor work, training American & Canadian airmen.

Mother remarked how thin he is, and he certainly does not look well. He was sleeping badly too. I hope he will get some sound sleep here, and that his appetite will improve – as we have no real shortage of anything but sugar.'

...Neurasthenia: chronic fatigue syndrome.

Vess crossed back to Liverpool on 24th June. John reported:

'...I do not think he is anything like so fit as I should like him to be: he does not seem to have that flush of vitality & spirit that I should call normal for him. The fact that the authorities did not send him to France implies expert opinion to the effect that he is not equal to hard strains of flying.

For our part we are thankful that they did not send him 'fit or not', as perhaps has been done in the case of many men.

On Friday two destroyers passed south, and north again shortly afterwards. They were six or seven miles off at sea.

We heard yesterday that the Manx boat sailed from Seacombe (near Liverpool), *as a large convoy arrived taking possession of the whole of the Prince's Landing stage.*

Daisy and the boy were here today; both well. The grass is cut, and I told him we would make a hay-rick. He went and got his 'angine' as he calls it, a wooden loco, and proceeded to load it with hay, and brought several loads together to make a hay-rick.

We went to Silverdale on Monday – they are busy despite Thompson's attempt to turn over Sunday School picnics this summer.'

Admiral Keyes made use of *H.M.S. Termagant* as one of the escort ships of the Dover Patrol during the summer of 1918 to transport many important people across the Channel. Dono wrote in his memoirs:

> *'On one occasion the ship led an escort for King George V and party on board another vessel, who were visiting the War Zone on the Continent.*
>
> *Two thirds of the way to Dover a problem ensued with one of the boilers, resulting in a fire on board H.M.S. Termagant due to contaminated fuel.'*
>
> ...Dono decided to continue at 27 knots (the best he could do) instead of the 30 required. The Royal party landed safely however.

George's son, the Prince of Wales and his Aide were passengers on another trip across to Boulogne, and were quite happy to make the journey at a slower speed – they had a nap in the Captain's cabin.

But on one occasion, Dono had taken *H.M.S. Termagant* to full speed, making the Dover to Calais route in 43 minutes: the wife of an American Colonel was particularly nervous about being torpedoed by German submarines which she believed infested the Channel in great numbers. Dono wrote:

> *'The lady asked if she could be given a ride on the highest deck above the water and please would we go fast?' [2]*

H.M.S. Termagant had been involved in some further raid on the Belgian coast in June and Dono was promoted. John wrote to Dono:

> *'We heard of you being gazetted – (Temporary) 'Acting Lt. Commander (Engineer)'; and found it in the Times on Wed Jun 26th – the promotion to date from June 22nd. We are very glad you have got this advance in rank, as the authorities may feel wary about giving promotion to men that have come in to the Service – until they find them exceptionally efficient!*
>
> *We were very glad to have your letter with your reference to recent action etc. I note your remark of approbation of your Commander, and remember what you said before of the same tenor. Daisy showed us the letter giving animated and excellent account of action of June 26th – a very serious affair – and satisfactory in a high degree considering overwhelming enemy force.*
>
> *I should say such an action – a very hard scrap: quite enough to get recognition from the authorities.'*

...June 26th also saw the end to the Battle of Belleau Wood, one of the most ferocious battles which U.S. troops fought in WWI.

Due to anticipation of more night raids by the German destroyers in the Dover Straits, and as a result of bad shooting and night shooting mishaps in the earlier sea battles of 1918, the Admiralty arranged some night firing practice for the ships of the Dover Patrol.

For the firing practice, a full-scale destroyer target made out of wood and canvas was towed into the Channel each night, and a division ordered into the target area and given orders to fire on the target with everything they had. The target was inspected during daylight hours for efficiency of hitting the target.

H.M.S. Termagant was in the first division, leading three other destroyers. After some heavy firing at the 'target', they retreated...

The morning papers reported 'heavy firing in the Channel'. The target was subsequently found to have not one shot in it, but... one of the gun-men maintained that he thought he hit something.

Subsequently, it was reported that three German destroyers had been in the Channel that night, one of them hit, causing them to abandon their mission... [2]

Later, John wrote to Dono:

'Your account of the action was excellent so far as you were able to go, without details. It was a very serious affair: bad as to odds, excellent as to results!

I heard quite independently that a Hun boat was sunk: I gather at least that hits were scored.

A man in a coast town near Dover wrote a clamorous letter to the press, asking that information might be given of heavy firing off there on night of June 30th; but nothing has appeared.'

John continued regarding Vess and Jack:

'Vess has had dentist trouble at Hoylake – 8 teeth stopped (filled) *and 2 new ones.*

Daisy and the boy are still at Raby Lodge (with Daisy's parents in Baldrine). *They were both up at Church this morning, but went back before dinner. The boy behaved fine in Church, but marched out when he was tired, with back as straight and stiff as if the institution existed for his convenience.*

I got him some 'wheels' in the bazaar in Douglas. He came up one day, marched straight in to my study and said, "Where are my wheels?"

Archibald Knox has a holiday from Knockaloe Camp, and is coming up this ensuing week to stay for a few days – when we hope to go and see some of the points important in the Roman Survey.'

...Canon Quine was working on a study into Roman influence on the Isle of Man: the 'Roman Survey'. Perhaps he threw himself into his work as a diversion from the strain of war news and worry of his family.

In 1916 Lord Raglan had been opposed to making reforms regarding the introduction of income tax in order to secure old age pensions, leading to his unpopularity with the Manx people and unrest.

Instead, attention was turned towards getting the Manx Government to grant a bread subsidy to bakers, as in Britain. As a result, a bread subsidy was introduced for six months on November 26th 1917, which enabled bakers to produce a nine-penny loaf (instead of one shilling).

When Lord Raglan announced in June 1918 that the Imperial Government would not allow the bread subsidy to continue beyond the end of the month, unrest followed.

On June 30th, John wrote:

'There is a sort of deadlock between the 'Keys' and insular Government. Uncle Thomas was one of a deputation from the 'Keys' to see the Governor at Government House. Lord Raglan explained the difficulty of his position, but Uncle Thomas said, "Nevertheless, you represent the Imperial Government, and we deal with you as their representative or agent – the only access to them, being you."'

The events resulted in the Manx people revolting against the removal of the bread subsidy, and a General Strike on the island from 3rd to 5th July 1918. Tynwald, scheduled for July 5th, was cancelled, as rioting was feared, and all public houses were shut down. John reported:

'This week there has been a sensational hold up of everything by a strike on the island; trams, trains and even boats ceased running. The question was whether bread should be, here, as in England.

The mob had possession of Douglas on Thursday; Captain Moughtin (and I hear, his daughter) were hurtled badly by the mob, mainly slum street women. Uncle Thomas got some yells howled after him, as a 'bread hoarder' – quite what he could afford to laugh at, as he did!

On July 4th I got a Government Office message to say there was no Tynwald on Friday July 5th – there will be a Court in Douglas on 18th.

A concession was promised on Friday evening, and the strike over: the Governor I hear, gone to London to lay matters before the authorities.'

Lord Raglan offered a 10-and-a-half-penny loaf, but this was turned down by the bakers, and so Lord Raglan capitulated and agreed to keep the nine-penny loaf. He was called to the Home Office in London to account for his action, and given orders to return to the island with a scale of Manx Income Tax. The British Government said they would impose income tax on the Manx people if this did not happen within one week. Two-thirds of the £20,000 bread subsidy could be paid from income tax collected, the remaining third from the revenue of the island.

Hence income tax was levied on the island for the first time! [3] John wrote:

'The contention is complicated: the 'Keys' having a part in it. They claim this right to vote a subsidy to bakers to enable them to supply a cheap loaf. The authorities do not recognize this as a Constitutional right vested in the 'Keys', and would not yield it. The crowd only called for 9d loaf and rather abused the 'Keys' as an obstacle to their clamoured object.

Apparently the strikers did not care a rap about the political liberty rights (their own included) for whom the 'Keys' were contending. The Governor gave them fair words and promised the loaf, and now they praise him up and abuse the 'Keys', who are quite right in their contention, even if their method of contending for it was to seize the wrong moment! ...All is peace and quiet again.'

John continued:

'The boy (Jack) *walked with me to Laxey yesterday, coming up on the tram. He saw a naval officer, (RNVR paymaster), and recognized that he was a sailor. He spotted things I did not notice, and kept up a lively talk all the time.*

There has been illness in the drome where Vess was stationed; on his return there, he was sent to the aerodrome near Salisbury to other quarters.'

John wrote to Dono on July 10th regarding Lardy who was also ill:

'We had a letter from Lardy of two days ago. He has had influenza. He had just received a package of quinine, sent a month ago, and his letter dated Jul 1 arrived here on 8th.'

...Over 120 men in Lardy's Company succumbed to the flu in June and July. [28] The summer months of 1918 showed a marked increase in the 'Spanish Flu' epidemic. This was a deadly flu, which attacked young people more often than the elderly.

During July, battles continued on the Western Front in the Champagne region and Marne, and later, Soissonais & Ourcq.

On July 21st, John wrote:

'The news from France is better towards the end of the week. It is good enough to make me hang on to the daily wires and papers again.

I fancy Lardy is at present near Ypres. He is asking for more quinine, which he finds useful, and almost necessary in the damp conditions he has to put up with.'

...Lardy was possibly not at Ypres, unless he was involved with some railway transportation there.

According to the War Diary for July 1918, the No.3 Monmouth Railway Company headquarters moved from Frévent to Conteville, just below Auxi-le-Chateau on 22nd July, although headquarters was soon moved again to Bernâtre in the same area; work continued in this region with Chinese labour force and prisoners of war, constructing a new water main at Auxi. There were days of very heavy rain. [28]

John told Dono of Vess's new work:

'Vess has charge of 'A' Flight, Training Depot Squadron, at Lake Down, Salisbury – a place he does not like: and he seems rather impatient about it.

Nan was on holiday at Powfoot with Marge since July 1. She had influenza there, and got home on Wednesday. Her holiday was spoiled and she is not wholly well yet.

Last evening we heard from Mary that Graham is in France – a surprise to us. This makes Mary cancel her arrangement to come to the island.

Marge has heard from Frank Sherriff, who is still at the same station in India – which I take to be a convalescent camp: but I understand he is on the active list.

Things are quiet here as usual. The political 'dead-lock', as they delight to call the recent frictions between 'Keys' & Governor, seems to have settled down again. Uncle Thomas told me there is to be a Tynwald at St Johns on August 1st.

Daisy and boy are well. He is rather fond of forcing his way into my study, and will not be put off by being told I am busy. He says, "Are you very, very busy?"'

Dono also succumbed to the virulent flu in July, and was sent to hospital.

Whilst Dono was in hospital in Dover, he met his cousin, William Quine (the Surgeon mentioned earlier).

...The crew of *H.M.S. Termagant* were hit badly by the flu; only 26 men out of 150 were fit for duty. [2]

One of William Quine's fellow medics at the hospital asked him:

"There's someone in hospital with the same queer name as you – would it be a relation?"

Dono went to stay with William and his wife in Dover to recuperate, and later saw Lardy coming back from France on the familiar shape of the Isle of Man Steam Packet boat with its jazzy zigzags of camouflage.

Wires were sent from William at Dover to Daisy at the Vicarage in the Isle of Man:

July 27th 1918: 'Dono's doing well is ashore with us probably up Sunday sends best love – Will'

July 29th 1918: 'Dono very much better good appetite certainly up tomorrow for lunch he sends love to yourself and Jackie – Surgeon Quine'

John wrote on August 9th to Dono:

'We are much relieved to hear from Daisy, as also from your note to Nan received this evening, that you are fairly well – though certainly we know that you must be suffering the persistent effects of your attack of influenza.

I hope that you will be able to carry on till your expected leave, some ten days hence, and that you are able to take care against any further cold or chill.'

Whilst Dono was ill, Vess stationed at Salisbury seemed under less strain and John wrote:

'I hope that Vess may have got that turn in the direction of recuperation, which takes a long time to arrive after the intense strain of his six months work in France. There was an investiture by the Duke of Connaught at Salisbury yesterday: the men who had won decorations to

be there; Vess said that he was one of those attending (for his Military Cross Award). He had otherwise meant to attend one in London, with the King investing.'

Meanwhile, there had been incident in the island regarding an aeroplane, in the vicinity of the Vicarage. John reported:

'On Sunday last, 11.30am, an aeroplane landed in the field before Mr Kelly's, Baldroma – right at the house – a bad landing – for if it had run on 20 yards, it would have crashed. The airman, Lt. Smale, had served in France, and I think was suffering from airman's neurasthenia. He was taking a plane from Bangor to Stranraer to be used as an instruction plane. He meant to fly over the island, not necessarily to land; but not finding it in the fog he got nervous, and when he made it out, he landed. He had a bolt sheared, and a strut useless. I recommended Mr William Knox, who came up and made the repair.

He got away 2pm Monday, and I had a good view of his flight from Baroose, where I chanced to be on business: first to the mountains east of Snaefell, where he encountered cloud and came back, and went to the west or left of Snaefell. We heard he reached his destination.

The news from France continues good.

I have not yet heard the most recent, as we had no paper this evening. But 100 guns and 7000 prisoners are reported on the British sector yesterday. Also cavalry are to some extent able to get into action.'

...During August on the Western Front, Morville was retaken by British forces, as was Albert on 22nd August.

On the island the annual August fete at Silverdale was planned for August 22nd, and a balloon (possibly a silk spotting balloon) was to go to Silverdale. John and his wife dried and aired the balloon outside the Vicarage.

Regarding the Fete, John wrote:

'There was a Red Cross and Hospital Show at Silverdale yesterday. Nan went to assist. The Governor & Lady Raglan were there. Mother did not intend to go, and I was laid up with a chill, which I partly thought might be influenza.

Uncle Thomas asked for the 'balloon' and we sent it over. He intended to inflate it with gas, but could not get a permit. He had an old smith's bellows, which he had bought years ago, and with this he inflated the balloon with air, on the sheltered slope between trees, to which the sheets were made fast. It was a source of much interest, and considerable profit to the Red Cross.

They took about £300 (with £100 cheque from a donor)... '

...Proceeds: £440.

John continued:

'Things are very quiet, except that there have been a very much larger crowd of visitors this August than at any time for the last four years. There does not seem much shortage of food: but it is better here than on the mainland.

The news from France is very much better.

It would seem that Marshal Foch is a man of capacity: and it only argues the old argument – that he was not entrusted with the direction of affairs long ago. But doubtless American reinforcements count for much in enabling him to do what he is doing.'

John told Dono that Frank Sherriff was a correspondence clerk in the hospital transport office at Bombay, dealing with sailings of hospital ships.

Jas Wilson, in active service in France, had been injured again, but was improving satisfactorily; his wounds were in the chin & thigh. He was in a London hospital.

Lardy was well again, and after a brief respite back in the U.K., his work continued on the Frévent to Conteville line and Auxi to Frévent lines throughout August. The constantly changing orders on the Western Front caused some demoralisation and uncertainty in his Company – noted in the No.3 Monmouth Railway Company War Diary:

'...Received advice that original scheme of long loops instead of doubling line was again to come into force; this means that 50% of work completed will be wasted... continuing works in an efficient manner is impossible... it is very hard to know what to carry on with and what to leave undone...' [28]

Late August saw the 2nd Battle of Arras – the Battle of the Scarpe. Roye was recaptured by British forces, as was Bapaume. The final three months of the war were known as the 'Hundred Days', during which, startling advances were made by the Allies, pushing the German army to the point where peace was their only option.

By the end of September the Allies had breached the Hindenburg Line – the heavily fortified German defensive zone on the Western Front, but German forces continued to hold.

Regarding Dono's expected refit of *H.M.S Termagant* in August, John wrote:

> *'We are sorry to learn that your refit is not to take place so soon as we hoped.'*

However, Dono did not return to *H.M.S. Termagant*.

On September 28th Dono was assigned to another ship – appointment as 'Temporary Acting Engineer Lieutenant Commander'.

Dono wrote on September 29th 1918 (in Glasgow):

> *'My Own Darling Daisy, I am very sorry that I have not had a moment to write to you. On my return to the Termagant I found that I had been appointed away and I had to close my accounts in a great hurry. I was relieved by an Artificer Engineer and the Captain was rather fed up.*
>
> *My orders were to proceed to the works of Messrs. Stephen & Co., Govan, and my appointment is to H.M.S. Vivid for H.M.S. Sycamore.*
>
> *I left London last night and arrived today, and although I went straight to yard and a man showed me the boats, he only knew them by their numbers, and did not know which was mine. He thought mine was on the 'stocks' yet and would not be ready till after Xmas. I will try to verify this tomorrow if I can... I cannot afford to live in a hotel at the terrible prices obtaining here at present (due to large no. of American Officers). This afternoon I must look for lodgings.*
>
> *I have left quite a lot of my things on the Termagant to be sent on to Lonan. I have also sent my gun packed in a box.*
>
> *It's rather cold in Glasgow and I have a cold myself – I was quite ill after my arrival in London – I had a suspicion when I was at home that I was not in perfect health...*
>
> *I ought to get some leave (at my own expense) before Xmas... With fondest love. Remaining your own Dono. Love to Jack.'*

On October 1st Dono wrote to his wife again regarding his ship:

> *'My own Darling Di, I went to the works this morning and found that my vessel is not due for completion until the middle of June 1919; it may be September before she completes...*
>
> *This will have burst my 4th, my last chevron...'*

John told Dono that he had been speculating on him getting another move or change of ship, and wrote:

'From your letter to Daisy, and wire, we suppose that you are to have a repetition of the 1915 job at Port Glasgow, and that the new ship is in a not very advanced state, or otherwise, that she is a larger class.

We shall be much interested to know, so far as you are free to say, what tonnage, speed, HP, etc. she is. Daisy says that as things are at present, lodgings are difficult to get and very expensive...

It seems to me that as engineer officers on active service, and even in the most important stunts, get so little recognition or none at all, that there is no professional disadvantage to an engineer officer in being on a supervision job ashore.

It seems to me to some degree an advantage to be in this job: for in active service your theoretical knowledge is apt to get rusty: this may be an opportunity to freshen it all up again. I would do that: because now you will, I hope, be able to get regular night's sleep.

Considering the 'strike' epidemics on the Clyde, it is a place of some responsibility.

The old rule: 'it is the unexpected that happens'.'

Mary had gone to Leicester to see Graham, wounded by a bomb dropped from an aeroplane. John reported:

'The wound is in his right arm. He is very cheerful, and will not be any use for soldiering for a very considerable time.

Marge heard from Frank Sherriff; he is well and has got a month's leave to go to Missouri in the hills.

Yesterday the war news was very good – so far as it went: it seems to be the early stage of a considerable offensive. If things go so well for a while, the Western Front will be a more hopeful outlook!'

On October 7th 1918, John wrote to Dono:

'We are glad to have your letter, though knowing from Daisy the general facts of things around you...

Of naval matters, you come with a vast amount of added experience, compared with when you took charge of a somewhat like job at Port Glasgow... Hoping that you get the hang of the work all right.

We are getting a permit to send Graham eggs and butter – as no eggs at least can be got in Leicester, nor at Worthing... Neither boat left here yesterday by account of heavy gale; also the elec. Telegraph communication was interrupted, and no wire today of war news.'

Daisy and Jack travelled up to Glasgow to be near to Dono. (Daisy was pregnant again – her baby due in January 1919.) John had not heard from Lardy for about a fortnight – rather longer than usual, but in October John wrote to Dono:

'We have heard from Lardy; he is well. They have been erecting a pumping station, already tested.

The locality I think is well to the north, but he gives no hint. There are plenty of partridges about where he is: so it must be back from the Front zone.'

The No.3 Monmouth Railway Company were working on the Domléger water supply, but also took over the work of erecting a water pump at Conchil near the west coast of France, north west of Abbeville, which was inspected towards the end of October. [28] John wrote later:

'Lardy last evening is troubled with neuralgia – I think partly from his teeth having suffered from the bad water in the Albert sector.

They have completed a pumping station, and his Co. has gone to another smaller job: but he has been detained to see how it works in the hands of those taking over the charge of it.'

On October 17th, King Albert and the Queen of Belgium along with Admiral Keyes entered the city of Ostend by sea. By October 20th, the coast of Belgium was back in the hands of the Allies, and the protective mines around Ostend and Zeebrugge were soon swept up. John wrote:

'The papers say the Belgian coast is being evacuated. There seems no doubt that the Western Front of the Germans is bending and even breaking on its present lines...

I took a philosophical view of Termagant being the ship that took the Belgian King to Ostend: you missed a Belgian decoration probably: but one never knows in the long run whether you were not as well in the move made.'

On October 21st John wrote to Dono:

'By this evening's Times, the line by Ghent to the Dutch frontier, and the whole coast is accessible from the sea. How strange that the Belgian coast work has undergone so soon, so complete a change: you practically stood the racket of it till it finished.

Mary does not have much to say very bright about Graham; he is very weak – the fracture in his shoulder causing trouble, though the flesh wounds seem to have progressed favourably. He is having a painful time: it is necessary to stretch his arm, after being kept so long in the same splints, in order to draw the muscles out of contracted growth – that if not stretched, would render the arm almost useless.

There is not much news locally.

The fighting is expensive: the casualty list very large, I understand. It seems to me the French are fighting with intense energy – having the hated enemy more and more at their mercy. They are making for Hirson, the railway communication ganglion. The Americans are having a fierce struggle north of the Argonne, in their attempt to cut across the other line of communications.

So far the Germans have succeeded in withdrawing without catastrophe. I am wondering if another American Army is to attempt an advance by Lorraine.

The heavy casualty list includes its proportion of Manx soldiers; someone told me 21 deaths were reported last week.'

On the Western Front, the newer tactics incorporated into the later ground battles of 1918 – tanks in particular, and the involvement of American troops, had made a difference. There were no further battles of note at sea, although plans were afoot for a battle between the Grand Fleet and the German Fleet, but on October 28th 1918, sailors in the German Fleet began to mutiny and resisted repeated orders to go to sea. Discontent spread through Germany, with rebellions and revolts.

John had a great deal to say about Germany, and on October 27th 1918, wrote:

'I do not think the Germans regard themselves as beaten, though they know themselves foiled: it is now for them a question of how to come off least badly for themselves and most badly for us. By the Germans I mean the 'possessors' of Germany: a group of Kings, the King of Prussia at the head of them, the rest including arch-dukes, dukes etc., probably 30 or 40, plus a landed aristocracy class. That monarchy as it exists in Germany should absolutely 'go' is all important: and it may seem a paradox, but yet may be true that it is far more important that all the petty Kings should go and be scrapped absolutely than that the Kaiser should go.

Monarchy in Germany and monarchy here in England or in the British Empire are two totally different things. Monarchy in England is but a symbol for the State, which is practically a democracy; monarchy in Germany is the Kaiser, embodying that idea...

To suppose that the privileged classes in Germany will give in, with the loss of all those things they have possessed and enjoyed, is so unlikely as to be incredible to me! And I expect all their votes are but for the purpose of gaining time and flattering public opinion in Allied countries.'

Dono managed to find lodgings for himself, Daisy and Jack. John wrote:

'We are glad to hear that you have found a fairly good house, or lodging.

We saw in the Times, Oct 25, the investiture list, Vess's name among them for his Military Cross. Vess has had malaria again, and bleeding of the nose several times, somewhat severely. He has been flying for nearly two years!

We hear that Lt. Col. Crellin has been killed in France, and that Capt. Harry, son of the Norton St Hotel people, has died in Africa. Crellin had remarkably rapid promotion. His wife was doing hospital work at Worthing along with Mary.'

Regarding Dono's new work, on October 29th John advised:

'...of all the things in the world not to do, it is to accept what others have done (or not done) as grounds for you doing (or not doing) it. I might rather say that the opposite would be a better rule.

The other engineers standing by their ships cannot set any precedent on which you are to be deterred from seeing everything that concerns your ship; nor can their not liking to go into the workshops (for whatever reason) bar you.

You have a professional obligation to see everything, and extend your acquaintance with any machine or device that goes into the construction of your ship! That the builders 'would not like it', is the weakest sort of excuse...'

John had noted the news in the London *Times* newspaper and wrote:

'It seems that the question now in Austria, and tending to be so in Germany, is, 'who is the Government?'

There seem to be half a dozen distinct Governments in Austria. In Germany the civil power has had no authority over army & navy: the Kaiser, who is pure & simple a military chief has had all power.

There is a certain measure of movement in Germany, like rats under straw, of a civil power asserting itself; that is, a new civil power struggling to come into existence – possibly not to come into existence except by revolution and class feuds.

But the Kaiser, as a military head pure & simple, can only say one thing or the other to the Allies – 'I fight, or I surrender!' His own theory is 'I am the army! I am Germany – that is the German Army & Navy!'

Germany is not a nation at all: it is one man...'

John wrote on November 6th:

'The news continues good from the Western Front, as from the others. The reference of all German overtures to Marshal Foch seems to imply that the Allied Council have ground to believe that Marshal Foch has the business potentially mastered.

Do you remember my repeatedly saying four years ago, that Sweden & Greece were our severest handicap and that eventually the way to Berlin was via Vienna?

We hope most sincerely that you may all three escape influenza, but in any case, be prompt to lie up, and continue for a fortnight to be extremely careful against chill etc...'

The months of October and November saw the highest number of deaths from the virulent influenza. Dono, working on *H.M.S. Sycamore* wrote:

'The virulent infectious influenza was still active, and the Engineer Officers of the new Destroyer H.M.S. Spindrift and H.M.S. Sabre, were both down with the illness. H.M.S. Sabre was ready for sea and anchored at the Tail of the Bank, near Greenock.

I was aware of prevailing conditions and somewhat surprised to receive orders from the Admiral Superintendent Clyde to proceed to the naval base at Rosyth on the north bank of the Forth, to join H.M.S. Sable as Engineer Officer. After packing my gear, I got my travel warrant, and proceeded by train from Glasgow to Edinburgh, and then across the Forth Bridge to the base at Rosyth.

On the journey I began to wonder if it were possible that it was the 'Sabre' and not the 'Sable' which I was to join, and wrote down the Morse dots and dashes for the two. I found there was only one dot difference between the 'L' in Sable: 'dot, dash, dot, dot', and the 'R' in Sabre: 'dot, dash, dot'. All the other letters were the same.

On arrival I was not surprised to be told that the Sable had an Engineer Officer on board, and received instructions to return to Greenock to join the Sabre!' [2]

The Kaiser abdicated on November 9th 1918 and there was a ceasefire on all Fronts.

Dono continued:

'I was fortunate to get a train to Edinburgh, and on to Glasgow, and arrived on board the Sabre at Greenock at exactly 11am on Saturday November 11th 1918, to be informed that not only had the Armistice begun, but also that the Engineer Officer of the Sabre had recovered sufficiently to take up his job – all this for one 'dot'!' [2]

John wrote later:

'We gathered from Daisy's note that the incident of your being called to Rosyth, Greenock, was some wire mistake at the Admiralty. I hope that you have settled down again, and are no worse for your rush about.'

Armistice

November 11th 1918 heralded the signing of the Armistice, and wireless message announcement from the Eiffel Tower, Paris.

The guns fell silent, and four and a half years of war were finally over, but the 'truce' was still to be signed by Germany! Unfortunately many men still died after the ceasefire as it took time for the news to filter through in some areas.

John wrote on November 18th 1918:

> *'The news is extremely scanty at present. I cannot form any idea of what is going on in Germany. It seems that the Kaiser is waiting for a 'Coup d'etat', or upset of the six socialists, in order to go back to Berlin.'*

Three days later on November 21st 1918, around 240 victorious ships of the Grand Fleet assembled in the Firth of Forth in line formation with captured German ships in the centre.

The Manx ship *S.S. King Orry* had a place of honour at the centre of this formation. There were three cheers as *H.M.S. Oak* came alongside. The spectacular parade of ships set sail for Scapa Flow, and Admiral Beatty proclaimed:

> *'The German flags will be lowered at sunset and will not be hoisted again.' [4]*

John wrote:

> *'I see that the Oak is the class of destroyer attached to the flagship of Admiral Beatty: this vessel took the German officer to the Admiral's ship.*
>
> *It would be interesting if you get a job on the German ships that are being surrendered – to examine their structure etc.'*

In Douglas a thanksgiving was called by the Mayor in the Villa Marina and this was attended by 3000 people including the Lieutenant Governor, Lord Raglan, and Manx novelist, Sir Hall Caine.

By November 1918 there were 24,450 prisoners in Knockaloe Camp on the Isle of Man. Only 16% of the internees took up residence again in Britain, and almost a year passed before the final men departed from the Camp: the last 175 marched out in October 1919.

All that eventually remained of the Camp in years to come was the sewage discharge pipe from Knockaloe Camp, and a mountain of old rusty tins contained by barbed wire in the sea caves at the foot of Peel Hill. During the war these tins were tipped over the cliff by the men in Camp, along with a great deal of other debris.

[See Knockaloe.im for further information]

The photo, showing the two Knockaloe farms, was taken from the direction of Peel Castle, and shows the open fields in the valley (left) where the Camp and huts once stood, as they are today.

Corrin's Folly is to the right, on top of the hill, and the hill and Folly would have been the dominant view from the Camp.

Photo by Julie Quine 2016

Thoughts on the War, & Aftermath

Following the war, John had a good deal more to say on the matter.

He wrote:

'Historians in the future will have much to say of the way in which the Allies have allowed the war to end: and perhaps if they had decided to end it in a more business like way, it would have meant 50 years added to the period of peace!

A League of Nations is absolute delusion! If one thinks what a 'Nation' means, it is a contradiction in terms, an impossibility – except for a brief and special contingency such as the present alliance.

There is a time when a new class of human passions will come into intense activity – that is the concern for one's future, and unconcern for others in a time of industrial & economic stress.

Personally I am absolutely dissatisfied with the way the war has been allowed to end: the knock-out blow so long promised was not made good when it was absolutely in the power of the Allied high command to administer it.

A profound disappointment and dissatisfaction has been my only feeling – or constantly predominant feeling! It is all so bad, so wrong, that it is inexplicable, except on hypotheses which imply that the English nation & the French are being sacrificed to financiers or politicians.

Talking of the country 'being regenerated by the war' – very far indeed from that – but the greatest mess made in history – or on the largest scale! However politics are only made for people in 'position', and one's own concerns are bitterly forced home on one as the only thing to mind!'

Lardy did not expect 'leave' and thought that his work would continue for six months or so. Vess decided to stay in air-service work. Regarding Dono, John wrote:

'The Board of Trade or Lloyds are possible directions for you – though perhaps it is not necessary to hurry. Or is it better to feel early in that direction?

I was in Ramsey on Tuesday; on Wednesday morning before returning I walked by the harbour and saw two salvage pontoons in the har-

bour, of the Ardrossan Salvage Co.; Telford Cain, a man I know at the Steam Packet Office, told me they had been there for 13 weeks unsuccessfully trying to lift a small steamer sunk about 300 yards from the pier head: big chains snapping etc. We hear that there are crowds of ships of different classes in the Tyne that have been raised on the east coast.

They are putting up a fete for naval & military war funds at the Villa Marina before Xmas, to raise say £2000. It was Aunt Eva's idea – to the extent of trying to raise £50 or so, by tea-table & stall.

The thing has this objection that a disappointed and cheated nation cannot rejoice! Also 'charity' in the common acceptance of the word is not the way by which these funds should be found, but the Government to provide, and to find it from Governor property territory, customs duties, or mines, etc.

Mother's Guild group are working for the fete... The Guild has raised £360 in two years past – over £400, if they count contribution of effort to a Xmas parcel stunt Nov 1916 – very good!'

...The Grand Fete took place on December 19th 1918 in the Villa Marina in aid of Manx and National War Charities.

John continued:

'I expect even in this parish and more in Laxey, some distress when the young women now earning (for this place) good wages at fabric work (Palace & Derby Castle – silk balloons, socks etc.) *are paid off. They have learnt the most deteriorating thing for a woman, bad for a man, worse for a woman – to spend money! They will be, not to say useless as servants – for people have got to do without servants – and places will not be easily found. We shall have to give poor relief to the homes where now there is much waste going on.*

I am wishful later at the first opening to get our war memorial on foot, and in occupation of the field here.'

On November 24th 1918, Lord Raglan sent his resignation as Governor of the Isle of Man to the Home Secretary in London, but did not announce this to the Keys until December 17th – in his last Government meeting.

At the beginning of December, John wrote regarding Vess:

'Vess writes fairly cheerfully. He is on the 'qui vive' he says, as to indications of employment. He is hoping for a leave about Xmas. He says the way the U.S.A. collected souvenirs prior to departure would have

done credit to the Crown Prince. He was fortunate in losing only a pair of flying gloves and an R.A.F. badge.

I see the number of submarines destroyed (or captured) totalled 200. I wonder how many of these were bagged in the 1915 campaign. The number of Manx casualties total about 1000, probably an average rate.

Things are very quiet, and news is chiefly of the English Elections.'

...Official records showed that 8,261 Manx men enlisted (82.3% of the male population of military age). Of these men, 1,165 lost their lives and 987 men were wounded.

John wrote to Dono on December 8th 1918:

'We are glad you continue to keep well. I am sure that this influenza is a 'poison malaria' – probably from the battlefields of Europe. I cannot understand indeed how the armies have escaped collapse from pestilence.

What you say about the expense of living I realized beforehand; I am glad that for some portion of the time of the war you were able to be under less expense through Daisy and the boy being here.

Lardy has been made a Second Corporal: promotion evidently very slow in that branch. On what principle promotions are made, no explanation exists...

Vess wrote from Bromwich near Birmingham – where he had gone to get a machine.

Graham is progressing and has been moved from Leicester to a hospital at Brighton: Mary hopes he will now get to Worthing hospital!

I hear the I.O.M. CO. have ordered from Lairds – two steamers – Ben-my-Chree type at £180,000 each.'

...Out of the 15 Manx ships in service, 11 were requisitioned by the Admiralty during WWI. Of these, 4 were lost: *Ben-my-chree*, *Empress Queen*, *Ramsey*, and *Snaefell* (torpedoed on her way to Malta in June 1918). 3 Manx ships were retained by the Government, and 4 returned to service: *Peel Castle*, *Viking*, *King Orry* and *Mona's Queen*.

Regarding further employment, John advised Dono:

'Should there be a demobilization of temp. Commissions R.N. you ought to retain a permanent honorary rank, either Lt. R.N. hon, or Lt. Commander R.N.R.; I think this is important. If you go out of R.N. Service, get by all means (if possible) into Lloyds or Board of Trade – because of the pension! Otherwise, ship building perhaps.

I see that mad things are being done – absolutely unjust to the soldiers.

Munition workers out of employ get for 6 months 24/- a week, whereas the soldiers are getting miserable doles, not at all as if their service was as good to the country as the munition men who had big wages – no risk – no wounds!'

Dono had been ill again; John wrote on December 29th 1918:

'We have heard that you were laid up, and are hoping you are better, or convalescent.

Vess got home on Saturday Dec 21st – after a Medical Board at Matlock on Dec 20th. The Board passed him 'fit'; he certainly looks more definitely fit than when he was at home a year ago, or in his short run home in the summer.

He is Disciplinary Officer of a camp at Boscombe Down, near Salisbury, a fairly good job. He is responsible for all the men in the camp (R.A.F.) of men who expect to demobilize; but as he knows, will not be demobilized for some time yet – say several months. To the question put to him (as to others) if he wanted to demobilize, he answered 'no': he intends to stay on in the R.A.F.'

At the beginning of 1919, Lardy finally arrived home at the Vicarage on leave, his first since the wearing action of March 1918. John wrote:

'He looks thin but very wiry and I should say very well indeed! He tells us of his experiences in the great avalanche of March. (See April 1918)

He has lately been on detachment, half a dozen on a pumping station 300' boring, for water for troops. This was quite away from the Front – about a dozen miles from Abbeville towards Bethune.

He speaks with the greatest scorn and contempt of the O.C. and of the officers generally; their knowledge nil and their inefficiency 100%: their only outfit, a certain amount of swank. Occasionally there was an officer who had intelligence and a certain amount of business manner to whom things could be explained... They employ natural responses covering their ignorance, and place that poor instinct in the place that ought to be occupied by a desire to know and understand!

He always found Canadians different: they stood more or less on the bed-rock of common sense and on attention to the facts of things; the same of medical officers. Fortunately there is none of that morbid sentiment which (if it existed) would make him regard with horror his three days fighting on the Ancre: he remains as cheerfully unaffected by it as if it had been shooting down an army of rats.'

Lardy crossed back to his Company. John wrote on January 12th 1919:

'I was rather sorry for him, after so long a period of hard work, going back to comparative drudgery with no certainty of demobilization, which may mean another year. He is a 2nd Corporal, a trifling difference superior to Lance Corporal, but with one arm stripe, and pay half-way between private & corporal, it is not very much after 4 years.'

...By the end of the war, there were 45 Companies engaged in Standard Gauge Railway Construction. At the end of the war there was still much line repair work to be done to restore lines of communication. Demobilisation didn't come for some until August 1919.

John continued:

'We hear that a recurrence of influenza epidemic is affecting Douglas: all schools closed again for a month. Mother and Nan keep very well. Things are very quiet. A good many young soldiers seem to have secured demobilization, but their having been in hospital may explain it.

I met a young man yesterday, formerly a clerk; a year and a half at Knockaloe Camp: subsequently 2 years in the army. Of them he spent 2 months in France – was wounded in hand & shoulder – the rest in hospital and convalescent hospital. He told me he is now as well as ever, and going to seek a job in Manchester. These young men philosophize: they have reduced and summed up things to one point: his was 'well the war has taught us one thing, that Englishmen cannot be leaders of men!' At first flash I took it to be mean Foch v. Haig; but found he meant that all the officers of his battalion were absolutely inefficient – swank their sole asset for their job.

One young officer in his Battalion knew his work and had spirit; but he was 'no class' with the others, having seemingly come from modest home environment etc. This sentiment, which I had no object in approving or disapproving of – merely to listen to, struck me as practically what I have heard from a good number of others – as if the impression was extensively affecting the soldiers.'

Dono's wife gave birth to their second child on January 14th 1919, and Dono's cold symptoms continued. John wrote to him on January 19th:

'It may be the reaction from strain of your three years active Service

at sea, and in part from the smoky and acid poisoned atmosphere of Glasgow. I wish you could have a few months rest in the country.'

John wrote on February 1st 1919:

'A cutting from a German paper, in yesterday's Times seems quite refreshing in its attempt to say what it thinks – to the German army. The German army, in spite of its organization, was in greater essentials, even worse than our own, and so lost the war!

I hear that at Havre there have been on two occasions, very serious outbursts of indignation on the part of soldiers – I was told – because they found themselves being embarked in a class of ship that led them to think they were being sent to Russia. The objection is not, I gather, so much because they are not demobilized, as because others are, with less claim than themselves.

Vess seems to see the outlook ahead very dark for the Country: he thinks a spirit, for which he can find no better name than Bolshevism, is fermenting, and will be in ebullition a year hence! I have no means of knowing or judging here, away from opportunity of seeing anything for myself.

Lardy's Company is being demobilized; the men who were in active Service in 1914 already off; the volunteers of 1914, of whom only ten including himself are left, to get off as soon as they have jobs. He wants to get an opening in Bibby's Line to Australia.

We see by today's paper that there has been serious trouble in Glasgow. The Times now talks of 'class' war being the motive.'

On February 11th 1919, John wrote:

'Vess seems to have got a job as a demobilization officer, which shows that some notice is being taken of his capacity for business... circumstances of the time are such as to increase the intensity of the scramble for employment.

Indeed the national, financial, economic, and political situation for the next 12 months is one of extreme uncertainty. The demobilized men will be in a reactionary state, full of dissatisfactions!

Even as influenza seems to be affecting the whole globe, so unrest seems everywhere!'

...In 1920 it was estimated that around 21.5 million people died from the 1918 flu pandemic, but later the estimate rose to 50 million, approximately one fifth of the world population. World War I claimed around 16 million lives.

[www.archives.gov/exhibits/influenzaepidemic]

On February 18th 1919, Lord Raglan had a farewell luncheon with the *House of Keys* in Douglas, and left the island a couple of months later.

The Peace Treaty of Versailles was signed on June 28th 1919 by delegates of the German Empire. On the whole, the English thought that the terms of the Treaty were fair but could have been more severe; German reaction on the other hand was negative causing resentment, as Germany lost 10% of its land, its colonies, 12.5% of its population, 16% of its coal and 48% of its iron industry. [31]

In the Isle of Man, the celebration of the end of World War I came on June 14th 1920, with the planned Carnival taking place in Douglas. Two navy ships also visited the island that day, and the Steam Packet boats were back in action!

The Douglas Victory Carnival on June 14th 1920: H.S. Cowin

Their Majesties the King and Queen and Her Royal Highness Princess Mary also visited the island on the 14th and 15th July 1920. [3]

The Impact of World War I

John was thankful that his family had remained intact throughout World War I. Regarding the impact of the war, in 1919 he wrote:

> *'...Two classes of people seem to me to stand out in contrast during the past five years – those who have found and made the war an opportunity to amass money, and those who have sacrificed five years out of the very core of their lives for their country!*
>
> *There is an intermediate class who in doing the latter have also gained development of themselves and secured some measure of status, so that in future they are in a very different position from the broken soldier, relegated back to tramp the mill round of toil, under worse conditions than before. The wealthy classes, at least those in finance & business, will be wealthier than before; the generality of the people will be far poorer than before! The intermediate class will have lost little, but not gained very much.'*

The Isle of Man suffered greatly in respect of loss of holiday makers and took years to recover from this. Many islanders never did. There were 2000 boarding houses in Douglas before the war began, but by the end of it, some 700 were abandoned. The collapsed economy of the island led to the realisation that to survive, diversification was necessary.

The cost to families and children during World War I was immense. Children suffered from the lack of a father figure during their early significant years (if their fathers returned at all).

Dono's son, Jack, was fortunate in that he had grandparents who were prepared to help his mother whilst his father was at sea. Many women were left to cope when their husbands did not return from war, and poverty was a new warfare for many families.

The complacent Edwardian work ethics were left far behind, and the reduced number of men available for work during and after the war meant that women became more widely involved in industry, replacing their days of servitude to the rich.

World War I caused great devastation and loss of life. However, the technological advancements made during the war years as a result of warfare on land, in the air and at sea, were rapid and immense.

Lonan & Laxey War Memorial Unveiling

War Memorial, All Saints Church Lonan

John was true to his word regarding erecting two War Memorials in All Saints Church, Church Road, Lonan; Archibald Knox designed both.

The unveiling of the first war memorial tablet (by Mr L. Goldie-Taubman) took place on Sunday afternoon, January 9th 1921. Over 300 people attended. The memorial was dedicated to the men of Lonan and Laxey who fell in the Great War; the inscription read: *'To the greater glory of God and in memory of the men of Lonan and Laxey who fell in the Great War, A.D. 1914-1919'.*

'A laurel wreath was placed on the central orbit of the tablet by Mrs Quine, and Mr Taubman placed a cross of flowers beside it. Rev. Canon John Quine referred briefly to Mr Taubman's distinguished work on behalf of Manx Sailors and Soldiers during the years of stress and agony entailed by the war.

The tablet, surmounted by the ancient arms of the Isle of Man (the Viking galley) is set on a hatchment, the emblem of mourning. On the tablet slab is the Sword of Man, enamelled in steel, the hilt in red coral enamel, with the guard and pommel bearing the Three Legs of Man.

The 41 names of the fallen are in gold letters in three columns on the main face of the white marble. The marble mason-work was by Mr R. W. Creer of Douglas'. [21]

The other Memorial, dedicated to the men of Lonan and Laxey who served in the Great War, was unveiled by the Lord Bishop of Sodor and Man on Sunday April 17th 1921.

John wrote the following Dedication Hymn for the occasion: (to the tune 'Wiltshire') [1: J60:39403/3]

Their names to live by valour's right
In adamant we place,
For other eyes in memory's night,
As starry orbs to trace.

A sword, their war companion,
Upon this stone is laid –
The symbol bright of victory won
In liberty's crusade.

By faith they fought a world to free:
This stone shall be a shrine
For men to read their agony
Here writ in every line.

Thou faint of heart, yet draw thou near;
And learn their sacrifice,
That knew in danger's hour no fear,
And pledged their life as price.

Oh noble hearts! Whate'er betide
Of wars from age to age,
You stood in battle side by side:
And our's the heritage.

Shall we in apathy forget?
Be lulled by dreams of peace?
When sun and moon must witness yet
Earth's woe till time shall cease.

'Not peace I bring, but sword and strife,'
Is still our Captain's call:
Then come, one hour of glorious life,
And in his ranks to fall! Amen.

A later addition was made to the memorial on the north side of the church in 1938 in the form of a teak carved shrine made by Mr Kelly (to use the remainder of the War Memorial Fund money). The new Lieutenant Governor accompanied by his wife, Lady Rose, unveiled the shrine.

It was inscribed 'How can men die better.'

What became of Dono, Lardy and Vess...?

The Future

1921 – (Left to right) Dono, Lardy, Jack (Dono's son), John Quine, Vess

The above photograph celebrates the fact that the three young men had survived the long years of World War I.

Dono:

Holding the distinction of Engineer Lieutenant Commander at the end of the war, Dono was relatively unscathed in terms of injury compared to his brothers, with the exception of his dose of the virulent flu.

A model of the gun-sight which Dono devised and submitted in 1916 to the Commander-in-Chief, Whale Island, Portsmouth, was thought to be displayed there and the design was possibly implemented.

The lack of any recognition for Dono's submarine net remained a disappointment to his father, but during those years of great stress, a great many decisions were made on the spot without thought of who, why or when; it was perhaps naïve to believe that he was the only person capable of designing such a deterrent to submarines.

> ...Some sources suggest that a Submarine Attack Committee was set up at the Admiralty in December 1914 and attention centred on the development of the net. However preliminary experiments had been going on for some time. The previous October, a scheme was suggested by Captain Doughty for the employment of nets and floating buoys with or without explosives – experiments with nets were made at Harwich – the original idea being to employ fishing-nets such as those used by

drifters. These developed into 'indicator nets', the submarine becoming entangled, fouling the propeller. [www.naval-history.net]

Dono remained in full-time Royal Navy work for a year after the end of WWI, and was appointed to *H.M.S. Spindrift* in March 1919. His next adventure was in the September of 1919 in *H.M.S. Valentine* as Engineer Officer, where he encountered a rather strange occurrence on an Island in the Baltic – a lady of high standing, in hiding on one of the islands – a lady whom he at first thought could have been Anastasia; a belief he sought to establish throughout his life. [2]

He was awarded the R.N. Long Service and Good Conduct Medal for his naval services, as well as the 1914-15 Star and British War and Victory medals. In March 1918 John gained the distinction, D.S.O., when he became a Companion of the Distinguished Service Order and allowed to use the letters after his name.

...The 1914-15 Star was awarded to anyone who had served in any theatre of war against Germany between Aug. 5th 1914 and Dec. 31st 1915, and was awarded alongside the British War Medal 1914 to 1918 and the Victory Medal.

[www.greatwar.co.uk/medals]

Dono had a lifelong interest in wireless (Morse signals were his hobby), and he wrote in his memoirs:

'After the war I applied for a transmitting licence again to resume my studies, as triode valves were available.

Unfortunately my application was refused by the Post Office and I accepted their decision – the disappointment not forgotten.'

Dono turned down the opportunity of naval experience on a submarine in favour of a few flying lessons; after moving to Hull and becoming a Chief Instructor at the Hull Technical College, he took a course in aviation, becoming a qualified pilot.

He was often referred to as Commander Quine, even after he fully retired from part-time naval work in 1931.

At the end of February 1940, shortly after the outbreak of WWII and death of his father, Dono gave up his job in Hull and moved back to the Isle of Man to be with his family; there he lived out his days (to the age of 93) with his wife Daisy in one of the ex-Knockaloe WWI huts, which he transported across the island in pieces when the huts were sold off.

Dono lived an eventful life as documented in the books:

'Odyssey of a Marine Engineer', & *'Engineer to MHK'*. [2] He became a member of the Manx *House of Keys* for a number of years, following in the footsteps of other Quine members.

Lardy:

It appears that Lardy had the toughest time of the three sons during WWI.

He was awarded the British War Medal and Victory Medal, as well as the 1914-15 Star.

However there was a tragic end regarding his Belgian sweetheart, Yvonne Armand, whom he had intended to marry when the war ended. It must have shattered Lardy's dreams, and disheartened him a great deal to learn that she was shot by Germans in some act of retribution during WW1. [30]

The truth regarding her death may one day be known!

Lardy returned to work on the Steam Packet ships after the war, married in 1927, and a daughter followed in 1933; he asked his wife if his daughter could be named Yvonne out of honour and respect to his sweetheart.

Lardy's previous experiences did not deter him from serving his country again during WWII. He worked on board the Manx ship *S.S. King Orry*, the same ship which had served during WWI as part of the Grand Fleet.

The ship *S.S. King Orry* finally met its end when it was bombed during the Dunkirk evacuation in 1940, but Lardy survived; after six hours immersed in the sea, he was rescued, though he was badly injured with a shattered heel, which remained an encumbrance for the rest of his life.

After WWII he returned to work on the Manx Steam Packet ships. Later he became a volunteer in the Naval Mine-watching Service along with other family members, reporting movements along the Manx coast.

In 1970, aged 83, Lardy tripped and sadly died from a head injury. Dono wrote the following:

> *'In WWI his practical experience of locomotive engines, track laying, signals, points and crossings, the curvature of rails and practical details of rolling stock for the ammunition trains was most useful.*
>
> *During the advance of the German army, the Royal Engineers took their place in the line using their rifles to repel the advancing enemy troops.*
>
> *Lawrence was a first class rifle shot and a marksman of note in the Quine family.'*

Vess:

Vess never returned to legal work, but remained in the R.A.F., living an action packed life. He married Hilda Toulouse in 1920 (Hilda was the friend to whom he wrote the many letters during WWI), and a son, William, was born in 1925.

Vess served as an instructor at the R.A.F. Electrical and Wireless School in the Middle East, and also worked in Palestine where he learnt Arabic.

Returning to the U.K., Vess became H.Q. Signals Officer. Then in 1932 he saw his childhood ambition fulfilled when he returned to Cairo and became Chief Signals Officer, ranked as Squadron Leader. He was back in the U.K. in 1935, and was promoted to Wing Commander of R.A.F. Driffield, Yorkshire in 1937.

Vess served again in WWII with involvement in top secret radar navigation, retiring as Group Captain in 1945. Having qualified as a Chartered Electrical Engineer whilst in the R.A.F., he then worked on the construction of new British power stations.

He returned to the Isle of Man in 1955 (with his second wife Lois, whom he married in 1949), and indulged in many hobbies and interests, including voluntary work, commanding Home Defence in parts of the island: observing movements of aircraft & measuring radioactive fallout. In 1961 he stood for the *House of Keys*, unfortunately at the same time as his brother, Dono. As the vote was split, neither of them gained a seat; this caused a very deep rift in their relationship: they never spoke to each other again.

An Old Comrades Association was formed when the WWI Manx Company was demobilised, with reunions around March 6th every year. In 1970, Vess took on the presidency of the group until his death in 1978.

All three brothers served their country with some patriotism; this should not be forgotten; they were the fortunate ones!

Graham and **Frank** both lived long lives. Frank returned to the textile trade as a Company Director, spent some time in Milan, Italy, with wife Marge and daughter Peggy, and died in 1952 aged 64. Mary's husband, Graham, died in 1956. They had one daughter, Betty.

The **Surgeon, William** (son of John's brother, Richard) died young aged 35 in 1923.

Final Word

I hope you found the adventures of the three young men enlightening: their activities, suffering and anguish, both in the Isle of Man and on the shores beyond.

What has been said here is only a fraction of what happened during the years of World War I, also known as the Great War. I found it a great surprise to learn of John's interest in the war and its technicalities, as well as his awareness of the impact of war on the island and on the wider fronts.

Canon John Quine lived an active and long life in the Lonan community. Of course World War II began in 1939, and John finally made up his mind to retire from Church life and move to a bungalow in Baldrine with his wife.

Unfortunately he died in February 1940 aged 82 years due to ill health, shortly after his announcement of his retirement in the Church magazine. He was greatly missed after his death, and many people paid tribute to him.

His grand-daughter, Betty Robinson, remembered:

> *'I was in the Island in May 1940 when Dunkirk was going on, and I met an old lady at the foot of the Church Road, and we talked about the Manx ships which were there ferrying troops back, and all the sad days we were experiencing. The lady said, "You know my dear, this is when we miss the Canon. He could have explained to us why this must happen and he could have comforted us."'*

~

If you have enjoyed reading this book, your views would be greatly appreciated. E-mail: books@juliequine.co.uk

Other Amazon eBooks edited/compiled by Julie Quine:

Odyssey of a Marine Engineer *(Merchant & Royal Navy stories): John Lindsay Quine. Edited & compiled by Julie Quine 2013 (Amazon). Paperback version available ISBN 9781540318121.*

Balnahawin, *&* ***Cross's Folly***: *(Canon) John Quine – historical stories based around the Isle of Man.*

Brassy Lass: *Julie Quine – a musical biography and history of a small village brass band.*

Acknowledgements

I am very grateful to Colin Kay (Grand-son of Dono), educated historian and author, who helped to iron out some idiosyncrasies in the book stemming from my inadequate knowledge of this subject area. Thanks are also due to Janet Tideman (Vess's Grand-daughter) for suggesting a few ideas and format changes.

My family maintained a great deal of patience and support throughout the book-writing process, my husband particularly, who helped keep things moving when I was overwhelmed by the enormous amount of work; he finally managed to read the book to the end, suggesting a number of changes on the way. My daughters also contributed: Christina made a great job of the book cover for which I was very grateful, and Teresa was great at solving technical problems.

Thanks to the Manx Museum and Manx Air Museum, who kindly allowed me to photograph a great deal of documentation.

Appendix

[a] 1910 Letter from Vess

April 1910 to Dono:

Dear Dono, I go back to College tomorrow and Marge also crosses to Whitelands. I enclose some cuttings which will I think interest you. They are about the London to Manchester flight. The photos don't give much of an idea of what the aeroplane is like.

I am going to make a model aeroplane at the College workshops this term. I hope you won't forget to see about designing that Helio for me.

I have a very powerful electric motor, which I got cheap from a fellow, and I am uncertain whether to use the motor or elastic...

(continued below)

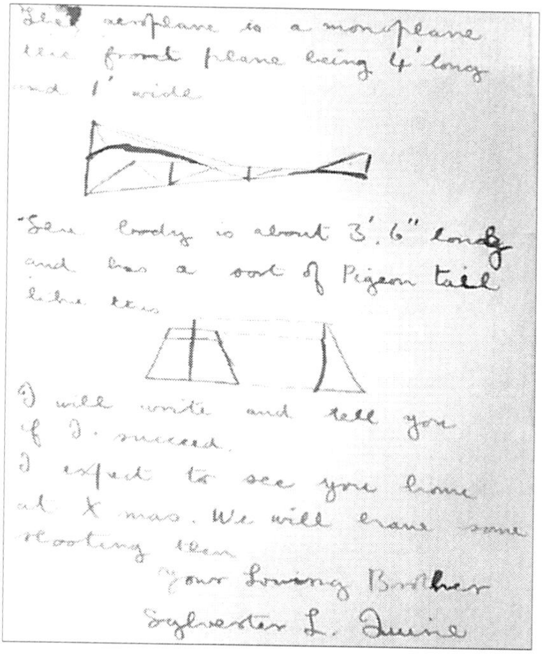

The aeroplane is a monoplane the front plane being 4' long and 1' wide

The body is about 3', 6" long and has a sort of Pigeon tail like this

I will write and tell you if I succeed.
I expect to see you home at X mas. We will have some shooting then.
Your Loving Brother
Sylvester L. Irvine

[b] 1914 Letter from Vess

February 1914 to Dono:

'Dear Dono, thanks for your letter & the information therein. I have for a long time been of the opinion that 'the Spanish Stn.' is Norddeich KAV. Perhaps our X might hear his call some evening about 10pm W.L. about 900m.

My coil is progressing favourably but of course slowly, as I am doing about 1 to 2 hours per night on my law now. I am insulating the primary by soaking it in shellac and when it is finally fixed in the tube I'm going to pour wax in until every crevice is full. The secondary is to be in one eighth sections insulated by filter paper soaked in wax. I have got a ripping rotary gap. Mr Needham turned it up on his lathe out of scraps I had at home. The shaft is mounted in ball-bearings and is fitted with a pulley in case the direct couple is not satisfactory.

It is to run at 3000 rev p.m. This will give a rate of vibration of 6000 p/m. or 100 per second. Base A on a piano has 27.5 vibrations per second. Top A has 3480 vibrations p/s. 7th C – has 4200 v.p/s. (Daisy will show you these. Daisy was a pianist) and musical notes (audible to human ear) range from 27 to 4000 v.p/s. From this you can calculate approximate tones (piano tones I suppose).

How about the Mercury Break? I understand the idea but how is it to be put into practice? I should like a diagram and an explanation. Can I dispense with a contact breaker (hammer break I mean)? I am making arrangements to have the 4" coil up on a shelf so that no one can touch it accidentally (or otherwise) and shall have an extra switch so that the current will be off. As to the earth, would a few zinc buckets buried in coke be any use? Alternatively would a piece of galvanise buried horizontally 2 or 3 feet deep with some lead covered cable soldered on in places & covered with coke be sufficient?

You might mention whether the key is in the primary circuit or in the electro-magnetic circuit when using a mercury break. I had thought of a Wehnelt Electrolytic Break but it would probably break down my insulation. I am swimming my coil in wax so it won't be pretty...'

[c] Prospectus of a Gun-sight for ant-aircraft guns

Jan 29 1916. Communicated by Rev. Canon Quine M.A. Lonan Vicarage, Isle of Man:

I This gun-sight is to act automatically, as the chief-gunner: who is observer and director of fire – orders the gun to be moved horizontally and elevated (or lowered) vertically, till he gives the order to fire.

II It consists in essentials of (a) a mirror; and (b) two wheels, deriving the movement from the trunnion of the gun – one directly, being attached to it; the second wheel, from the first: the second wheel carrying an observers eye-piece bearing on the mirror, but in a manner which constitutes one of the features of the device, as also the setting of the mirror constitutes an essential feature.

III The director of fire does not look up at the field of the sky, but downwards at that field as seen in the mirror. Such observer can work much more easily in this posture; and experience has shown that he can see an object – viz. air-craft target – more clearly, and can have better control of the movement of such object, in the mirror field than in the actual sky field.

IV For calibrating, 'range-finding' reliance is placed on the use of the 'spotting shell' – which the observer will note in the mirror: but this does not preclude additional observation of the burst of the 'spotting shell' by an assistant looking direct for range.

V The function of this gun-sight is to enable the observer:

To see as on a plane the path of the moving target.

Order timely spotting shells to try for range.

Anticipate the target's approach to a point which he decides to make its danger point.

Simultaneously – by such simple orders to his assistants as 'up', 'down', right', 'left' – train the gun on the selected danger point.

Finally, give the word to fire.

VI This gun-sight could be used detached from the gun – connection to be by circuit. With such arrangement one such sight could direct a battery.

VII Probably anti-aircraft gunnery might most successfully be employed – but not to say limited so – for elevations say from 45 to 90 degrees. Gunners may by this device at least specialize for accurate work on a defined sky field. For effective work sub-division of the whole sky field is important: each gun, or each battery, to control its section (all round the compass), viz. – create its section of field a danger-zone provided for a target entering it.

VIII The employment of this gun-sight is not confined to anti-aircraft guns.

[d] 1916 Letter to Lord Raglan & reply

Copy of John's letter to Lord Raglan regarding a new gun-sight for ant-aircraft guns:

Feb 24 1916 – Lord Raglan, Guards Club, 70 Pall Mall, London.

My Lord,

Your Lordship will remember the submarine net memorandum of Oct 1914 – through your kindness and that of Mr Sargeaunt, conveyed to the authorities: the result a great achievement, long ago matter of fact, though not yet written history! My son, the author of that device, has now solved a problem of almost equal importance, viz. has evolved a 'gun-sight' for anti-aircraft guns, which by automatic mechanism etc., will enable a gunner to hit the moving air target.

There is in the respect of his position a difficulty... He is a naval officer on active Service: and in this consists the difficulty, as it is essential that he should have the opportunity to submit the device in person – to ensure that secrecy which its importance demand, and also to protect his own rights as its creator!

In your Excellency's absence from the island I called on Mr Sargeaunt who most kindly promised – after telling me what he had done in Oct 1914 – to now write to the same personage as on that occasion, stating that the 'author' of the submarine memorandum has now evolved a new gun-sight as above.

What may result from this I do not know... My son had a wish that I should at least write to mention it – as undoubted a solution of a problem up to the present unsolved. Anti-aircraft gunnery is so far simply random shooting, for the most part without result, except the chance hit once in 5,000 shots or so.

The newspapers mention that Lord Derby is to take charge of anti-aircraft defence: if so, this matter may possibly come under his jurisdiction.

I have the honour to remain, my Lord, Your Excellency's most obedient servant, J.Q.)

Reply from Lord Raglan: 28.2.1916

My dear Canon, Your son is a real genius. I am so glad to hear that he has now turned his mind to anti-aircraft guns. I sincerely trust that he will be as successful in getting this device adopted as he was in the case of the submarine net. As Lord Derby is now apparently to take charge of the anti-aircraft defences perhaps I could be of use with him. I hope to be back in the island next week; perhaps you could come and talk with me if I can help in any way. Yours Sincerely, Raglan.

[e] 1916 Letter to House of Commons

'Private and Confidential Feb 28 1916

Sir,

Referring to the question asked in Parliament Feb 23rd as to whether the Admiralty still retains the services of 'the person or persons who devised the defensive methods which have been effectively employed against the so called submarine blockade etc.' the following may interest you:

One person and one person only, devised the methods used as well as the 'device' employed: and this 'device' and its employment for defence and offence (by destroyer and trawler activity) were set forth by this one person, though partly with the collaboration of another.

Outside the Admiralty (Oct 1914) only four persons had any knowledge of the creation of this device in question...

No stipulation was made by the author of the device: there was no bargaining or bartering; no price was asked: none has been paid in any form.

It was done in the Service of the nation by one capable of estimating the nature of the menace, and with capacity and training to solve the problem as to how the menace could be check-mated!

The solution of the problem had already been thought out by this person prior to the war and was submitted to the Admiralty after some early incidents of the war made it likely that it would be considered! The action of submitting it to the Admiralty was a voluntary act quite distinct from being 'employed' to do so...

This statement is made not for any public use; the object, to let you know the actual facts as one of the four persons above referred to, but not as the creator of the device. I have the honour to remain Sir your most obedient servant, J.Q.'

Bibliography

Some photographs and information in this book came from the private Quine family collection. The sources listed below provided invaluable information. No infringement of Copyright intended.

[1] Manx National Heritage Museum (M.N.H.) & archives (letters written by John Quine & photographs: MS11835: Quine family papers) Photos from imuseum.im

[2] Odyssey of a Marine Engineer (Merchant & Royal Navy stories): John Lindsay Quine. Edited & compiled by Julie Quine 2013 (Amazon)

[3] The Isle of Man and the Great War: B.E. Sargeaunt 1922

[4] Island at War: Margery West 1986

[5] www.naval-history.net: WWI timeline information & ship information

[6]westernfrontassociation.com/component/content/article/121-aerial-warfare/876-bombing-britain-war

[7] The Crisis of the Naval War: Viscount Jellicoe of Scapa G.C.B, O.M., G.C.V.O., 1920

[8] www.vlib.us/wwi/resources/britishwwi

[9] National Archives – WO 95-4052-6 (1916)

[10] www.firstworldwar.com/battles/zeebrugge

[11] A Sailor's Odyssey: The Autobiography of Admiral of the Fleet Viscount Cunningham of Hyndhope K.T, G.C.B., O.M., D.S.O. 1956

[12] www.submarine-history.com/NOVAthree.htm

[13] www.monmouthcastlemuseum.org.uk/historymenu/coys-railway

[14] www.longlongtrail.co.uk/

[15]www.mi5.gov.uk/home/about-us/who-we-are/mi5-history/mi5s-early-years/carl-hans-lody

[16] www.nas.gov.uk/about/090320.asp

[17]paperspast.natlib.govt.nz/cgibin/paperspast?a=d&d=DOM19141128.2.27

[18] www.historyofwar.org/articles/raid_scarborough1914

[19] www.1914-1918.net/asc.htm#depots

[20] War Letters 1914-1918 Vol.1 Wilbert Spencer 1897-1915

[21] Manx Notebook – Edited by A.W.Moore: online document created by F Coakley www.isle-of-man.com/manxnotebook

[22] Tynwald Hansard: www.tynwald.org.im

[23] The Dover Patrol: Reginald Bacon 1919

[24] War in the Air: Walter Raleigh 1922

[25] Log books of Sylvester Quine and Scrap book of letter memoirs (written to his friend, Hilda, who later became his wife) – Manx Air Museum, Isle of Man

[26] British Army Service Records (National Archives)

[27] www.airshipsonline.com/airships

[28] National Archives: WO95-4052-7 (1917/18/19)
[29] National Archives: WO95-4052-5 (1914/15)
[30] Memoirs of Yvonne Bodey (nee Quine)
[31] www.nationalarchives.gov.uk/education/greatwar
[32] I.W.M.: Imperial War Museum

22310481R00179

Printed in Poland
by Amazon Fulfillment
Poland Sp. z o.o., Wrocław